REA

Y0-ABI-538

**DO NOT REMOVE
CARDS FROM POCKET**

Marty Jerome
Wendy Taylor

THE STREETWISE GUIDE TO PCs

Secrets for Getting Your Money's Worth

Addison Wesley Publishing Company

Reading, Massachusetts · Menlo Park, California
New York · Don Mills, Ontario · Wokingham, England
Amsterdam · Bonn · Sydney · Singapore · Tokyo
Madrid · San Juan · Paris · Seoul · Milan
Mexico City · Taipei

THE STREETWISE GUIDE TO PCs

To a year in San Francisco and to each other.

Many of the designations used by manufacturers and sellers to distinguish their products are claimed as trademarks. Where those designations appear in this book and Addison-Wesley was aware of a trademark claim, the designations have been printed in initial capital letters.

Library of Congress Cataloging-in-Publication Data

Jerome, Marty, 1960–
    The streetwise guide to PCs : secrets for getting your money's
worth / Marty Jerome, Wendy Taylor.
      p. cm.
    Includes index.
    ISBN 0-201-60839-1
    1. Microcomputers--Purchasing. 2. Computer software--Purchasing.
I. Taylor, Wendy, 1966–   II. Title.
QA76.5.J46 1992
004.165'029'7--dc20

92-10944
CIP

Sponsoring Editor: David Rogelberg
Project Editor: Joanne Clapp Fullagar
Technical Reviewer: Ed Tittel
Production Coordinator: Vicki Hochstedler
Cover Design: Jean Seal
Text Design: David F. Kelly
Set in 11-point New Century Schoolbook by CIP

1 2 3 4 5 6 7 8 9-MU-9695949392

First printing, October 1992

Should You Read This Book?

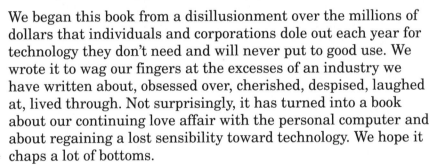

This is a book of heresy. It maintains that the personal computer—marvelous tool that it is—has been overhyped, overwrought, oversold. It suggests that behind the marketing and journalistic fog that enshrouds PCs today lurk people who will relieve you of money you'd ultimately prefer to keep.

We began this book from a disillusionment over the millions of dollars that individuals and corporations dole out each year for technology they don't need and will never put to good use. We wrote it to wag our fingers at the excesses of an industry we have written about, obsessed over, cherished, despised, laughed at, lived through. Not surprisingly, it has turned into a book about our continuing love affair with the personal computer and about regaining a lost sensibility toward technology. We hope it chaps a lot of bottoms.

This book is for you if you're relatively new to computers, if you rely on your nebbish cousin Cliff, a professional programmer, for computer buying advice—or if you're seized with angst whenever a computer salesman slithers toward you, jibbering about 80-nanosecond DRAM or 16-bit VGA boards.

Our advice will help you evaluate your computing needs from the consumer's, not the chiphead's, point of view. It will show you how to avoid buying more—or less—technology than you need, how to avoid getting fleeced, how to save a buck. It will navigate the backwaters of mail-order, the treacheries of retail shops, and the hidden pitfalls of used computer brokers.

This book is also for nerds, geeks, computer cowboys, technoweenies, and micro-managers—the people with bad posture and bad breath who keep the industry honest and the rest of us on our toes.

Even if you know a lot about technology, you may be surprised by the advice in these pages. We offer streetwise tactics for negotiating a deal, for inventing your own bundling arrangements, and for fighting back when you've been burned. We'll show you the mark-up on various PC components, what your current system will be worth five years hence, and how to get the most for technology you wish to unload. We realize that buying a hard disk should be as easy as buying a toaster, but that's not the way things are.

Finally, this book is for managers, whether of multinational corporations or of home businesses. We offer it with a dare: Cut the revenues your company or department spends on information technology by 30 percent next year. Productivity and market share will not drop as a result. Quality and communication will not suffer. You will spend *more* time managing people, ideas, and assets. You will spend *less* time managing paper and technology bureaucrats. Your life will get better. We dare you.

Contents

Elite Computer's 486SX Racehorse Sets the Pace

For sheer speed and processing brawn, Elite Computer's PowerLine IV is a must-have. Power users will find it impressively fast and versatile, yet priced to compete against machines with half its muscle.

An upgradable PC, the 486SX/25 speedster turned 18-millisecond hard drive seek times in the Technoweenie Lab benchmarks—30% faster than the comparable Dragon Tail LE25. The PowerLine IV performed nearly as well in CPU-intensive tasks, turning 31 in the Aggregate Performance Index. With this amazing performance you get a 120-MB IDE hard drive (upgradable to 650 MB), a Sapphire Plus Super VGA video adapter with a full megabyte of memory, one parallel and two serial ports, a small footprint design, ergonomic "SmartVu" LED diagnostic display of system functions, and a responsive 101-keyboard.

The only caveat to this otherwise top-notch performer is its mere three free expansion slots. Also, the power switch is a reach. But, at $2,999, the PowerLine IV combines high speed and upgradability with the latest in technological design at prices serious computer users can't afford to pass up.
—Ed Bitt

The PowerLine IV's sleek profile cuts a suave image on any power user's desk.

Put Your Wallet Away

Lo! Men have become tools of their tools.—Henry David Thoreau

In May 1986 an issue of *Fortune* featured a barren photograph of a personal computer on its cover. The headline asked, "So Where's the Payoff?"

It was a dour report from an otherwise heady era. By the mid-1980s the personal computer came to symbolize the mythos of that roiled decade: twenty-two-year-old vice presidents who drove Porsches to work, million-dollar businesses grown out of spare bedrooms, empires toppled by upstarts. The lecture circuit teemed with consultants and B-school professors who evangelized about the coming Information Society. With the PC at its vanguard, a revolution in productivity thundered on the horizon. Expectations would know no limits. Profits would spiral eternally upward.

But as *Fortune* noted, reality begged to differ. White-collar productivity stagnated between 1976 and 1986; by 1992, it declined. After pumping billions of dollars into microcomputers, software, and training, corporate managers saw their departments—often their whole companies—taken hostage by technology bureaucrats, while profit margins sagged. Educators who championed the vapid notion of "computer literacy" graduated a generation of adults highly skilled at computer games, despite their inability to read the software manuals. Americans spent ever more hours at the office, ever fewer enjoying the rest of their lives.

1

To blame the personal computer for flagging productivity is absurd, of course. Almost everyone recognizes the efficiencies, savings, and conveniences the PC brings to the office. And as its overpaid apologists in the media routinely suggest, we probably don't yet know how to measure the computer's true benefits, anyway.

But in the early 1990s it's pretty clear that the PC isn't the miracle those apologists preach. For every hour saved by producing a professional report with a fancy word processor and laser printer, two hours vanish as a secretary fiddles with fonts on a memo about parking privileges. For all the collaborative genius a computer network brings to a group of workers, a whole company seizes when the network goes down. Computer training typically gobbles as much time and money as computer proficiency saves.

Primitive technology, bad implementation, inept management—the usual excuses for computing's failures all ring with at least some truth. This book doesn't explore those theological issues of computers and productivity. Far too much of that blows through the computer press already. Its stale platitudes and mindless boosterism have picked the pockets of corporations, small businesses, and individual consumers for more than a decade.

The Streetwise Guide to PCs takes a less-lofty, somewhat heretical view of computers: technology as a means, not an end. Fact is, most people *don't* need a larger hard disk, a faster video card, or more fonts. Most people need to get work off their desks. The naked assumption that more computer whizzies yields more time on the golf course or a faster track to upper management is patently ridiculous. Yet this is exactly the dogma that drives computer magazines, computer merchandisers—the computer industry in general.

It is both hilarious and enraging, though mostly it's just expensive. This is a book for people who've paid and paid for computer equipment and gotten little in return. It's for people who want their technology to work for *them*, not the other way around.

Software Bloat

Consider software. Despite the flood of new programs that wash onto dealer's store shelves each year, remarkably few advance productivity in any practical way. Desktop publishing programs have evolved into cost-saving tools for a highly limited market. Electronic mail brings welcome convenience (also overwhelming distraction) to millions. And there are other scattershot programs and utilities that simplify or expedite work.

But the applications that legitimized the computer in the first place—spreadsheets, word processors, and databases—aren't significantly more useful today than they were seven years ago, despite the features, add-ons, and kitsch they've accumulated. Worse, no new application has arrived to equal or better these three.

Today technical splash and commercial success come from programs that solve computing problems, not work problems: DOS shells, hard disk utilities, graphical interfaces, file managers, memory managers, and font managers. With all the windowing, file managing, and font rendering preoccupying expert computer users today, it's a marvel they accomplish anything at all. If these programs contribute *anything* to your job, they also add another layer of complexity to your computer system, another set of incompatibilities and conflicts, another way to squander two hours tweaking a WIN.INI file or remapping your upper memory area. If they giveth at all, they taketh twice in return.

Meanwhile programs that actually accomplish work have largely grown bloated, inefficient, and cumbersome. They're similar to the overweight and barely controllable automobiles of the 1960s, in which technological "innovation" meant bigger engines, longer wheel bases, and push-button gadgetry. A typical word processor now includes page-layout tools, a grammar checker, a scientific equation editor, and a graphics-import engine. Computer magazines purr at all this flashy, innovative capability. Though word processors now take months to master, they can do just about anything anyone would ever want to do to text—except, of course, manipulate words with the ease and efficiency of word processors produced five years ago.

Unlike automobiles, word processors don't wear out. And, unlike the past decade, eight or nine million new computer users aren't marching into the software market each year eager to buy their first word processor. These concurrent trends have begun to squeeze profit margins at software publishers everywhere. To keep revenues flowing, publishers must either invent new programs for customers to buy or entice existing customers to throw away the old version of a program in order to buy the "upgrade."

Upgrades are far cheaper and less risky to develop than new applications. Slap a few whizzies and what's-its onto an existing program, and a gleaming new product emerges. Never mind how useful those new features are. Simply offer the upgrade to existing customers at one-half or less the cost of the program's purchase price. They'll buy it as reflexively as they'd renew a magazine subscription (a purchasing decision that software marketeers rightly call a "no-brainer").

It's quite a racket. Publishers sell upgrades on the vague promise that more typefaces, prettier menus, or grammar checkers will magically boost productivity. Customers buy on that same mysticism. After all, companies want their employees to have the most powerful tools available. Unfortunately this arrangement ignores the obvious: most upgrades have nothing to do with innovation or productivity. They have everything to do with marketing and a publisher's overextended profit margins.

Hardware: More, Bigger, Faster—Now

The same is true of hardware. For years computer makers have lorded the specter of obsolescence over customers to encourage sales of top-of-the-line PC systems. Computer salespeople gloomily caution customers that today's mid-range PCs will be obsolete in three to five years; such is the meteoric state of the technology. Better to buy a high-end system now, they'll suggest brightly. It guards against obsolescence.

Even computer dim-wits quickly recognized that three years from now that same high-end technology will cost one-third its current price. For a much smaller total investment, you can buy a mid-range computer today, then move to the more powerful technology when (and if) you need it. Get two computers and twice the warranty in the bargain.

Not to be out-smarted by cretin consumers, manufacturers dreamed up the idea of "upgradable PCs." Pull yesterday's processor from your aging machine, then plug in tomorrow's space-age chip, and, presto, a new computer rises from your old bomb. It protects your investment, right? But already consumers smell the marketing flimflam in this. Upgrade boards cost nearly as much as a new PC. Besides, they protect against chip obsolescence only. Disk, video, and memory subsystems evolve more quickly—and less predictably—than microprocessors. Five years hence you may discover that your Ferrari processor is pulling a pick-up truck.

Not that you'll need all that power, anyhow. The mythical day when software publishers write programs that run exclusively on high-end computers keeps failing to arrive. Publishers would *love* to free their software from older, slower machines. It would let them produce far more sophisticated programs with far greater ease. Unfortunately it's financial folly. Tens of millions of computer owners are perfectly happy with their old chugging, clunky PCs, thank you. Theirs is a market too large for most publishers to snub.

Software will certainly make greater demands of hardware in the coming years. (Microsoft Windows, for example, has already given millions of people the first practical reason to buy an 80386-based PC.) However, the urgency to buy faster processors, bigger disks, and more memory grotesquely outstrips any real need. It is a product of technology fashion, superstition, media hype—and marketing fraud.

This should come as little surprise. These days computer makers are at a perilous loss about how to shore up sagging revenues. With consumers' sad but wise realization that computers are nothing more than commodity electronics—as reliable and unremarkable as toasters—PC makers have found their once-exalted and lucrative marketplace transformed by price wars, wholesale discounts, and marketing tactics inspired by K-Mart. Gone are the days when IBM, Compaq, or Apple could charge extortionist prices for PCs in the name of "quality." No-name Taiwanese clones perform just as well, last just as long, and cost far less.

Fog

This is good news for consumers, except that computer makers continually find new ways to slip yet another dollar from their fists. One proven method is simply to turn up the marketing fog. The alphabet soup of industry standards, acronyms, and buzz words provides endless opportunities for shysters. Advertise that a PC comes with an "8-bit CGA video card," for example, and few consumers will recognize this as a slow and grainy, decade-old technology long abandoned by the industry—or that the word "card" is an unintended tip that the monitor costs extra. Nestled deep into advertising copy, such babble sounds positively inspiring.

Failing technical gobbledygook, manufacturers can cloak their products in euphemism. Thus a "home computer" typically describes a low-powered (cheap) PC with a $100 modem and perhaps a "software starter kit" thrown in to hand-hold the un-initiated. The "home computer" label enables manufacturers to slap a premium onto the system's price—and to prey on the naiveté of novice computer buyers.

Makers of "multimedia computers" have taken a slicker course. Last year a consortium of manufacturers fashioned a "Multi-media PC" logo (emblazoned with the letters "MPC") that now appears on both computers and software. Neither a certification of quality nor a guarantee of satisfaction, the logo means only that your official multimedia PC can run official multimedia software. That is, it means nothing at all. The same hardware à la carte typically costs a fraction of the price. And virtually any software program that squeaks, shimmies, burps, or sings can call itself "multimedia."

No less, a "WinStation," the lowly PC's latest sequined disguise, is remarkable for how poorly it suits its role. The logo carries a guarantee from the Microsoft Corporation that the machine can run Windows. But because manufacturers expect the logo alone to sell their machines, they typically stock their PCs with the bare minimum memory and storage capacity required to meet Microsoft's specification. To fully avail Windows' multitasking capabilities, its fonts, and graphics, you'll want as much memory and disk space as you can afford. Most WinStations toss bread-crumbs at a bear.

Legitimizing a PC with a logo, a costume, or a merit badge are relatively new gimmicks to computer merchandising. They supplant the time-worn strategy of simply hiding costs. Once upon a time, makers would advertise a PC at an eye-popping low price. Only after the consumer grabbed the bait did he realize that the hard disk, the monitor, and DOS cost extra—or that a machine otherwise well suited to a specific task may lack adequate memory. Extra memory, he discovers, costs $979 per megabyte. These days such deceits are more inclined to incense consumers than to sell PCs. Computer manufacturers shy away from them.

Not so computer add-on makers. Modems often lack the communications software that makes them usable. CD-ROM drives, scanners, and tape drives routinely sell *sans* controller card—as if you'd buy the device as a desk ornament. Laser printer makers profit richly from extra printer memory (required for desktop publishing and graphics, two key reasons for buying a laser printer in the first place) and often charge exorbitant amounts for a plastic paper tray. Cables, batteries, cases, and rechargers on *anything* generally cost extra. As corporations have reluctantly learned about computer training, the PC's largest costs are often invisible. They gouge you from behind.

The Trade Rags

This nickel-and-diming of the consumer is probably no worse in the computer business than in any low-ball electronics industry (which, after all, now includes computers). But given the colossal dollar investment in the technology from corporations, schools, small businesses, and individuals, one would expect some kind of industry watchtower to emerge. Unfortunately there is no nerdy equivalent of a Ralph Nader for computers—not yet, anyway. Goodness knows, the computer press doesn't play this role. The feeble notion that PC magazines help expose industry swindlers, sham, and snakeoil is wishful thinking at best.

Like all special-interest publications fueled by advertising, computer magazines are part of the industry they cover. They're owned heart and soul by the computer business, by advertisers.

This doesn't diminish the wisdom in their pages, but behind that wisdom lurks a gloomy, unfortunate motive: whatever a computer magazine's duty to the reader might be, its ultimate goal is always to help advertisers sell their products. Publishers will bray in moral outrage at such charges. But don't kid yourself about these things.

This is not to suggest that computer magazines prostitute themselves (perish the thought). In some ways a magazine's business objective *reinforces* editorial virtue. After all, if a magazine publishes articles that openly pander to advertisers, readers smell sham and stop renewing their subscriptions. Circulation drops and advertisers flee. This doesn't stop advertisers' influence, of course. But the actual effects on a magazine's articles are subtler, multifarious, and bewildering.

The oft-levied criticism that computer magazines only publish cheerful product reviews as a way to glad-hand advertisers is certainly true, but in oblique, unsuspecting ways. Even the lowliest writer on the editorial food chain understands that writing negative product reviews does not advance one's career. When a review offends a manufacturer (who, after all, is either an advertiser or a potential advertiser), the manufacturer shows up at the publisher's doorstep, presses his thumb against the publisher's nose, and says, "inaccuracy."

The publisher then demands that the writer defend the article—in the name of "accuracy"—usually in a formal memo. Whether or not the writer's career gets hammered, the whole process casts a chilling effect across the entire staff (and is so intended). It's highly effective.

The larger reasons that computer magazines beam with such tedious happy news, however, aren't quite so venal. Laziness is a big factor. Criticizing a product in print requires double-checking of facts, extra phone calls, worry. Far from winning you friends, it usually just provokes unwanted attention from the ogre in the corner office. It also alienates important sources of information. Stuffing a magazine's pages with sunshine and butter requires far less work. Everyone stays happy.

Also, competition among computer magazines for an early look at a new product creates a cozy climate between the press and the industry. Journalists who routinely write kissy-face reviews are repaid with advance glimpses of new technologies, tips about forthcoming upgrades, and interviews with corporate overlords. Their careers soar. As vile as this may seem, the same greasy rapport connects national politicians to the Washington press corps. Journalists everywhere strive to keep their well waters flowing—even at the expense of truth.

Tools of Our Tools

Consumers who recognize that computer magazines are toadies to advertising still often succumb to the hype, the smoke, the technoweenie's sensibility that informs the trade magazines. Whatever the problem, the solution is always to buy, buy, buy. State-of-the-art computing is something you *need*, not something you merely want. More computer toys are justified, admirable, even righteous. Smarter computing means smarter work—the trademark of a smarter worker. And so forth.

Browse through any computer magazine, however, and you'll be astonished at how little it has to say about actual work. Computer reviews are about speed, capacity, interoperability, compatibility, expandability, feature sets, interfaces—about computing as an end in itself. Usefulness doesn't much matter. Neither does warranty, dollar value, technical support, nor any of the other issues consumers most need to know about when buying a tool, whether it's a lawn mower or a microcomputer. To write about such issues reduces glamorous high-technology journalists to mere consumer affairs reporters. Worse, it rankles advertisers.

Slowly this sensibility is beginning to change (at the keen insistence of both corporations and consumers). Computers are losing their mystique—not because they're no longer marvelous, empowering tools. They are, they are. But consumers are beginning to demand a practical and *accountable* return for their technology dollars. Prettier pie charts, better memory management, and bigger hard drives don't improve profits. They don't grant you more time at your daughter's soccer practice. This message has failed to reach computer manufacturers in the past, but slowly it's getting through. It's becoming clear as can be.

The PC Oscars

Whatever a computer magazine's duty to the reader might be, its ultimate goal is always to help advertisers sell their products.

Nothing reveals the cozy rapport between computer magazines and their advertisers quite like the ads themselves. You can't flip through more than one or two advertisements without finding a computer magazine's logo popping out. It's more suggestive than you think.

A magazine logo in an ad means the publication once reviewed one of the advertiser's products and awarded it some kind of technical excellence merit badge. Such awards provide a marvelous lubricant between the computer press and the industry. They repay both parties richly.

Every issue of every computer magazine reviews dozens—sometimes hundreds— of products. As many as a dozen of these products wind up getting awards. Given the number of computer magazines in circulation at twelve (or more) times per year and the number of awards they ladle onto products in each issue, the odds of an advertiser *not* winning some kind of award are rather meager.

Look Closely

Once a magazine has tapped a product with its wand, the product's manufacturer gets legal right to use the magazine's award logo in its ads. This arrangement makes for lots of happy advertisers, and it bolsters the magazine's editorial authority in the bargain. Product awards ostensibly help readers make informed buying decisions, to distinguish great products from dogs. But what results is a confusion of another kind.

Look closely at an award logo, and you'll notice how little—if anything—it tells you. Product awards are conferred on specific products from specific tests. None of this information appears in the logo, of course. Advertisers quite often plop the logo in some vague corner of the page like a magisterial seal. Dozens of products might float on that page, but it's anyone's guess to which gizmo the award actually belongs.

Notice, too, how the date on the award (if it appears at all) disappears when the logo is reduced to the size of a postage stamp. You'd need a magnifying glass to determine that the award is nearly five years old—a couple of lifetimes in PC technology.

You won't learn much about the company behind the product, either. (*Computer Shopper*, a large-circulation PC magazine, once bestowed an award on a mail-order dealer that was in the midst of bankruptcy proceedings.) Product awards honor performance, speed, feature sets, and other whiz factors. They seldom take into account service, support, or the solvency of the company. →

For Sale

What awards do best is *sell*—both computer products and magazines. So much so, in fact, that advertisers aren't above using a little creative advertising, rightly guessing that magazines will turn their obsequious heads.

Manufacturers often drop award logos into ads, even though none of the specific products mentioned has won the award. They'll reproduce the award logo multiple times in a single ad to give the impression that the company has won multiple awards. Award logos often adorn whole computer systems, even though only a component of the system—a monitor, say, or a hard disk—was the actual winner. A product that won an award three years ago quite often still wears its award logo, even though different products are current winners in its category.

Better still, sometimes advertisers cobble together their own award logos. Lift a phrase from a product review—"honorable mention" or "excellent value"—run it with the magazine's masthead logo, and, voilà, you've got a winner.

Comfy Bedfellows

Naturally computer magazines set "guidelines" for how their award logos can be used in ads. They just neglect to police them. Almost all computer publications publicly insist that advertisers must publish the product name, version number (in the case of software), and the date the award was conferred alongside the logo. But browse through virtually any computer magazine, and you'll see for yourself how poorly these guidelines are enforced.

None of this is surprising, of course. That a magazine issues awards at all is enough to woo advertisers. It's no wonder that an award logo for a product will often turn up in both the review article and the advertisement—each running in the same issue. This isn't peculiar to the computer industry (even the hallowed Good Housekeeping Seal of Approval, for example, isn't bestowed on products unless a manufacturer commits to running at least $60,000 worth of ads in *Good Housekeeping* magazine).

This chummy relationship between the industry and the trade publications is only part of the problem. Because magazines are so promiscuous with their awards—often doling out several hundred a year—enforcing guidelines about how to publish the logos is nigh impossible.

Indeed, awards are largely a terrible sham. They sell ads. They tell *you* nothing at all. ❏

"Interactive menus" means that your software stays in your face as you work, and that printing a document requires you to answer six questions. Software as electronic gnat.

An indecipherable blob at the top of your screen that's ironically supposed to make a program easier to understand.

What! No photo touch-up tools, no flowchart module, no Veg-O-Matic?

MultiQuikSoft MicroWord 3.5 for Windows

Take advantage of our special limited upgrade offer* today and watch even everyday documents come alive. You won't believe the difference.

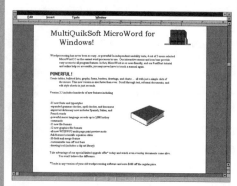

*Trade in any version of your old word processing software and save $100 off the regular price.

INTUITIVE!

Word processing has never been so easy…or so powerful! In independent usability tests, 4 out of 5 users selected MicroWord 3.5 as the easiest word processing software to use. Our interactive menus and icon bars provide easy access to all program features. In fact, MicroWord is so user friendly, and our FastStart tutorial and online help so accessible, you may never have to touch a manual again.

POWERFUL!

Create tables, bulleted lists, graphs, forms, borders, drawings, and charts…all with just a simple click of the mouse. This new version is also faster than ever…you can scroll through text, reformat documents, and edit style sheets in just seconds.

Version 3.5 includes hundreds of new features:

- 85 new fonts and typestyles
- Expanded grammar checker, spell checker, and thesaurus
- Improved dictionary, including Spanish, Italian, and French words
- Powerful macro language that records up to 3,000 hotkey commands
- 35 new file formats
- 12 new graphics file formats
- All-new WYSIWYG multipage print preview mode
- Full-featured scientific equation editor
- 20-field mail-merge feature
- Customizable tear-off toolbars
- Drawing tool (includes a clip art library)

So you can design your own indecipherable blobs. This is an astounding waste of time.

You've been burning for one of these, right?

Pronounced "whizzie-wig." Sounds like a hair piece. Previewing pages might save printer paper, but is it worth the cost of an upgrade?

What's not mentioned is that with clip-art libraries, drawing tools, spell checkers, thesauruses, fonts, blah, blah, blah, the program consumes 16 megabytes of hard disk space—about $100 worth.

Might as well write your own software. If you need more than eight to ten macros, your software's probably too complicated. Also, watch out, those macros might not work with the next upgrade.

CHAPTER **2**   CODE . . . . **Software**

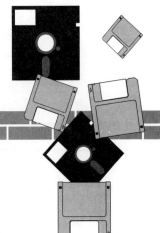

Let software inform all computer decisions. You won't be sorry.
By itself, the box of electronics on your desk accomplishes
generic, abstract tasks, but the work you do is specific and personal. If you're lucky, it both demands and reflects the very best
that's in you. A good tool can augment your work skills and habits, your abilities and limitations. It can hedge time and financial constraints. With computers, you'll find this tool in software.

That's a ticklish proposition. No commercial word processor,
spreadsheet, or database manager will ever completely fulfill your
expectations. Work a week with a program that proves delightfully
useful, and you'll quickly dream up ways to improve it; new chores
it ought to accomplish, but can't. Software publishers spend
their time dreaming likewise. In trying to meet every whim and
work tic, however, today's major applications have become slow,
overburdened, and laughably convoluted. Accomplishing even
rudimentary tasks often forces you to navigate many miles of
menus or to build huge libraries of macro commands.

Print a one-paragraph memo, and your word processor officiously demands that you first answer a half-dozen questions
about how you want it printed. Screen fonts, display modes, and
graphics styles invite endless adjusting and tweaking. Program
features designed for convenience often require incessant fid-
dling and fuss, and hours of leafing through the manual. The
very concepts and language that describe a program's functions
("Dynamic Data Exchange," "embedded objects," and "tear-off
toolbars,") have grown abstract and increasingly removed from
the work they were designed to accomplish.

Something is backwards in this arrangement. Like any smart technology (the bicycle, for example, the toothbrush, or the lock washer), a good software program should remain true to a single idea. Its design should be elegant, even simple, and impressive only in its efficiency and lucidity. It should accomplish one broadly defined chore exceptionally well…and it should stay out of your face as you work.

Good luck finding those programs. Although they do exist, if obscurely, such simple, useful applications typically lack the baroque technical wizardry that fetches attention from the computer press. Also, the computer magazines' self-congratulatory ritual of picking winners from various software categories in-

Software Lite

Expensive, lumbering, feature-crammed software applications sell so well because they play on two human foibles: techno-snobbery and the fear that one fine morning you will wake up to discover that you actually *need* a scientific equation editor or a database report publisher. Even software makers readily acknowledge that most people use only about 10% to 40% of the features in any given program.

What publishers don't tell you is that if you can overcome snobbery and fear, you'll find some of the best software programs at the cheapest prices available. Many turn up as "lite" or "personal" versions of major applications. Stripped of their more fatuous features, such programs typically require less hard disk space and memory. What's more, they're faster, easier to learn, and easier to navigate. Finally, they cost 40% to 90% less than their corpulent cousins.

Lite software can be found in integrated packages as well. A single program that includes word processor, spreadsheet, database, and (usually) communications modules, most DOS-based integrated packages share data between modules as easily as Windows (some packages come in Windows versions as well). They're especially handy for laptop users who rarely need the muscle of full-featured applications on the road anyway. Most integrated packages provide file compatibility so that the tubby, full-featured programs in your office computer can read data created in your svelte integrated package while you were traveling. →

variably heaps high praise on programs that further computing as a fine art, not as a way to get work done.

The very idea of a "winner" program is odd. Because work and work styles are subjective, you should seek the advice of co-workers and colleagues about software. Get the opinion of people who understand the *work* you do. Look to computer experts and trade magazines only to explain a program's general features and capabilities, its hardware requirements, and where to call for a brochure. Let the work you do dictate which of those features you need.

What do you lose in a "lite" software package? Not much. Slenderized word processors usually lack the ability to create footnotes, tables, indices, or three-column documents. Spreadsheets may (though not always) lack charting features, macros, and publishing tools. Lite database managers are non-programmable and may accommodate only limited-sized databases. With lean and mean desktop publishing programs, forget page-to-page column wraps, multiple layouts, and color separation.

Even if those features seem too important to lose, you can almost always find crafty ways to work around them without sacrificing whatever it is they ultimately produce. Software publishers, ever eager to hook you into their more expensive programs, usually provide some kind of discounted upgrade path. Outgrow your software lite, and you can buy its full-calorie version cheaply. In fact, it's often cheaper to buy a lite program and upgrade to the full-featured version than it is to buy the jumbo version outright—a testament to the perversity of software pricing.

Software publishers created software lite to tap a secondary, less lucrative market. Once aimed at small businesses on tight technology budgets, hobbyists, and students, integrated packages have now begun to attract increasing numbers of Fortune 500 buyers, a trend that has software publishers cursing in their sleep. Corporate managers bewildered by the high software costs, hidden hardware costs, steep learning curves, and low payoff of full-featured applications are beginning to look for leaner, meaner, and cheaper ways for their armies to accomplish the same work. Software lite might not be the complete solution to this problem, but it's definitely a step in the right direction. ❐

Price

The value of any software program rides entirely on its concept and design. After all, its diskettes and manuals typically cost less than $10 to produce, whereas the program sells for hundreds. This is because developing a full-featured software program is a colossal enterprise. It requires fanatical dedication to an idea, thousands of programming hours, casino financing, weird hunches, and marketing pugnacity. The rewards occasionally make a handful of unlikely social misfits filthy rich.

Unfortunately the price tag on a program reflects the whim of the endeavor. That is, software pricing tells you nothing about value. An application that costs $600 has no inherent advantage whatsoever over a similar program that costs $99. The only person qualified to assess the better of the two is *you*. Even software reviews tend to ignore the caprice of pricing (it's too risky and it infuriates advertisers). Why any good commercial application costs less than $1,000—or more than a paperback novel—is anyone's guess.

By all means, find the cheapest price possible on your favorite application, but don't let a cheap price seduce you into buying a different, half-baked program. Software more directly affects the work you accomplish than any other aspect of computing. You needn't spend a fortune on code; the industry still brims with low-priced gems. When you find an application that can truly make a difference in your job, don't whine about the price—just pay it.

But make sure you can get your money back. Don't even touch your credit card until you've asked about returns. Most software programs come with a 30-day, no-questions-asked, money-back guarantee from the publisher; better manufacturers offer 90-day guarantees. Consider this probation, a period for the application to prove its worthiness and good manners to you. Don't think twice about returning a program for reasons that seem as fickle as its price (it's slow, it's ugly). You don't owe *anyone* an explanation for returning the thing. Also, inquire about the software dealer's policy on returning software. Whenever possible, let your salesperson fight the software publisher about getting your money back.

Upgrades

Software pricing is not entirely devoid of meaning. A sudden drop in a program's cost, for example, might presage an upgrade (it might also augur a liquidation sale for a doomed product). The software industry has enjoyed remarkable success in getting customers to buy software on a subscription-like basis, to ante up $20 to $200 or more for upgrades that appear every six months or year. In fact, many publishers issue upgrades on just such a schedule, unconcerned about the planned obsolescence it implies.

Over a ten-year lifespan of any program, expect only about three upgrades to be significant enough to affect the way you work. Not nearly enough scrutiny is given to buying upgrades. In *not* buying them, you can often find terrific bargains in timeworn older versions of a program. A whole category of retail stores has sprung up that sell obsolete versions of software as if selling day-old bread.

However, you can also get scalded. When buying an application, make sure you know its current version number. Software dealers—especially mail-order houses—quite often sell old versions of a program at full price, either through fraud or ignorance. Correcting the mistake is a hassle—it will cost you shipping charges, arguments, and multiple phone calls.

A more galling scenario is to buy a program at full price, drop the registration card in the mail, and *then* find out that the upgrade was six days away from store shelves. The upgrade, you discover, fixes defects in the release that you now own, and it costs $99, please. Software publishers typically confront such plights with all the sympathy of the IRS. To avoid this, look for four signs that suggest that an upgrade is imminent:

1. Has the current version been on the market for more than a year and a half? Publishers accustomed to plump profit margins seldom wait much longer before issuing an upgrade.

2. Have the program's competing products issued *significant* upgrades recently? Software publishers become remarkably innovative when the competition heats up.

3. Does a Windows version of the product exist? If not, it will.

4. Has the price dropped dramatically? If so, find out why.

Bugs

Even simple programs contain many thousands of lines of program code. As such, defects, bloopers, inconsistencies, boo-boos, and bugs are an inevitable woe of computing. They simply happen. Because bugs can tarnish a software publisher's reputation immeasurably, publishers tend to test their products rigorously and to exhaustion before shipping them. For all the self-policing care, however, bugs still emerge.

On the whole, the computer press does a pitiful job of reporting bugs. On the other hand, computer user groups and online software forums are terrific places to find out about bugs before you buy an application. Defects tend to appear in poorly designed interfaces, in features hastily cobbled together, or in upgrades rushed to market. There's no fool-proof way to screen for bugs yourself, but you can test for their likelihood:

- Command the program to save a file to a floppy diskette. As soon as the drive light comes on, yank the diskette from the drive. The program should report the error to you and prompt you for action. If the software simply hangs, it's poorly designed.
- Command the program to print a report. Just as the printer gets to work, turn its power off. Again, the software should report the error.
- Look for a consistent command set throughout the program. Menus invoked with function keys in some parts of the application, but with ALT-key or CTRL-key combinations in others suggest hurried design.
- Check the manual for selecting and changing printers, tailoring reports, building macros or scripts, and importing foreign file formats. If these chores are difficult or impossible to accomplish, they might be hiding more serious shortcomings.

Microsoft Windows

Throughout this book, we avoid naming specific products except where absolutely necessary. Discussion of Microsoft Windows is absolutely necessary. Its towering presence in DOS computing inspires near-religious debates between proponents and detractors—debates that tend to distort the practical issues with philosophical rhetoric about how humankind is supposed to compute.

Like it or not, Windows owns the foreseeable future of DOS computing. IBM's rival product, Presentation Manager, which runs under the OS/2 operating system, is ultimately just a Windows clone. In growing flocks, software publishers have begun churning out Windows versions of their applications, a trend that will continue for at least the next five years. If publishers can make their programs run under Presentation Manager too, that's terrific. However, no publisher is betting the farm on the success of PM.

Windows brings both benefits and drawbacks to computing, none of which matters as much as the quality of the applications that run under the program. Applications should guide your decision about whether or not to buy Windows in the first place since they most directly affect your work. Keep in mind that any DOS program can also run under Windows, though it gains nothing by doing so. At least it enables you to stock your system with both Windows and DOS programs.

Also, be aware that DOS is hardly dead. Even manufacturers who swear allegiance to Windows aren't about to ignore the tens of millions of people who still prefer their contentious C: prompt. DOS applications will flourish for many, many years, rest assured. For millions of people, Windows' high hardware costs, slender selection of applications, and complex design and configuration make it an expensive date.

Windows is an "environment," or "user interface," that runs on top of DOS. It enables you to launch your applications and manage your files through its menus instead of through the puzzling and forlorn C: prompt. Graphical in design, Windows incorporates much of the Macintosh's appearance and functionality, including pull-down menus, multiple typefaces, desktop tools (clock, calculator, and notepad), and the ability to move data between applications with relative ease. Windows programs have these same capabilities. The benefits they bring to your work are subtle:

- Shared information—select a long list of numbers from a financial spreadsheet you've worked up, and then copy it automatically into a memo you're composing in your word processor. This saves retyping the numbers and reduces errors. It's also a far more natural way of working with information.

- A familiar face—applications written to run under Windows conform to a standard set of menus, commands, and protocols. All Windows programs tend to look somewhat alike. This makes learning them quicker and easier—much easier.

- Central heating—Windows manages files, printing, fonts, video, and other computing housekeeping ordinarily handled piecemeal by each application you use. This saves you from futzing with printer and video drivers, resolving memory conflicts, and handling other problems each time you add a new software program to your system.

- Multitasking—sometimes handy, multitasking (the ability to run more than one program at once) deserves more praise for its technical achievement than for its productivity payoff, neither of which, when the hype has finally settled, will make a tremendous dent in your workload.

- Memory management—applications that run under DOS can claim no more than 640K of memory, which is a terrible constraint for today's porky programs. Windows provides crafty ways for applications to sidestep this barrier. Programs written to run under Windows tend to be more elaborate, but not necessarily more useful, than their DOS counterparts.

Not surprisingly, the chief drawbacks to Windows are cost and complexity. The program itself costs only about $90 and is generally thrown in for free with a 386-based system. Windows' hidden costs, however, can be staggering: Expect to fork over at least $1,000 or more for the extra RAM, hard disk capacity, processor speed, mouse, and video you'll need to keep the program—and its applications—from gagging (see Chapter 3). Software written for Windows generally costs more than its DOS equivalents, too.

Getting Windows to run peacefully on your system can be as much fun as oral surgery. Get your hardware dealer to install the program when you buy your PC. You should also try to reckon—realistically—how much help you can expect from your dealer months later when you add new software or peripherals to your system. Unless you're willing to rack up large long-distance phone bills to Redmond, Washington, don't expect Microsoft Corporation to be of much help.

Windows plays strongly in both the hardware and software you'll buy. It deserves careful deliberation. In turn, the applications most likely to help you decide whether or not to use Windows are the big three: word processors, spreadsheets, and databases.

Word Processors

"Word processor" is quickly becoming a misnomer. Today's mainstream text editors are actually desktop publishing and page layout programs, tools as devoted to the appearance of words as to their manipulation. Even a basic word processor can now bedeck printed pages with multiple columns of text, multiple fonts and type sizes, graphics, borders, pictures, and symbols. It can build indices and tables of contents. It can check your spelling, grammar, and arithmetic. It can help you find that recalcitrant word on the tip of your tongue.

What it can't do is make your sentences smarter, your thinking clearer, or your meaning more direct. Tools intended to improve prose rarely do (the dictionary is a fine exception). Today's feature-bloated word processors often lull their owners into a foolish self-satisfaction about the quality of their writing. This is one reason they sell so well. The same is true of the publishing and design tools that word processors now include. Unfortunately, not everyone is brilliant in the fine art of page layout and design. Used poorly, these tools can sabotage your document's message and waste remarkable amounts of time.

The real value of a word processor lies in expediency, the ability to manipulate words quickly and freely before committing them to print, and to produce finished, professional-looking documents from your desk. Expedient editing often succumbs to pretty pages, however, and every word processor tends to excel at one capability over the other. When evaluating a package, try to decide whether it's a better editor or a better publisher. At the same time decide which talent more closely complements the work you do.

Windows tends to make that distinction plain. Marvelously well suited to working with graphics, it brings desktop publishing capabilities to word processing without the complexity and →

The Business of Viruses

Anyone who watches television or reads a newspaper has almost certainly heard of computer viruses, rogue software programs that sneak into PCs, attach to legitimate software, and wreak mayhem. Viruses, we're told, threaten national security, the solvency of corporations, the international phone networks, and—especially—the data in your PC. They make terrific headlines.

Software publishers have been quick to capitalize on the public's fascination and paranoia about them. Hundreds of antivirus software programs for detecting and destroying viruses fill software dealer's shelves. Viruses, it seems, have become big business in their own right. That's not to say that they're epidemic—or even that you're likely to get one. The risks are grossly overstated.

Viruses *can* delete whole directories of files, render floppy diskettes unusable, or reformat your hard drive, but few actually do. Most viruses aren't malignant; infections typically result in little more than your PC announcing "Your computer is now stoned" or "Legalize Marijuana," before it returns to its normal behavior.

Your Odds

So what are your odds of getting a virus? That depends how on promiscuous you are with programs and data. If you seldom exchange files with other computer users, you'll probably never see a virus. Add several new software programs a month to your system or pirate programs from friends or computer clubs, and you have a better (but still by no means certain) chance of infecting your PC.

To put it in perspective, you're far more likely to lose data to a defective hard drive, a software bug, a power surge, or—most commonly—by hitting the wrong key on your keyboard. Add to those low odds two precautions and you can cut your chances of infection to almost zero: avoid booting your PC from floppies, and keep your diskettes out of communal PCs. Booting from an infected diskette loads the virus in memory. Each time you insert another floppy in your PC, it too becomes infected. This is the primary way viruses are transmitted.

PCs used for training, print servers, software lending libraries, or PCs simply sitting in the open for office workers are also excellent places to catch a virus. Avoid them. By the same logic, don't stick co-workers' diskettes in your machine if you can avoid it.

Of course, you *can't* always avoid it and none of these measures cancels your odds of infection altogether. Should you acquire an infection, you'll want to turn to an antivirus program. Be aware, however, that this category of software is largely a scam. →

A Shot in the Arm

The antivirus program that can detect the most viruses wins, right? Wrong. Antivirus programs differ primarily in packaging and price.

Because there's no agreed-upon definition of an identifiable virus, the number of viruses a program claims to detect is meaningless. There are at least 40 known variants of the Jerusalem virus, for example, all of which exhibit similar characteristics. Where some antivirus software publishers list this as one virus, others list each variant as a separate virus. Another common practice is for publishers to list viruses that aren't even active; they're merely test viruses created by research teams.

Most antivirus programs detect, kill, and/or prevent viruses:

Detect   The most important feature in an antivirus program is the scanner, a utility that searches all files for the signature code of a particular virus. There's little practical difference between manufacturers' scanners. Some use a menu interface; some you must command from the DOS prompt. Both get the job done (though the one with the interface will probably cost more). The only other difference is that some can scan network drives. If you store files on a network, make sure the one you get scans network drives; you won't pay extra for this capability.

New viruses purportedly turn up every day, and software publishers, quick to profit from the hysteria, issue frequent updates—for a fee. Although scanners occasionally need to be updated for new virus signatures, most updates are extortionware: programs to allay fears, rather than eliminate danger. Ninety percent of all infections result from the same handful of viruses, and one update a year is generally adequate.

Kill   Some antivirus programs also have features for killing or removing viruses once they're detected. They typically work by chopping out viral code in an infected program. The alternative is to manually delete the infected file with DOS's DELETE command. Since it's difficult to ensure that a virus has been completely purged, however, it's better to delete the whole file if possible and then restore it from backups or the original program disks. (Viruses do not infect data files, only program files.) This feature is superfluous.

Prevent   A few antivirus programs also include features to intercept viruses before they have a chance to spread. Although this sounds easy enough, prevention features are generally more trouble than they're worth. To enable these features, you have to have the antivirus program running at all times. Unfortunately they hog memory. They also conflict with other software and have a tendency to sound false alarms. They're irritating. You probably won't use them. ❐

expense. In fact, unless you're a professional designer, there's no need to buy a full-blown desktop publishing or page-layout program. Coupled with a laser printer, most Windows word processors can competently produce sophisticated newsletters, technical documents that include scientific equations, charts, photographs, schematics, outlines, and extensive footnotes, endnotes, appendices, and other front and back matter.

You pay for this wondrous capability in speed, complexity—and cash. On the same PC, DOS-based word processors scroll through documents, manipulate text, and execute other functions far faster than Windows programs can. Their command sets tend to be quicker to navigate, quicker to put to work. They require less memory and less disk storage (typically 1 to 3 megabytes, compared to 15 megabytes for many Windows word processors— about $100 of disk space). They run on older, cheaper equipment, and they typically cost about half the price of a Windows word processor.

For correspondence, business reports, doctoral dissertations, literary manuscripts, and notes to your nanny, a good DOS-based word processor is more than adequate. Better packages can manage fonts, build indexes and tables, create footnotes, and headers—do anything a Windows word processor can do—except work with graphics. No drawing tools, no borders around graphs, no graphs, no clip art, no pretty pictures. Quel drag.

Only through long hours and a diversity of chores with a word processor will you discover how much you love or hate it. But, for tire-kicking a program—in either DOS or Windows versions—several tests can tip you off about the program's design.

- Use the Search-and-Replace command to search for a tab or a return in a document. Is this possible? Does the feature maintain capitalization when it changes words? Can you search by wildcard characters (such as "r*n", to find every instance of "run" and "ran")? Can you search backwards?
- Try to redefine the tabs to line up a column of numbers along a decimal point.
- Try to set the default for hyphenation to "Off."
- Open a second document while the first one is still loaded.

Does it require more than five keystrokes? Does it require more than five keystrokes to cut and paste text from one document to another? Can you open a third document?

- See if the spell checker recognizes the following words: abrade, coven, defenestrate, exanimate, funicular, horny, lexis, maculation, oodles, ripsnorter, tyro, wino. (Consider five out of twelve acceptable.)

- Check the manual for "mail-merge," the process by which you produce personalized form letters to a long list of people. How easy is it to use the feature? Even if you don't use mail-merge, it often showcases the program's overall quality of design. Can it skip an incomplete record without stopping the merge? Can you print data fields on the page in an order different from their actual file layout? Can you add conditional statements (for example, for printing letters only to those people with the title "Ms.")? Will it print mailing labels?

- Footnoting also says a lot about a word processor's design. Better programs automatically renumber footnotes when you delete or add one. They also provide for a variety of numerical styles (including symbols). They should let you create endnotes as well.

Spreadsheets

Like word processors, spreadsheets increasingly find themselves in the publishing business. Marvelously malleable tools for analyzing virtually any form of numerical data, this category of software helped legitimize the personal computer as a business tool in the early 1980s. Unfortunately the analytical capabilities of spreadsheets have advanced little at all since then.

Most spreadsheets have grown fat in charting and graphics features. They can now add fonts, labels, borders, shadows, clip art, colors, and doilies to the charts they produce. Those charts now dominate business presentations—so much so that the eyes of seasoned businesspeople tend to glaze over at the very sight of a bar graph or a pie chart in a handout. More and more business charts today illustrate less and less. That they make information easier to grasp doesn't make that information more significant or useful. As a business tool, charts are grotesquely over-used. They're quickly losing their ability to communicate anything at all.

Nevertheless, almost anyone who uses a spreadsheet eventually winds up producing charts. The amount of time you devote to chart making should help you decide whether or not to go with Windows. As with word processors, Windows brings tremendous graphics capability to spreadsheets. You can view how your charts will appear before you print them. You can make scores of changes to fonts, borders, shapes, and sizes with unsurpassed ease. You can zap your charts into documents created in a Windows word processor or a Windows presentation graphics program with little pain at all.

None of this helps with simple number crunching, however, and Windows hardly enhances the spreadsheet's core function at all. It would be difficult for any technology to improve on spreadsheet basics. Because they're used for both quick-and-dirty scratch-pad calculations and for extensive financial modeling, spreadsheets don't elegantly lend themselves to the highly specialized features that clutter other applications.

This hasn't stopped publishers from tacking on financial subroutines, customizable "floating toolbars," "Autoformat" style sheets, spell checkers, and other useless frills. Not surprisingly, most spreadsheets have become confusing, forbidding, and impossible to master. Features designed to expedite report and equation writing send you running to the manual. Byzantine database capabilities promise profound financial insight, yet squander countless billable hours as middle managers vanish into an enchanted forest of hot-linked worksheets and 3-D what-if equations.

If you're buying a spreadsheet for a single complex chore, you should become current in the so-called features wars raging between the various programs. Try to discover which spreadsheet's zoom feature and Scenario Manager best suits the task, which chart gallery and color wheel will do more for your company's bottom line. Bon voyage.

Most people, however, use a spreadsheet for a variety of fairly general chores. Better packages allow them to quickly cut through the claptrap to add rows of numbers, multiply columns, and print simple reports. They're *accessible*. As with all software, your personal work habits should guide your purchase, but a few simple tests can help you evaluate a spreadsheet:

- Use the tutorial in the program's manual to create a macro with the "record" feature and then with the macro programming language. Entering data into a spreadsheet is typically repetitive and tedious. Macro commands execute dozens—often hundreds—of sequential keystrokes with a single command. They alleviate the drudgery of data entry. Computer magazines tend to laud highly sophisticated macro programming languages, but you should also be able to create them with as little pain as possible.

- Add 25 rows of random numbers down, and then across. Find the mean value of each of these rows and columns. Sort the mean values of the columns in descending order. The whole process shouldn't take you more than a few minutes.

- Browse through the program's "functions." All spreadsheets have some manner of built-in functions, prerecorded formulas that perform common mathematical and financial calculations such as straight line depreciations or future values. How easy is it to look up functions and drop them into your worksheet? Look up a function in the manual. Is it explained in English?

- Try to print a worksheet sideways. Are the results readable?

Database Managers

Recipe filers and Fortune 500 accounting systems, electronic rolodexes and spare parts inventories for Boeing jets all share a common core technology: database managers, software programs that can sort and search through dozens—or millions—of records of information. No other PC technology spans as much technical sophistication.

The simplest database managers come dressed as special-purpose applications such as programs that manage your daily schedule (personal information managers), balance your checkbook (personal finance software), or track your sales calls (contact management programs). They wear hundreds of costumes and usually cost less than $300. Some prove eminently useful (financial packages, in particular, which include not only check writers, but tax preparation programs, portfolio managers, and small-business accounting programs, can save you many times their price in both time and dollars).

Others, such as personal information managers (PIMs), tend to suffer from too much concept and inadequate delivery. Using one turns you into an employee of your software. The endless data entry and maintenance that most PIMs require rarely pay off with better time management. PIMs appeal to compulsively fastidious personalities. People who use them iron their underwear.

A non-programmable database manager, which is more sophisticated than the special-purpose variety, is a *tabula rasa*. As with spreadsheets and word processors, you decide which information you want it to manage, structuring and naming the information as you see fit. For bringing order to a large body of unruly information—everything from a list of clients to a warehouse inventory of brass bedroom fixtures—a non-programmable database manager is typically all anyone needs.

Their malleability and versatility come at a cost, however. Non-programmable database managers take time to learn. They can cost as much as $500. Using them to build databases requires creativity and forethought so that you don't have to restructure your data after it's entered (which can be a nightmarish undertaking). People new to this genre of software typically build a couple of hard-to-search, poorly designed databases before they catch on to the obscure art of good database design.

Although some non-programmable database managers include so-called relational capabilities, which let you search for information across several databases at once, most are a "flat-file" variety, which let you search only one database at a time, a process akin to sorting through a single stack of index cards. Most "relational" database managers (a somewhat misleading name) are programmable. They occupy the high-end of sophistication among database managers.

Tremendously powerful, programmable databases are really development tools—applications for writing your own applications. They're complex; indeed, careers are made in mastering them. They're also expensive, typically $750 or more. Most of the people who buy them don't need them, but when shrewdly applied, they can pay for themselves many times over. If you've got a burning need for a relational database, a programmable database manager can make sense. Better packages now come with menus and coherent, fairly friendly interfaces. You needn't be scared off by their programming capabilities.

Windows brings little benefit to database managers, save some efficiency and sophistication in designing reports you plan to print. If you plan to include graphics or images in your databases, you'll have to go with a Windows-based database manager. You'll also need to bone up on your programming skills.

When shopping for a database manager, plan to spend many hours scrutinizing feature sets and capabilities among the various programs. Their sheer immensity can take months to conquer—enough time for a career to languish—before you find the database manager best suited to your work. Most publishers provide demo disks of their database managers, which can help you evaluate their interfaces. Use the following tests to evaluate a database manager:

- Look for a logical transition between menus, uncluttered screens, and a coherent set of options in each menu.
- Test the online help facility by looking up "Boolean Operators." Writing help screens to be intelligible to both programmers and shipping clerks is no small feat. It's often indicative of the program's overall design.
- Check the manual to see that the program can import data from your particular spreadsheet as well as from ASCII and .DBF formats. These cover most bases.
- Find out if you can define a graphics field in the program. Many packages force you to buy a separate module for handling graphics.
- Make sure you can add a memo field to your records. These are indispensable.

- View several records at once. A good program lets you tailor the way you view them.
- Look up "filter" in the manual's index, and read how you define one. The process should be simple and flexible.
- Go into the report writing menu and press the help key to find out how to eliminate "trailing blanks." These are the spaces that appear when you print fields in a record side by side. Better packages let you eliminate them through menus rather than with programming codes.
- If you're eyeing a programmable database, find out if the applications generator is menu driven. Find out if you have to buy a "run-time" license for applications you develop or whether it's included for free. This is a crafty way for the publisher to bilk you months after your initial purchase.

Utilities and Workware

None of the preceding tests offer more than a few simple tricks for spotting incompetent program design, technical shortsightedness, and bad implementations. Keep in mind that software demos, advertisements, and reviews in the press won't tell you very much either. Until you've installed a program on your system and applied it to the stack of work on your desk, you won't really know how useful it is.

That makes things difficult indeed. With thousands of DOS applications vying for space on your hard disk, finding useful programs ought to be easier. (See "Ten Totally Weenie Software Programs.") As some consolation, many of the memory managers, print spoolers, data backup utilities, systems diagnostics—the programs that solve computing problems—now come built into DOS and Windows. You don't need to pay for them at all.

This lets you focus on applications that solve work problems. All software purchases should flow from these. In turn, all hardware purchases should flow from software. It's as fool-proof a method as you'll find.

Ten Totally Weenie Software Programs

Anyone with a few crude programming skills can cobble together a program that makes lists or calculates basic math. Dress it up with a clever concept, and you can market it as a daring new genre of software. Some of these programs are whimsical, a few are even vaguely useful, but judge for yourself.

Calories Savant (Diet) That's right, spend an hour a day logging the details of every last soda cracker, carrot stick, or Snickers bar you've eaten in the last 24 hours. Then get *really* depressed.

Lottery Trend Analysis Expert (Lottery) This program happily cons you out of $40, or you can spend it directly on lottery tickets. Which odds are better?

Flow Charting 3 (Flow Charting) This is for people who like to draw boxes and connect them with lines to show a progression of events. Did someone say dweebola?

After Dark (Fritterware) One of dozens of gimmicky programs called screen savers that profess to prolong the life of your monitor. Mostly they're an excellent way to waste hours tweaking the colors and graphics on your monitor.

Home Inventory (Nonessential Lists) For cataloging those souvenir backscratchers, perhaps? Or how about that lawn ornament collection?

LoveTies (Astrology) Finally a program that tells you what to do when her Mars is in your fourth house. This one calculates the tropical or sidereal zodiac, the geocentric or heliocentric coordinates, and any of thirty-nine house systems. Yah.

Micro Cookbook (Recipes) People who have time to type in their recipes, catalog them in a database, and print them on special index cards don't have enough going on in their lives.

Marriage Planner (Niche Scheduling) People who like to type recipes into a database can now plan their marriages with software. It's very romantic.

Overcoming Depression (Therapy) *Overcoming* depression? Turning a PC into a shrink is pretty depressing.

User Friendly Exercises (Ergonomic) This gem monitors your work patterns and periodically emits a "low frequency tone" to remind you to take a break. We're waiting for the advanced version that throws you a bread crust when you sit up and bark. ❑

Intol, Schmintcl. Get the system you need. Forget about designer labels.

Meatloaf by any other name .... Worry about price and service; brand-name components don't mean a thing.

Are these vague enough for you? With all the awards computer magazines dole out each year, it's hard not to be a winner.

$2,299!!!

Lightning-fast speed is yours with the FireBall WinStation 386/33 from MicroFast Computers. Our award-winning system turned in top marks in all the major benchmark tests.

The FireBall WinStation doesn't skimp on anything—except the price! All of our systems are solidly built with unsurpassed attention to detail and only premium brand-name parts. We even include deluxe features and extras such as our 32K MeteorCache and a dazzling 16-bit SuperVGA card so your software displays up to 32,000 brilliant colors.

Power. Quality. Support. You simply can't find a better deal anywhere—we guarantee it!

This unbelievable bargain features:

• Genuine Intel 386DX/33 CPU
• 2 MB RAM (expandable to 64 MB)
• 80 MB 20 msec IDE Hard Drive
• 1.2 MB 5 1/4" and 1.44 MB 3 1/2" floppy drive
• 16-bit 512K Super VGA card—up to 32,000 colors
• 1 parallel, 2 serial ports
• 101 enhanced keyboard
• Full 256K MeteorCache
• Math coprocessor socket
• 30-day return policy

You also get:

• MS-DOS 5.0
• MS Windows 3.1 and Hi-Res Mouse
• Lifetime technical support

MicroFast Computers

1-year onsite service option available for just $75

Whose lifetime? Yours—or the manufacturer's?

"Onsite" doesn't mean instantaneous. You can waste the livelong day waiting for a repairperson to show. Such "options" are rarely worth the cost.

Super VGA is a catch-all term for any graphics resolution above the standard 640 by 480 VGA. If higher resolutions matter, get the details before you bite.

Notice that the monitor isn't included. Add $400 for a cheesy VGA monitor, $700 for one that makes the most of the video card's higher resolutions.

Chips, Boxes, and Systems *Complete*

Ultimately price is everything. At least with computer systems it is. Once you arrive at the configuration you need and recognize the telltale signs of competent design and technical support, the purchasing issues become arrestingly simple. You can measure them in dollars.

The name of a computer tells you diddly about the components inside its case. This is a disguised blessing, actually. In its rush to market, IBM built the first DOS PC entirely from off-the-shelf components. (Big Blue didn't even manufacture the metal box that housed the electronics.) Almost overnight a rag-tag industry of clone computer companies emerged, each assembling machines in like fashion to IBM's uninspired design. Its legacy is with us still.

The distinction between *assembling* PCs and actually *manufacturing* them is significant. Microelectronics expertise matters very little in the PC clone business; deal-making and sales savvy drive the train. Clone makers buy black-box components on the open market, assemble them into bigger black-box PCs, and pipe them out the door. Starting a computer company today requires little more than a telephone; a two-person, unskilled assembly line; and an ambitious sales representative. You could do it from your living room.

As a result, there's no telling which component brands fill your computer. Even if Blipo PCs, Inc., manufactures the motherboard in its systems, it most assuredly doesn't make the hard drive, memory, video chip set, drive controllers, monitor, support

33

chips, and myriad other components. Buy a Blipo Speedster 2QR-4u this week, and it comes with Chipster memory. Buy it next week, and it comes with Cheapster memory because supplies are cheaper—or more reliable.

Even when a computer maker promises that its machines will include a Lucky Tiger hard drive, for example, there's no telling where Lucky Tiger bought the drive that bears its name. Such is the faceless, many-handed bazaar of wholesale electronics.

All this is terrific news for the consumer since fierce competition between suppliers drives prices ever earthward. It's also a testament to the wide, though hardly perfect, interoperability and reliability of computer components. That you can plug just about any maker's hard drive into your system says worlds about how far computer compatibility has come. However, it should also make you a little cynical the next time a salesperson gasses at you about the inherent quality of some overpriced brand-name PC.

Solid-state electronics are tremendously reliable. Yes, add-in boards occasionally short-circuit; and memory chips sometimes fail, but most defects rear their heads in the first six weeks of use. Because you can't know—and shouldn't worry about—the component brands inside your box, simply make sure that defects and incompatibilities become your dealer's headache, not yours. Worry about warranty, service, and support. After these, your only concern will be landing the lowest price possible on a suitable configuration.

Processors

Computer pricing is informed first and foremost by the central processing unit (CPU), the chip or brain that drives a PC. Until recently, the Intel Corporation designed and manufactured almost all CPUs for DOS computers, but legal fist fights within the industry have lessened that company's imperious monopoly. Today a handful of manufacturers offer variations on Intel's designs. CPUs for DOS machines now come in more flavors than Italian ices do.

Anywhere confusion exists in the computer industry, someone profits from it. Computer manufacturers delight in the menag-

erie of new CPUs now arriving on the market because each offers its own avenue for hype, new ways to distinguish one commodity PC from another. This is nothing to dread; consumers
stand to benefit as well—not from perceived design improvements,
but rather from cost savings. The competition among CPU makers
has already begun to tow prices downward, a trend that should
accelerate as more manufacturers jump into the chip business.

Differences between CPUs entail less than you might imagine.
Generally speaking, five families of Intel processors define DOS
computing. Each represents an ascending level of sophistication,
and each is entirely backward compatible, meaning that software designed for a less sophisticated family of processors will
also run on the more sophisticated chips—but not necessarily
the other way around. Meanwhile, design subtleties *between*
processors in a family inspire great advertising copy. In terms
of moving work off your desk, however, their distinctions are
typically—often ludicrously—irrelevant.

Whatever name Intel assigns a chip, the last three digits in the
name indicate the family to which it belongs. Manufacturers
who clone Intel CPUs sneak these three numbers into the names
of their chips as well. Incidentally, many PCs now come with a
sticker that proclaims, "Genuine Intel Inside," as if certifying
your Jordache jeans. This is twaddle. The name of the chip
maker signifies nothing at all.

As with other computer components, choose a processor according to the software you want it to run.

8088 (also the 8086 and V20)

Think of an 8088-based PC as a sophisticated typewriter, splendid for simple word processing and spreadsheets, games, recipe
filers, check-writing programs, and other "homeware"; but woefully underpowered for graphics, page-layout designs, or financial modeling. For that matter, even many games now require
more horsepower. The selection of software that runs on the
8088 is shrinking, and by anyone's standards it's slow.

Nonetheless you can buy one for well under $500 (monitor and
hard drive included), and this price has completely, absolutely
bottomed out. Be aware, however, that next-generation 80286-

based systems typically cost only about $200 more. Because the 286 is vastly superior, it's generally a better buy.

80286

For more than three years now, major computer magazines have belittled the 286 chip, contemptuously insisting that its flawed memory management and its inability to switch between real mode and protected mode without rebooting make it utterly inadequate for today's high-powered programs. Unfortunately software publishers continue to write programs that run quite nicely on the 286. Because you can buy a full system for well under $1,000, individuals, small businesses, even major corporations continue to buy them. For most mainstream DOS applications, the loathsome 286 is an excellent bargain.

Its power begins to hit performance limits with Microsoft Windows, which it runs slowly and only at great expense and trouble. The same is true for desktop publishing, for computer-aided design and other sophisticated graphics programs, and for math, science, and statistics packages. Finally, prices for 386-based systems have plummeted so quickly in the past year, their additional cost can be worth the protection they buy you. Even if you despise Windows, it's the platform that will pilot computing for the foreseeable future.

80386

It comes in more than one dozen varieties and has lorded over computing as the preferred family of processors longer than any other CPU. The 386 churns data in 32-bit chunks (at least internally). This means that it can run any commercial software on the market today. It also will run any that comes to market in the next five years. Its processing power is largely overkill, but slumping prices on the chip ensure that you won't get soaked for capability you don't need. The 386 is a wonderful CPU.

Not much of practical importance distinguishes its many subspecies. The 386SX and 386SXL fetch some of the best dollar bargains in systems. Because they communicate with your PC's other components only in 16-bit blocks, they bog down Windows NT and other 32-bit programs (see "Architecture" later in this chapter). The 386SL and 386SXL come with power management features that *can* prolong battery charge in portables (see Chapter 6). New variations on the 386 chip seem to arrive daily.

With the introduction of the 586 chip in 1993, prices on 386s are heading south at a tantalizing pace; but they won't hit bottom for at least another year. Although bargains abound, beware of two trends: a 386-based system will cost appreciably less by next year, and its resale value will tumble further than that of a 286-based PC.

80486

More than one million transistors crowd the 486's silver-dollar-sized wafer. Like the 386, the 486 processes data in 32-bit gulps. It also comes with 8K cache built right onto the chip as a kind of holding trough for data so that the processor can gorge itself on new instructions as soon as it processes the old (see "Speed" later in this chapter). The 486 also comes with a built-in math coprocessor. Because the CPU and math chip pass data between them directly, without trucking it through a slow system bus, they produce processed data more quickly than PCs that use an external math coprocessor (see Chapter 5).

Who needs all this resplendent capability? Any application that requires or benefits from a math coprocessor (primarily graphics, engineering, and statistical programs) is a candidate. A 486 is a great CPU for driving a file server on a network, though a fast 386 will hold up just as well. Otherwise, most software applications are a full generation behind the chip. They'll need at least two years to catch up with the chip's capabilities.

Several companies now have 486 processors on the market. More will follow. To take advantage of the chip's muscle, make sure that a math coprocessor and at least some cache (even if it's only 1 kilobyte) is integrated on the CPU. Last year Intel introduced a version of the chip called the 486SX, an identical copy of the full-featured 486DX, except that the math coprocessor was disabled. In other words, the company crippled its own CPU and sold it at a lower price in order to bring more consumers into 486 systems while not undercutting sales of its exorbitant, full-featured 486DX. Is marketing *everything* in this business, or what?

Prices on 486-based PCs have already slipped into the near-reasonable lower stratosphere. The 586 chip will push them down faster. However, they still have a way to drop before they're outright bargains.

80586

Ha! Don't even kid yourself about this one. Unless you're writing your own software—and extremely sophisticated software, at that—you don't need this chip in the DOS computer on your desk. It's a great CPU for a network file server. Just make sure it's not coming out of *your* pocket.

Speed

When a computer magazine slavers over some PC's "performance," all it's really talking about is speed, how fast the system tallies numbers and finds answers. For want of anything more significant to talk about, computer publications obsess over speed, heaping high praise on systems that outrace other PCs by as little as one thousandth of a second in benchmark tests (see "Benchmarks and Black Magic"). Computer magazines worry about the length of gnat's teeth.

System speed buys convenience, not productivity. Certainly no one relishes interruptions in thought as the PC loads a program into memory, redraws a pie chart, or saves a file to the hard disk, but what price convenience? If you're careful, you can get it for free.

Many factors influence system speed, though chief among them are the sophistication of the CPU and its clock speed. All things being equal (though they rarely are), 486-based PCs work faster than 386-based systems; 386s are faster than 286s, and so on.

But within each family of CPUs, the computer's clock speed, as measured in millions of cycles per second, or Megahertz (MHz), determines how fast it is. Most system clock speeds range between 8 MHz and 50 MHz (though 100-MHz 486s lie on the very near horizon). A PC running its 386 chip at 25 MHz is faster than a PC running the same chip at 16 MHz.

Generally, the faster the PC, the more it costs, but a few rules of thumb can save thee from getting bilked. →

Benchmarks and Black Magic

The computer industry thrives on many forms of black magic, but none incorporates as much sorcery as performance benchmarks, tests that "objectively" evaluate the true speed of a system or its components.

Computer makers crowd their ads with benchmark results, each inscrutable number scientifically validating that the system in question is *absolutely, positively the fastest computer money can buy* (or similar understatement). Computer magazines stake their reputations and their technical authority (not to mention their ad rates) on benchmarks. Without magical numbers to augment their reviews, computer journalists would have little to talk about, no device for distinguishing one commodity product from another.

Benchmark results can destroy a new product in a gasp. They can make the phones at a two-person company ring with sales for months. They mystically broker billions of dollars across the computer industry. Unfortunately they suffer from two minor drawbacks: they're meaningless, and they're irrelevant.

When six system makers each claim they have the fastest 486SX system on the market, *PC/Nerd Magazine* claims a seventh is fastest, and *Geek Week* claims yet an eighth, who's right? Everyone—and everyone has the benchmarks to prove it.

Measuring computer performance is a slippery business. Benchmark tests, developed by hardware makers, computer magazines, and third-party software developers, span the spectrum in reliability, consistency, and competence. There are hundreds of them. Some test raw hardware capabilities: how fast a CPU pushes data at a video card, for example, or the time it takes a hard drive head to travel to the appropriate sector on the disk. Others simulate several types of common hardware functions: finding, reading, and then transferring information from the hard drive to memory, for example.

This is a shell game. Depending on which benchmark you run, you'll get different results. Use the Norton SI to measure a hard disk's seek time and transfer rate, for example, and you'll get one number. Use the Core Test to measure the same thing, and you'll get a faster—or slower—number. Which do manufacturers publish? Take a guess.

You can even get different results from the same test—on the same system. Run a benchmark, pour yourself a cup of coffee, and then run the benchmark again. Zingo, different numbers! Test two identical hard drives in two identical systems, and you →

get different results. Technicians try to control extraneous forces that affect benchmark performance, but humidity, dust, lunar phase, or the technician's mood can alter a test that, after all, measures thousandths of a second.

This ambiguity is great news for hardware makers. It means that, depending on the results you want to achieve, you can modify your test bed accordingly. Furthermore, because the benchmark tests that computer magazines use are available to anyone who wants them, PC makers can design their hardware (or, more commonly, tweak their software drivers) to perform well on the specific tests. After all, high marks in the right trade magazine make the cash register ring.

Computer magazines put so much emphasis on benchmarks because they have to. Confronted with hundreds of new computer products each month, they must find a way to evaluate them in a way that seems authoritative and fair. Quite often this means distinguishing between a drive that finds data one-thousandth of a second faster than another drive, a video card that redraws a pie chart one-hundredth of a second faster than another card. When an advertiser squeals about a bad review, the magazine need merely point to their sacred benchmark scores to take the heat off.

That benchmark tests measure things that have no practical value at all seems unimportant to the industry at large. Benchmark black magic still works splendidly at peddling generic hardware. Some day, however, a benchmark test will emerge that measures price, service, warranty, and *value*. It won't be as slick or mysterious as today's tests, but it will be a lot more relevant and much more useful. ❑

- Never pay extra for a PC that runs only 5 MHz faster than a similar, cheaper system. The difference in speed is nearly imperceptible, and there are tricks for goosing the slower system's real-world performance. Any good book on DOS explains how. For starters, look up RAMDISK and FASTOPEN in the index.
- A 33-MHz 386 is typically a better buy than a 16-MHz or 20-MHz 486. That is, it will run most Windows and DOS applications as fast as the 486 will. But shop around; you can find bargains in both families of processors.

- If you're on the fence about whether or not you want to run Windows, get a slow 386 over a fast 286. A 386SX is an excellent compromise. You'll find 386SX-based systems for only $100 more than comparable 286 systems, and they run Windows quite nicely.

- The fastest rated chip in a family of processors usually commands a premium. Thus a system running a 50-MHz 486 costs more than it should. Ditto for a 40-MHz 386-based PC. Generally, the second fastest chip in the family delivers better value for the dollar.

- A few crooked manufacturers will run a chip faster than its rated clock speed. This can give your computer schizophrenia and burn out your CPU (though there's no harm at all in running a chip slower than its rated speed). If you have any suspicions at all, pull off the cover and check for yourself. The rated clock speed is printed on the CPU.

A fast clock speed isn't the only way to stoke CPU performance. Some 386 and 486 processors have a "memory cache" built into their chips, which acts as a kind of telepathic waiter for the processor. When the CPU orders up a piece of information from memory, the cache takes the request, runs back to memory, and grabs not only the information the CPU is looking for, but several additional chunks of information lying next to it.

The cache is guessing that the CPU's *next* request will be for one of those additional chunks of information. More often than not, the cache guesses correctly. Because the new information is already on hand, the CPU doesn't have to wait for it. This eliminates what are appropriately called "wait states." It's somewhat like McDonald's.

Cache is a snazzy technology, but with the skid in CPU prices, you're often better off buying a system with a faster clock speed or a more sophisticated processor. In other words, don't pay extra for an external cache. Also, don't be hoodwinked by half-baked implementations. They are everywhere. If the cache isn't built directly into the CPU—as it is with many 486 chips and some 386 processors—make sure it's based on "static random access memory" (SRAM), which is far faster than standard memory. Also, better caches are driven by Intel's nimble 82385 controller chip. You don't need more than 128K of cache for a 386-based PC, no more than 256K for a 486-based system. Larger sizes don't make your computer go faster.

One other hot-rod technology merits some attention: Intel's clock-doubling chip, the DX2. Currently available only for Intel 486-based systems (though soon to appear in other chips from other manufacturers), the DX2 doubles the internal clock speed of 25 MHz or 33 MHz processors. In a 25-MHz system, for example, the CPU processes data at 50 MHz, but traffics the information at the standard 25 MHz. In a 33-MHz system, the chip churns data at 66 MHz. Real-world performance of DX2-based systems ranks a little higher than midway between the internal and external clock speeds, but it depends mightily on the program it's running.

You can buy the chip yourself and pop it into the "OverDrive" socket in your 486 system, or you can buy a PC with the chip already built in. Intel designed the DX2 as a canny way for either a manufacturer or a consumer to increase an old computer's speed tremendously. Be aware, however, that long-term reliability is a formidable issue with this processor owing to the peculiarities of its technology. We won't know for a year or so. If you buy one today, make sure it comes with a "heat sink," a ribbed plate that fits over the processor to dissipate heat. The DX2 gets scorchingly hot, and many PCs may lack adequate fans to prevent disaster.

There are hidden costs with this processor. To make it sail full mast, you'll need fast video and memory subsystems: an external cache and a graphics coprocessor (see "Video Adapters and Monitors" later in this chapter) at the least. These add several hundred dollars to what is, after all, an investment in convenience. It's typical of most all high-end PC components. The obsessive hunger for speed can squander more of your dollars than just about any aspect of computing. Just when your racer seems tricked to the max, one more whizzie or what's-it appears on the market promising yet another performance boost. Speed is a bad drug.

Memory (RAM)

As with choosing a processor, the amount of memory or RAM (random access memory) you need depends on how gluttonous your software is. Most DOS-based word processors, simple databases, and spreadsheets can live on a lean 1 or 2 megabytes. Factor in a graphics program, desktop publishing, sophisticated math, or computer-aided design programs, and you'll need two or three times this amount just to load the software, never mind getting work done. Windows programs, which by definition are graphics programs (even a Windows word processor), require at least 4 megabytes of RAM and will greedily gobble more if it's available.

Although the software you run should dictate the specific amount of memory you'll need, you can gauge this indirectly by the CPU that drives your PC:

- 8088 PCs need 640K. This is sufficient for word processing and simple text-based software.
- 80286 PCs need 1 MB. This runs almost any DOS-based software that doesn't require graphics or Windows. By the way, if your software requires more than 1 megabyte of RAM, you're a good candidate for a 386 CPU (and 386SX-based systems typically cost as little as $100 more than 286-based PCs).
- 386s and 486s need at least 4 MB to run Windows, more for memory-craving Windows programs. Desktop publishing, for example, needs at least 6 MB; get 8 MB if you can spare an extra $100.

Of course, your system may not come dressed with as much memory as you'd like. RAM costs less than $45 per megabyte on the open market (dealers, of course, pay one-third this or less), and prices are steadily dropping. A dealer who charges more than $50 per megabyte is swindling you. Ditto for high installation charges. Memory chips snap onto motherboards like Lego pieces. If your dealer's installation charge is more than $20, roll your eyes, then purse your lips in a "You've-*got*-to-be-kidding" glare. He'll back down.

Once you determine how much RAM you need, you should consider some other specifics: whether your PC uses SIMMs or DIPs, whether it uses standard or proprietary memory, and what your upgrade alternatives are.

SIMMS or DIPS?

Memory chips come in three shapes: DIPs, SIPPs, and SIMMs. PCs manufactured around 1986 and earlier require memory chips called DIPs (dual-inline packages). They're a hassle. Adding just 1 megabyte of memory to your system means adding nine separate chips to your motherboard, each no bigger than a Chiclet. The chips plug into the motherboard with hair-fine wire pins that are easily bent or broken. They make upgrading your PC's memory (or worse, replacing defective chips) a pain.

If the computer you're eyeing uses DIPs (as all 8088s and many older 286s and 386SXs do), either make sure you get a rock bottom price on it, or better yet, look elsewhere. PCs that use them are closeout material.

Newer computers use SIMMs (single-inline memory modules), which combine the nine DIPs onto a single wafer. SIMMs slide easily into a socket on the motherboard, and you can add them without special tools. (Another kind of memory chip, called a SIPP (single-inline pin plug), is similar to a SIMM except that it uses pins instead of a slot connector. Since these chips are only slightly less problematic than DIPs, they should be avoided too.)

SIMMs come in capacities ranging from 256-kilobyte to 16-megabyte chip sizes, though not all PCs will accept all capacities. In general, look for a system that accepts 1 MB (or larger) SIMMs and that comes with 1 MB (or larger) SIMMs installed. This will make adding additional memory or replacing defective chips later a lot easier. (See Chapter 7.)

SIMMs range in speed from 53 to 120 nanoseconds (nsec). The lower the number, the faster the memory. For 8088- and 286-based PCs, memory speed is largely irrelevant, but for 386- and 486-based PCs, fast memory becomes palpable. The most common speeds for 386 and 486 PCs is 70 and 80 nsec. Don't pay more for a system with faster memory, but always get the fastest you can.

Make sure that the memory sits on the motherboard, rather than on an add-in card. Add-in memory slows down your system. Besides, it's a flag for obsolescence and bad design.

Proprietary or Standard RAM?

Because the mark-up on memory can be quite lucrative to PC makers, many better known companies design their systems to hog-tie customers to their design of memory. For years, Compaq, AST, NEC, and IBM, among others, forced you to buy their namesake memory chips, insisting that their proprietary design ran faster and more reliably. Wrong. Proprietary saves neither time nor repairs—but it will cost you a bundle, typically three to four times the cost of industry standard SIMMs.

To find out if the memory is proprietary, ask the dealer its price for upgrades. More than $100 per megabyte (including installation charges) means it's proprietary—or that you're being mugged. Either way, head for the door.

Upgrade Insurance

One last consideration is upgradeability. Make sure that you can add at least 8 megabytes (16 or more is better) directly to the motherboard should you need it. A 386-based system should hold at least 16 megabytes (32 or more is better). If you have to add this much memory to your machine, you're probably running the wrong software. However, such upgradeability ensures that your machine was designed within the last year or two.

Hard Drives

Like any good warehouse, a hard drive must, above all, protect your goods and then let you move stuff in and out of it quickly and efficiently. That's all it does. Bury yourself in volumes of snoozy technical articles about hard drive "latency," "zone-bit recording," "data coding," "caching intelligence," and other natter, and you may learn enough technobabble to impress your computer-illiterate friends, but you won't learn how to select the right drive. Only four things matter on this score: reliability, capacity, performance, and price.

Reliability

Hard drive technology today is extraordinarily sophisticated (hence the tide of technical articles about it). That they function at all is a marvel given their dainty size. Their vast gains in reliability are utterly astounding. Unfortunately there's no way to evaluate, distinguish, or otherwise divine one drive's reliability from another. Hard drives crash suddenly—often without notice. Drive failure is computing's most common catastrophe. Curse the spirits on a rainy Tuesday in March, and your drive dies. There's seldom a better explanation.

The name of the manufacturer won't tell you anything about reliability. Drive makers buy, relabel, and then sell each others products more promiscuously than any other segment of the industry. Slicker salespeople will point out the drive's "mean time between failure" (MTBF) estimate, the published number of hours a drive should operate before crashing—according to the drive maker. Pull out your calculator, however, and quite often you'll discover that the drive is estimated to last longer than the company has been in business.

MTBF is not arrived at through rigorous testing. (Officials from hard drive companies typically smile in disparaging silence when asked how they calculate their MTBF.) It's a highly misleading number, even for comparison purposes. Give it not an ounce of weight in your purchase decisions. Instead, just make sure the drive is covered by your dealer's warranty (see "Warranty, Service, and Support" later in this chapter). Everything else rides on providence.

Capacity

Running out of disk space is a pathetically disheartening experience. You'll kick yourself for the flintiness that made you select a small drive when you bought your system. Adding a second drive is expensive and bothersome. It devours an afternoon and will make you crabby.

Today's software applications insinuate themselves into ever larger spaces on a hard disk. Common sense suggests that the volume of information you want your PC to store can only grow; it never diminishes. A universal truth in the computer press maintains that more drive capacity is always better, but this platitude is a one-armed bandit.

Most data files on a drive ultimately end up as archives, never touched except as references. There are ways to pack this information into less space (see Chapter 7). If you perpetually add new software applications to your system on a monthly basis, say, perhaps you should reexamine the way you work. There are probably better uses for your time and money.

The capacity you need depends on the number and type of applications you use, which is loosely reflected in the type of CPU you've chosen. Bear in mind that graphics files (including desktop publishing) and database files slurp three to four times as much disk space as text or spreadsheet files. Also, many Windows programs now arrogantly appropriate as much as 25 megabytes of drive acreage. These are ballpark drive capacities that typically suit each processor family:

Processor Family	Drive Capacity (megabytes)
8088	20–40
80286	30–80
80386	60–120
80486	120–300

Performance

A slow hard disk will dog a fast CPU like nothing else can. On the other hand, lightning-fast hard drives tend to command unjustifiably lofty prices. Though drive makers crow tirelessly the intelligence of the cache on their drives or their unique single-platter architectures, the scheme behind a drive's performance doesn't make a twit of difference. All that matters is how fast the thing reads and write data.

Judge a drive's performance first by its "average access time," the time the drive takes to locate both the right track on which a piece of requested information is stored and the specific place on the track where the information lies. It's usually described in milliseconds (msec). Just as important as access times are "transfer rates," the speed with which the drive can deliver the information from the disk platters to the CPU, as described in megabytes per second.

Always look at these numbers *together*. Drive makers and dealers alike quite often tout a drive's fast access times with no mention of the transfer rate—a very common ruse in computer advertisements. Unfortunately, fast access plus a slow transfer rate gives you slow performance.

The lower the access time, the better. Manufacturers fudge their numbers, of course, but generally not by much. Just make sure that your dealer quotes the *access time*, not the *seek time*, a convenient confusion that makes a drive appear faster than it is. Consider the following access time guidelines:

Processor Family	Access Time (milliseconds)
8088	<80
80286	40–28
80386	<20
80486	<20

Meanwhile, the *higher* the transfer rate, the better. Use these rates as guidelines:

Processor Family	Minimum Transfer Rate (MB per second)
8088	0.8
80286	4
80386	4
80486	4

Transfer rates depend on the drive's interface, the way it speaks to the computer. There are four types of interfaces, only two of which truly concern most users: ST506 and IDE. For an 8088 PC, an ST506 drive is perfectly fine. Despite its low capacity (typically only 10–20 MB) and slow speeds, it's cheap to manufacture and will not bog the 8088 CPU.

Not so any other family of processors. Consider an IDE (integrated drive electronics) drive for 286-based PCs and better. IDE drive performance now approaches that of more sophisticated and troublesome SCSI (small computer system interface) drives, and the IDE helped nail the now-moribund ESDI (enhanced small device interface) standard. Tremendous gains in reliability and economies of manufacturing have made the IDE's price/performance the best you'll get.

A dealer trying to liquidate an old ESDI drive or yearning to sell you an expensive SCSI drive may allude vaguely to compatibility problems with IDE. These snags vanished six years ago. IDE compatibility is virtually universal.

One final note about drive interface performance: yes, SCSI is faster than IDE. It also squeezes more capacity from smaller drives, supports very-large capacity (650 MB or larger) drives, and offers other benefits as well. It's ideal for PCs that function as network file servers and for some very high-powered scientific and engineering applications. However, SCSI is a free-floating standard with a half-dozen variations. It's expensive. It can be insanely difficult to make work with your system and peripherals. Furthermore, for most DOS applications, its advantages amount to zip.

If your drive's too sluggish, add a software disk cache. It duplicates part of the information on your hard drive to memory (RAM), which in turn shovels information to your CPU far faster than a hard disk. Like a memory cache, disk caches try to anticipate your program's requests for data. They're both larger and more versatile than RAM disks, but be aware that disk caches can present incompatibilities with some applications. Don't pay extra for one.

Microsoft includes a disk cache called SMARTDRV.SYS with DOS 5.0 (or higher) and Windows. Both commercial and shareware disk caches are available as well, but you might have to add memory to your system to take advantage of them. You can also add a caching disk controller, which is an add-in card that can cost as much as $1,800. Besides their obscene expense, caching controllers aren't noticeably faster than simple software caches. They're whizzies.

Price

Drive pricing is a cinch. For comparison purposes, you'll want to calculate the price per megabyte, which can range from a sweet $4.50 to a galling $9.00, with $5.50 per megabyte a reasonable deal. Even if your system comes with a 60-MB hard drive, say, and $150 extra buys you the optional 80-MB drive, the cost per megabyte comes to a rather lofty $7.50. Negotiate this downward—or shop elsewhere. Also, remember that speed costs. Be willing to pay $.50 more per megabyte for a drive with access times under 18 msec. Be ready to pay $1.00 more per megabyte for access times under 15 msec.

Video Adapters and Monitors

With so much hype surrounding system speed, it's easy to overlook the item you'll actually spend your day looking *at*: the monitor. Make sure it's included in the system price. When it's not listed in the ad copy, expect to lay out a few hundred more than the price quoted.

A display that's out of focus or that flickers makes working at the computer akin to passing idle hours with your least favorite in-law. Be aware that cheesy monitors quite often accompany otherwise respectable systems. A few tips should help you recognize the signs of chintz.

Display Size

A monitor's size, referred to in inches, measures the diagonal length of the display. Basic monitors range from 13 to 15 inches. A few systems now ship with 16- or 17-inch monitors, but you'll pay between $1,000 and up to $3,000 for the luxury. You'll want one only if you run high-resolution graphics, typical of engineering and scientific programs. Monitors with 19-, 20-, and 21-inch displays used for professional desktop publishing and very sophisticated graphics programs start in the $2,500 neighborhood. They move uptown quickly from there.

Incidentally, the advertised display size refers to the size of the glass tube, not the size of the image you'll see. Subtract 1 to 2 inches from the official number to estimate the actual image size.

VGA, Super VGA, or XGA?

Closely related to display size is image resolution, which is measured in pixels, where each pixel represents one dot of light on your screen. Manufacturers express resolution as the number of pixels displayed horizontally and vertically on a monitor. Thus the most common graphics resolution, VGA, displays 640 by 480 pixels. Virtually all PC software supports this resolution.

Many newer monitors, however, also support so-called Super VGA, a nebulous term that encompasses any resolution above 640 by 480, including 800 by 600, 1024 by 768, and even 1280 by 1024 pixels. Monitors that can support more than one video resolution are called "multifrequency" displays.

Unless your video card, monitor, *and* software support these higher resolutions, however, you can't use them. Generally only sophisticated desktop publishing, computer-aided design, and graphics software (that demand a lot of detail) take advantage of them. For most mainstream software, VGA is just ducky.

Windows and the applications that run under it are possible exceptions. Windows can support 800 by 600 resolutions—and higher. If your monitor and video card also support these higher resolutions, you can cram 50 percent more information on a screen. That is, several applications are visible at once. In one corner of your screen, you can work on a letter to your accountant in a word processor. In the other corner, you can display some expenses in a spreadsheet that you intend to reference in your letter. Hardly a revolution in personal productivity, but higher resolutions under Windows bring convenience to your work. Monitors and video cards that support higher resolutions typically cost only a few hundred dollars more than their VGA cousins. Just make sure they're capable of 800 by 600 pixels or higher.

In the world of DOS and Windows, resolutions higher than this rarely make sense. The next step, 1024 by 768 pixels, is only practical on expensive 17-inch (or larger) monitors. Otherwise, text and thin lines disappear. Monitors and adapters that support this resolution cost as much or more than the computers that drive them.

Older CGA, Hercules, and EGA graphics standards still occasionally appear in advertisements (particularly with 8088-based

PCs), even though they're nigh dead. Hardware manufacturers no longer build to these standards, and many makers won't even support the products they've already built to these standards. Nevertheless, you may find a tremendous deal on an 8088-based PC with a CGA or EGA video card and monitor. Make sure you inspect the display before you buy. Depending on your tastes, CGA can be perfectly adequate for word processing, or terrifically hard on the eyes. Monitors and adapters that support VGA (particularly monochrome ones) are only slightly more expensive and produce infinitely sharper images.

Color or Monochrome?

Most software today yearns for a color display. Menus pop out in chartreuse, error signals flash in crimson, teal patinas wash background screens making them restful to the eye. This isn't to say, however, that software *requires* color, but as PC luxuries go, it's a pretty common one. It is, after all, how we see the world.

Color monitors are relatively expensive. For less than $100, you can get a monochrome VGA monitor that runs all the software a VGA monitor does except that it translates colors into 64 shades of gray. The lowliest VGA monitor costs $250–$400. Monochrome monitors also produce much sharper images than their colorful equivalents. For word processing and simple spreadsheets, monochrome is easier on both the eyes and the wallet.

Monochrome monitors come with green, amber, or white pixels. The color you choose is a matter of personal preference, but white is the most popular.

Otherwise, get a color monitor. They're far more pleasing, far more fun. The colors a monitor can display depend on the video card that drives it. In some cases the video circuitry doesn't come on a "card," but is integrated onto a PC's motherboard. There's no difference in performance. Just make sure that if the circuitry is on the motherboard, you can disable it to install a video board of your own choosing later on.

Video cards come in four flavors:

- 4-bit cards display up to 16 colors simultaneously.
- 8-bit cards display up to 256 colors simultaneously.

- 15-bit and 16-bit cards display about 32,000 and 65,000 colors, respectively.
- 24-bit cards (also called true color cards) display up to 16.7 million colors for photo-quality images—about as many as the human eye can discern.

More isn't necessarily better, however. Most software programs need no more than 256 colors. More than this, and your screen often slows to a crawl as the video card labors to generate them. Even if a board supports 32,000 colors or more, it may not be able to produce them at all resolutions. Just make sure the card comes with software drivers that support all the color levels at all the resolutions you plan to use.

Video cards that support 16.7 million colors are designed for very high-end color graphics, cost more than a good PC, require sophisticated 17- or 20-inch monitors, and are generally sold separately (see Chapter 7).

Video memory also affects the colors a card can display. Most cards come with 512K of RAM right on the card. This supports 256 colors at standard VGA (640 by 480) resolution but only 16 colors at higher resolutions. For 256 colors or more at all resolutions, you'll need a board with at least 1 MB.

Video Speed

For software that runs under DOS, video speed is unimportant. Switch to Windows, however, and a fast video card makes as much or more of a difference than a fast processor. Two things that affect video speed are the type of video memory and whether or not the board uses a coprocessor.

Video cards generally come with either DRAM ("dynamic" RAM), which is similar to the memory found on your PC's motherboard, or VRAM (video RAM), which is specifically designed for video. VRAM is marginally faster than DRAM, but it's also a lot more expensive. Don't pay more for it.

A few systems now ship with video cards called "accelerators" or more specifically, "Windows accelerators." They include their own processor chip designed to take over some of the graphics functions that slow down your PC's CPU. You'll pay a few hundred dollars more for an accelerator, but they can raise the speed with which Windows redraws screens three to ten times. If you work only in Windows, an accelerator is a worthwhile investment.

"Local bus," another video technology, boosts video zip by moving data to the screen via quick and clever shortcuts. There's no standard implementation of local bus, however, and not all local bus designs improve graphics performance. Eventually all PCs may use some form of the technology, but today it's someone else's science project. Stick to graphics accelerators; they're cheaper and faster, and they work in any PC.

The Image Test

You'd never guess it from monitor reviews, but how an image *appears* is important. Plan to spend some time looking at a monitor before you buy. Check first for glare. The unit should come with a tilt-and-swivel base for adjusting its angle. It should also have controls for adjusting the size, image, and positioning of the image—preferably on the front where they're reachable.

Examine the text. Is it sharp and focused, even when displaying small type? Next look at geometrical figures. Rectangles should be perfectly parallel to the sides of the monitor. Circles should be round, not oval. Also, look for flicker, a wavering of the image. It is the stuff of migraines and nausea. You can check flicker by studying the monitor out of the corner of your eye—particularly when a white image illuminates the screen.

A little trick for testing a monitor's durability is to rap the thing on its side—hard (try not to be distracted by your salesperson's bulging eyes and gaping jaw). If the image quivers, the magnets and wiring may not be well designed or manufactured.

If you can't examine the monitor (when buying by mail-order, for example), a few questions will tip you off about image quality. For example, a monitor with a "vertical refresh rate" of 70 hertz or higher is fairly flicker-free, even to sensitive eyes. The "refresh rate" describes how often a screen image is redrawn or refreshed. Make sure that your video card supports the higher refresh rates. Also, make sure the monitor is "non-interlaced." Interlacing is a cheap way for a maker to boost resolution—at the expense of screen flicker and image quality.

Finally, a monitor's "dot pitch" can give you clues about how sharp its image will be. Expressed in millimeters (mm), it refers to the distance between the dots or pixels on the screen. A smaller dot pitch produces a sharper image; look for 0.31 mm or less.

However you buy your monitor, inspect it carefully the moment you uncrate it. Monitors are sensitive, and carting them around can knock the color guns out of alignment. Make sure you can return yours for any reason whatsoever.

One final issue to consider is radiation. Studies about the effects of monitor emissions are inconclusive. If you're worried about radiation, look for a monitor that meets MPR-2, the Swedish low-emissions guidlines. You shouldn't have to pay extra for it.

System Design

The modularity of DOS PCs makes them inexpensive, expandable, configurable, cheaply fixable, wonderfully useful, ugly machines. Know which components to stock your box with, and you're mostly home free. PC design is astonishingly generic. However, even within its cookie-cutter format, makers have found ways to fleece you. Here are a few things to watch out for.

Architecture

Motherboard architecture typically refers to the system bus, the highway within the computer along which data travels between the CPU, the video card, the hard disk, and other components. Three architectures now dominate DOS PCs: Industry Standard Architecture (ISA), Extended Industry Standard Architecture (EISA, pronounced "Eesa"), and MicroChannel Architecture (MCA).

In the late 1980s, the computer press made a tremendous and tedious fuss about the impending war between EISA and MCA architectures. Whole forests died for the magazine pages used in dramatic speculation about which architecture would finally supplant the aging ISA. The predicted blood-bath, however, never materialized. The vast technical differences between bus architectures amount to so many pencil shavings in terms of real-world benefit, and consumers wisely ignored the issue. The world did not stop.

Some day advanced architectures such as EISA or MCA will make a difference in the work we do (multimedia applications will be the first to urge these buses along), but today they simply slap $300 to $1,200 onto the price of a system as a vague and unlikely hedge against obsolescence. Your best bet is to stick with the simple ISA architecture, unless you find an irresistible deal on a 386- or 486-based EISA system. For the time being, forget MCA entirely. It is IBM's proprietary design. Overpriced and inferior to EISA, MCA is IBM's sad, petulant effort to maintain at least some influence over the computer industry.

Be wary of said irresistible deals on EISA systems. Quite often a manufacturer will offer an EISA and an ISA version of otherwise identical machines for the same price. Begin dissecting the components, however, and you'll likely find that the EISA version skimps on cache, memory, disk storage, the monitor, or some other component. EISA costs more to build, plain and simple. One way or another those costs fall to you.

Expansion Slots

Inside your box, you'll find several rows of adapters, called "expansion slots," into which you can plug expansion cards (see Chapter 5), for scanners, extra memory, fax boards, and other attachments. Typically, the bigger the PC's metal box, the more slots in the machine. Regardless of how many slots are advertised, however, you should find out how many are *available*. Some machines come preconfigured with video cards and other boards already occupying slots. Make sure your system has at least three 16-bit slots free. It's all the expansion you're likely to need.

Floppy Drives

The computer industry wants desperately to kill off the wide 5¼-inch floppy diskette in favor of the now-standard, hard-plastic-coated 3½-inch variety, which is more compact and durable, but the bigger floppy refuses to die. At least once in the life of every computer user will come the absolute need for that 5¼-inch drive. Your system should come with the smaller floppy drive as standard equipment. The additional larger drive makes a terrific point for haggling prices. Don't pay more than $100 for it, try to get it for free, and settle somewhere between the two.

Keyboard

A cheap keyboard can help a system maker lob $100 or more off
production costs. It's an obvious corner to cut. At retail, keyboards
cost between $31 and $260. Price has absolutely nothing to do
with keyboard quality (some of the best boards you'll find cost
less than $50). If you're dissatisfied with the board that comes
with your system, shop around.

The layout, pressure, and travel (the distance the keys move) of
a keyboard should suit your particular typing habits. In this re-
gard, brochures and sales hype won't tell you anything. In addition, pay attention to the clatter a keyboard makes, which can
become a form of water torture if you're sensitive. Give some
thought to the slope and curvature of the board; many wrist and
finger aches develop from these, rather than from the pressure
of the keys themselves. Above all, insist on a 30-day full refund
policy with any keyboard you buy. Only by pounding on the
thing for a full day will you truly be able to evaluate it.

Drive Bays

Once your system has a hard drive and two floppy drives installed, simply make sure your box has one "full-height" drive
bay free to add a second hard drive or internal CD-ROM drive
should you need it later on.

Ports

All DOS PCs should come with one parallel port (to which you'd
connect a printer, typically) and at least one serial port (for a
mouse or modem). Some systems come with either two serial
ports or one serial port and a "PS/2 mouse port." The additional
port should not cost extra, but don't forgo a system because it
lacks one. They cost about $30 and require an expansion slot.

Size and Construction

Larger PCs generally house more drive bays and expansion slots
than "slimline" or "small footprint" models that sit primly on
your desk. The extra space of larger PCs makes them easier to
work on. (Small PCs may require you to remove the power sup-

ply, expansion slots, or a disk drive to add memory or a math coprocessor. This is perturbing.). Larger boxes are also more generic and hence house more generic components. Replacement components are readily—and cheaply—available. Buy a PC in a dainty box, however, and you may find that it requires odd-sized components; you'll pay dearly for them.

Good construction shows up in computers that come with cross beams to reinforce the walls of the unit (you'll have to remove the cover to see them). Make sure that the cover slides on and off with ease and that it fits snugly against the unit when you screw it down. This ensures proper air flow for cooling.

Software

Computers can't run without DOS (disk operating system) or some other operating system, the software that tells your PC how to work with other software. Make sure that it's included in the cost of any PC you buy—and that it's the most recent version.

The 386 and later-generation PCs should also include a copy of the latest version of Windows and a mouse. Microsoft nearly gives both away to PC dealers, so don't pay extra for it.

Many systems also come bundled with other software. It's often junk. Try to get your dealer to substitute some software you'll actually use, or negotiate a hefty discount on other software you're eyeing. If you're interested in the software that's included, make sure they're full working versions of the programs—not merely crippled demo versions.

Warranty, Service, and Support

Given their choice, PC makers would ship their products out the door like cheap telephones: idiot-proofed electronics that you throw away when they break. Providing service, warranty, and technical support costs money—in an industry that earns pennies on the dollar. It's little wonder that both dealers and manufacturers provide these "extras" begrudgingly, if at all. Yet these are the qualities that truly distinguish one brand of computer from another. In many cases you may have to fight for them. Use the following rules as your battle creed:

Rule 1: If it doesn't come with at least a one-year warranty, don't buy it. PCs are tremendously reliable. Most defects appear in the first month of service. Afterward, only wear and tear forces repairs. So why, then, insist on a full year of coverage? A dealer who won't take such easy odds is hiding something from you.

Rule 2: The warranty should cover *everything*. Grill your dealer about the terms of the warranty to ensure that it covers the entire system: hard drive, monitor, video card—the whole enchilada. This means parts *and* labor on all repairs. Let your dealer point out exactly where in the written warranty you'll find this guarantee.

Rule 3: The warranty is your dealer's problem. Shun dealers who try to slough responsibility for the warranty onto the manufacturer instead of honoring it directly. You'll wind up in repair purgatory, and only a lawyer can set you free.

Rule 4: Get the dealer to install it. This includes extra memory, software, fax/modem cards—anything you buy with your PC. Let the dealer worry about setting interrupt switches or negotiating hardware conflicts. You should be able to take a PC home, plug it in, and start hacking.

Rule 5: Ask about the turnaround time on repairs. Then perform a little undercover work. Call the dealer anonymously from home and ask how long it will take to repair a dead floppy drive on a system you bought from the company. Salespeople will promise anything; repair technicians are realists. If a repair so simple takes more than a few days, keep looking.

Rule 6: Look for a dealer who replaces (rather than repairs) dead components. If your monitor or hard drive fails in the first month, you don't want to have to wait for the dealer to send the monitor or drive back to the manufacturer to be rebuilt. Better shops swap out a dead component immediately and square with the component maker on their own time. If you bought the PC by mail, some companies can ship out replacement parts overnight and talk you through repairs on the phone—this is the best arrangement. Others require you to return the part before receiving a replacement— or worse, make you return the entire PC. Both are unnecessary bureaucratic delays.

Rule 7: Service contracts are overrated. Many dealers offer the option of onsite service contracts with the PCs they sell. If it's free, fine. If not, think hard before you shell out for it. Onsite service is typically limited to certain geographical locations—make sure you live in an area that qualifies. Also, "onsite service" isn't necessarily convenient. You may have to wait around for hours (days) for a repairperson to show. Be sure to read the fine print; many service contracts only cover a few components.

Rule 8: Promises of unlimited tech support are worthless if you can't get through on the phone. Make sure technical support is free and unlimited (good for as long as your PC or your dealer remains in business). Ask about the support office's hours of operation (weekends? after 5:00?). Test it by calling at times when you're likely to need help. Check their expertise by posing questions to which you already know the answers. If it's not a local shop, make sure the 800 number is good for tech support, not just sales.

Rule 9: Always pay with a credit card. It's the best leverage you have against a dealer who turns out to be a sleazeball. You get 60 days to stop payment if a dealer recants on a service agreement, sells you a lemon, or fails to deliver. Despite the sign in your dealer's window, no sale is final if you pay with plastic. It has other advantages as well: some credit card companies will double the warranty on your purchase or cover the cost of replacing your new toy if you drop it enroute to your car.

Rule 10: If you can't return it, don't buy it. A dealer who bills all sales as final or offers only store credit on refunds is likely caught in a cash squeeze. The company may not be around when you need service or support. Don't get soaked by someone else's financial straits.

Rule 11: You're allowed to change your mind. Insist on a 30-day unconditional money-back guarantee. Weeks after your purchase you may decide you don't like your new PC (the monitor flickers after an hour's work; the fan's too noisy; the keyboard feels like Jell-O). You should be able to take it back, no questions asked. Get this guarantee from the dealer in writing and make sure it's unconditional. Many outfits only accept returns on defective equipment or charge a 15 percent restocking fee for returns—a pirate's toll.

ALPHABET SOUP

Average Access Time: Measured in milliseconds, average access time reflects the amount of time it takes for a hard drive to locate and retrieve data on a hard disk.

The Lowdown: For this number to mean anything, you also have to consider a hard drive's transfer rate. A slow transfer rate can drag down even the fastest access time.

Benchmarks: Tests used by manufacturers and computer magazines to measure system or PC component speed.

The Lowdown: Because they tend to measure imperceptible differences in speed, they're meaningless and irrelevant. Ignore them.

Caching Disk Controller: An add-in card that speeds hard disk performance by copying data from your hard drive into special memory chips on the board.

The Lowdown: Caching controllers are outrageously expensive and often present compatibility problems with your drive. Software caches are far cheaper and work at least as well.

CPU (Central Processing Unit): The brains or main chip in a computer. The five main families of CPU chips are the 8088, 286, 386, 486, and 586.

The Lowdown: There's no such thing as Gucci for CPUs; choose a chip by its family and clock speed, not its brand name.

Clock Speed: Measured in millions of cycles per second, or megahertz (MHz), clock speed determines how fast the CPU runs. Most system clock speeds range between 8 and 50 MHz.

The Lowdown: Never pay extra for a PC that runs only 5 MHz faster than a similar, cheaper system. The difference in speed is negligible. Also, the fastest clock speed in a family of processors tends to command an unnecessary premium.

Coprocessor: A processor or chip that performs calculations or instructions that assist a PC's main CPU. The most common coprocessors help with math and graphics calculations.

The Lowdown: To use a coprocessor, your software must be written to take advantage of it.

Disk Cache: A technology that speeds hard disk performance by copying part of the information on your hard drive to a special area of memory (RAM).

The Lowdown: Disk caches occasionally create incompatibilities with your software. Never pay extra for one.

Dot Pitch: The distance between the dots of light or pixels on a monitor expressed in millimeters.

The Lowdown: Usually (but not always), the smaller the dot pitch, the sharper the image. Ultimately trust your eyes, not the numbers. →

DIP (Dual-Inline Package): A memory chip found primarily in 8088 PCs and older 286 and 386 PCs.

The Lowdown: It's prehistoric, expensive, and fragile technology. Look for a system that accepts industry-standard SIMMs instead.

DRAM (Dynamic Random Access Memory): The type of memory that makes up a system's main memory or RAM. "Dynamic" means that as soon as you turn your PC's power off, all the data in memory vanishes.

The Lowdown: Don't pay extra for speed, but get the fastest memory possible (80 nsec or lower).

DX2: A chip technology that doubles the internal clock speed of a PC's CPU.

The Lowdown: A chip that processes data internally at 50 MHz doesn't deliver true 50 MHz performance because it communicates with the system's other components at 25 MHz. For full performance, the DX2 requires fast video and memory subsystems—its hidden costs. Also, the long-term reliability of this chip is questionable.

EISA (Extended Industry Standard Architecture): An advanced system bus design that moves data along a wide 32-bit data path (compared to the standard 16-bit ISA path found in most PCs).

The Lowdown: For now, few software programs can take advantage of the wider data path, and it adds $300 to $1,200 to a PC's price. You don't need it.

ESDI (Enhanced Small Device Interface): An older hard drive interface.

The Lowdown: R.I.P.

Expansion Slot: An adapter on a PC's motherboard that holds expansion cards such as internal modems, video cards, and drive controllers.

The Lowdown: Your PC should have at least three 16-bit expansion slots *available* for adding peripherals.

Interlacing: A video technique for boosting monitor resolution by only refreshing or redrawing every other line of an image.

The Lowdown: Interlaced monitors flicker; avoid them.

IDE (Integrated Drive Electronics): The most common hard drive interface. Its controller circuitry is built directly on the drive.

The Lowdown: It's fast, reliable and quiet; it's your best bet for a hard drive. Period.

ISA (Industry Standard Architecture): The most common system bus for DOS PCs today. It moves data along a 16-bit data path.

The Lowdown: It's almost always your best bet unless you write your own 32-bit programs.

Kilobyte: Abbreviated as KB, K, or Kbyte, 1 kilobyte equals 1,024 bytes. →

The Lowdown: One thousand kilobytes equals 1 megabyte.

Local Bus Video: A video design that boosts video speed by moving data to the monitor through several clever shortcuts.

The Lowdown: If you need better video performance, stick with a low-end graphics accelerator—it's cheaper. There's no standard yet for local bus video, and you may or may not get faster performance.

Math Coprocessor: Sometimes called a floating-point unit (FPU), a chip or processor that speeds up math and graphics calculations.

The Lowdown: Unless your software is written to take advantage of a math coprocessor, you won't see a performance gain.

Megabyte: A common unit of measurement for a PC's memory and hard drive capacity. It's also written as MB.

The Lowdown: 1,024 kilobytes equals 1 megabyte.

MCA (MicroChannel Architecture): IBM's proprietary system bus design that traffics data on a 32-bit data path.

The Lowdown: For now, don't even think about this one. It's an overpriced and inferior competitor to another 32-bit bus design, EISA.

MTBF (Mean Time Between Failure): A manufacturer's guess at the number of hours that will elapse before a hardware component fails.

The Lowdown: Many drives are predicted to live longer than their manufacturers have been in business. This number is typically an engineer's fantasy. Ignore it.

Motherboard: A computer's main circuit board that typically holds the processor, system memory, and other integrated circuits that drive your PC.

The Lowdown: The cleaner the motherboard (meaning the fewer chips, circuits, and resistors on the surface), the more advanced the design.

Pixel: Short for *picture element,* a pixel is a single dot of light on a computer monitor.

The Lowdown: A monitor's resolution is measured by the number of pixels it can display horizontally and vertically.

Parallel Port: A connector on a PC to which you typically attach a printer.

The Lowdown: Every PC should have one.

RAM (Random Access Memory): A computer's main memory expressed in K (kilobytes) or MB (megabytes).

The Lowdown: The amount of memory your system needs depends on your software's requirements. You'll need at least 4 MB to run Windows.

Refresh Rate: The speed at which a monitor's displayed image is redrawn by the video card. Both the monitor and video card must support the same refresh rates. →

The Lowdown: The higher the refresh rate, the less likely you'll notice flicker or a wavering of the onscreen image. Most people notice flicker if the refresh rate is below 70 Hz.

Seek Time: The time it takes a hard drive's read/write head to find the physical location of a piece of data on the disk. Seek time is only one component of access time.

The Lowdown: A drive's seek time tells you only how long it takes the drive to find the data—it doesn't include the time it takes to retrieve it. Many manufacturers publish the seek time, hoping you'll confuse it with access time.

Serial Port: A connector to which you typically attach a modem, mouse, or other peripheral to a PC.

The Lowdown: Every PC should have at least two (though a dedicated mouse port will suffice for one).

SIMM (Single-Inline Memory Module): A tiny circuit board with memory chips on it. SIMMs come in 512K, 1 MB, 2 MB, and 4 MB (and larger) chip sizes.

The Lowdown: The newest type of memory chip, SIMMs are inexpensive and simple to install. Look for a PC that accepts SIMMs in at least 1 MB sizes.

SIPP (Single-Inline Pin Plug): A memory chip similar to a SIMM except that it uses pins instead of a slot connector.

The Lowdown: An older memory design, SIPPs make adding memory a hassle. Avoid them.

SRAM (Static RAM): A very fast (and expensive) type of memory typically used in cache.

The Lowdown: You want it only for a cache.

ST506: An older, slow, low-capacity (10 to 20 megabytes) hard drive standard.

The Lowdown: It's fine for 8088 PCs but get IDE for later generation systems.

SCSI (Small Computer Systems Interface): Pronounced "scuzzy," an interface for connecting peripherals and hard drives to your PC.

The Lowdown: SCSI hard drives are fast, contentious, and, above all, expensive. It's a good interface for high-capacity hard drives used in network file servers, but for most applications it's not worth the premium.

Super VGA: A vague term for any video resolution above standard VGA (640 by 480 pixels), including 800 by 600, 1024 by 768, and 1280 by 1024 pixels.

The Lowdown: Ask for specifics about the resolutions that a monitor or video card supports before you buy.

System Bus: A shared data highway that connects different parts of a PC, including its CPU, video, and disk drive controller. There are three main bus designs: ISA, EISA, and MicroChannel. →

The Lowdown: For most people, ISA will do.

Transfer Rate: The speed at which a hard drive can deliver information from a hard disk's surface to the CPU, measured in megabytes per second.

The Lowdown: Always consider a drive's transfer rate with its access time; a fast access rate plus a slow transfer rate equals slow performance.

VGA (Video Graphics Array): The most common video graphics resolution, VGA displays 640 pixels horizontally and 480 pixels vertically on a monitor.

The Lowdown: Virtually all software supports this standard; for simple text-based DOS applications, it's also all you'll ever need.

VRAM (Video RAM): Memory designed specifically for video cards. VRAM is slightly faster than DRAM, the other kind of memory found on video cards.

The Lowdown: The slight performance gain from VRAM generally isn't worth the premium it commands.

XGA (Extended Graphics Adapter): Technically a term for the graphics adapter in IBM's 486 PCs, XGA is sometimes used as a general term for a resolution of 1024 by 768 pixels.

The Lowdown: 1024 by 768 pixels is only practical on a 17-inch monitor or larger—you'll go blind using this resolution on one of the 13- or 14-inch monitors that comes with most PCs. ❐

Shopper's Checklist

The questions that you ask your dealer depend on the chip that powers your PC. For each family of processors, our recommendations are as follows:

8088 PCs

Hard Drive
- ❑ 20 to 40 MB hard drive
- ❑ IDE or ST506 hard drive
- ❑ 80 msec or less hard drive access time
- ❑ 0.8 MB per second or higher hard drive transfer rate

Memory
- ❑ 640K of memory (RAM) included

Video

❑ Monitor/video card included

❑ Acceptable image quality (bright colors, sharp text, no glare)

80286 PCs

Hard drive

❑ 30 to 80 MB hard drive

❑ IDE hard drive

❑ 40 to 28 msec access time

❑ 4 MB per second or higher hard drive transfer rate

Memory

❑ 1 MB of memory (RAM) included

❑ Accepts industry standard SIMMs

❑ Motherboard accepts up to 8 MB of RAM

Video

❑ Monitor/video card included

❑ Monitor/video card support at least 640 by 480 (VGA) resolution

❑ Monitor/video card support 70 Hz refresh rates

❑ Monitor dot pitch less than 0.31 mm

❑ Acceptable image quality (bright colors, sharp text, no glare)

80386 and 80486 PCs

Hard drive

❑ 60MB to 140MB hard drive for a 386; 120 to 300 MB for a 486

❑ IDE hard drive

❑ 20 msec or less hard drive access time

❑ 4MB per second or higher hard drive transfer rate

❑ Optional external cache: Maximum of 64K external cache for 386s, 128K for 486s

Memory

❑ Minimum of 4 MB of memory (RAM) included

❑ 1MB SIMM memory chips (not DIPs) rated at under 80 nsec

- ❏ Accepts industry-standard SIMMs
- ❏ Motherboard should hold at least 16 MB (32 MB is better) of memory

Video

- ❏ Monitor/video card included
- ❏ Monitor/video card support at least 800 by 600 resolution
- ❏ Monitor/video card support 70 Hz refresh rates
- ❏ Monitor dot pitch less than 0.31 mm
- ❏ Acceptable image quality (bright colors, sharp text, no glare)
- ❏ 512K of memory on video card for 16 colors at 800 by 600 and 1024 by 768; 1 MB for 256 colors.
- ❏ Graphics accelerator optional

General Questions

Use the following information to formulate questions you can ask about all PCs, regardless of the chip that drives them:

Design

- ❏ ISA System Bus Architecture (generally)
- ❏ Two serial ports
- ❏ One parallel port
- ❏ Three free 16-bit expansion slots
- ❏ Both 3 1/2-inch and 5 1/4-inch floppy drives
- ❏ Acceptable keyboard
- ❏ At least one full-height drive bay available

Software

- ❏ DOS 5.0 included
- ❏ Microsoft Windows included with 386 and later CPUs

Service and Support

- ❏ One-year warranty
- ❏ Warranty covers parts and labor
- ❏ Warranty covers *all* components
- ❏ 30-day 100% money-back guarantee
- ❏ Accessible tech support (toll-free if it's not local)

Oh, boy! Think of all the time you can spend primping your documents with fonts that won't make your message any smarter, clearer, or more interesting.

Amazing? Hardly. Six pages per minute at 300 dpi is standard for any run-of-the-mill laser printer.

Ad man speak with forked tongue: At this price, you're certainly not getting PostScript. The word "compatible" is a tip that you'll be able to upgrade your printer to PostScript—which may cost as much as buying a PostScript printer outright.

G • E • N • U • I • N • E
PostScript-compatible

LASER PRINTER

You pay only
$799!!

Manufacturer's suggested price: $1,299

The LAX-1419 genuine Adobe PostScript-compatible printer from Laser, Inc., offers the full features of an office laser printer at a very personal price. At speeds of up to six pages per minute and up to 300 dpi output, the LAX-1419 is truly amazing!

The LAX-1419 gives you 22 built-in fonts as standard features. But that's not all. By combining fonts, character sizes, and enhancement modes such as bold italic, underline, subscript, and superscript, you can create over 5,500 type styles. It also comes with two slots for optional custom font cards.

Other features of the LAX-1419:

• 512K RAM expandable to 4.5MB
• HP LaserJet Series II and Diablo emulation
• Full 50-sheet paper tray with manual feed bypass
• Optional legal, A4, and envelope trays also available
• Small footprint—and weighs just 28 lbs!
• Easy front panel control with LCD display
• One year limited warranty

...and many other features too numerous to list.

To Order or Info Call USA1-500-333-2223

⬥ LASER INC

"Optional" means you'll pay dearly for it; "custom" means you're hog-tied to a manufacturer's prices. Beware of euphemisms like these. They have their fingers in your wallet.

Diablo emulation? This is like buying a stereo with an eight-track tape player. Is your salesperson wearing bell bottoms?

So you can't take your printer backpacking. Who totes these things around, anyway? Weight is a consideration only if you have to ship your printer to a repair house.

This claim plays on the widely held confusion between fonts and typefaces. Once you consider underline, bold, and italic versions of a font in its various point sizes, you wind up with only three or four typefaces.

CHAPTER 4

MOVABLE TYPE . . . . **Printers**

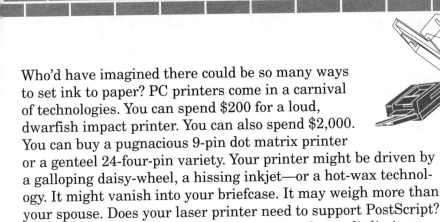

Who'd have imagined there could be so many ways to set ink to paper? PC printers come in a carnival of technologies. You can spend $200 for a loud, dwarfish impact printer. You can also spend $2,000. You can buy a pugnacious 9-pin dot matrix printer or a genteel 24-four-pin variety. Your printer might be driven by a galloping daisy-wheel, a hissing inkjet—or a hot-wax technology. It might vanish into your briefcase. It may weigh more than your spouse. Does your laser printer need to support PostScript? Should it emulate PCL 5? Did you mention the credit limit on your MasterCard?

The finer distinctions between printers dissipate in the clickety clack of marketing hype. Computer magazines will slavishly recommend the fastest, coolest, whizziest (most expensive) printer they can find. Or, in sober moments, they'll steer readers to a printer that seems vaguely well suited to a highly specific task, such as business charts or mailing labels. The assumption, one supposes, is that you'll buy separate printers for each of your printing chores. Computer magazines will bleed your wallet dry.

Printing needn't be so confusing—nor its costs so exorbitant. Design studios, engineering firms, and biotechnology laboratories may require special-purpose printers. But the vast majority of us merely need to print words and simple images. We can get by with a reliable general-purpose printer in one of two varieties: dot matrix or laser. Each technology suits a different set of needs; each has its own cost/benefit tradeoff. When selecting a general-purpose printer, keep seven (somewhat jaded) guidelines in mind.

1. **Daisy-wheels are dead.** For that matter, so are inkjets (except color inkjets). Daisy-wheels clatter and shake; inkjets require expensive, messy cartridges. Both technologies are slow and stubborn. As these dinosaurs succumb to faster, high-quality dot matrix and laser printers, they'll become more expensive to feed and repair. Don't get stuck with one.

2. **Emulation standards are mostly fog.** (See "Alphabet Soup".) Trouble yourself with only three: laser printers should emulate the HP LaserJet II (officially dubbed "PCL 4 emulation"); and dot matrix printers should provide IBM ProPrinter and Epson emulation. Ninety-nine percent of all software programs can print to these.

3. **Printer consumables cost more than the printer.** Ultimately you'll spend more for ribbons, toner, and other disposables than you paid for your printer. Calculate the per-page price of these consumables before you buy your printer. Use this number to compare printers as you shop. Make sure you can buy consumables from a third-party manufacturer. You'll get a better price. Also, you won't find yourself without supplies should your printer maker bite the dust.

4. **You *can* have too many fonts.** Most people don't need PostScript (see "PostScript and SanSkrit"). In fact, most people don't need more than a handful of typefaces—even for professional newsletters. The whizzie mindset that says otherwise has unleashed some of the most aggressively offensive, aesthetically jarring reports, presentations, and newsletters humankind has ever seen. Your message is clearest when the reader focuses on the meaning, rather than the appearance, of words. Devote your energies to content.

5. **The steering wheel costs extra.** Printer makers almost universally refuse to include the cable you'll need to hook their printer to your PC. Battle-worn to consumer wrath about this, computer salespeople stubbornly refuse to throw one in as part of the deal. You'll typically have to pay extra for it. If your dealer charges more than $15 for a parallel cable, glare menacingly (or sit in stony silence on the phone) until he or she flinches on the price.

6. **The proof is on the page.** Spec sheets and sales spiels won't tell you anything about print quality. Even if you're buying a printer by mail, first visit a showroom to look at a page of text and a page of graphics that the printer actually produced. Examine text for jaggedness in oval letters, unintended splotches on the page, and overall consistency. In graphics, look for subtle contrasts and evenness of shading.

7. **When you need a pro, hire a pro.** A $15,000 color PC printer can't even approximate the quality you'll get from a professional printing house. Don't kid yourself. If dazzling graphics are crucial, professional printing costs are worth it.

Lasers First

Laser printers now dominate PC printing for a single, predominant reason: value. You can buy a hearty laser printer today for $800 or less. In the bargain you get speed (four to six pages per minute), professional—and gorgeous—300 dots-per-inch text and graphics, highly consistent print quality, and mechanical reliability. You also get office tranquility, which you won't get from a screeching dot matrix printer.

Nothing beats a laser for publishing text in *any* professional document, from correspondence and reports to newsletters, fliers, and prospectuses. Coupled with the right software, lasers can produce sharp typeset-quality fonts, foreign language characters, mathematical symbols, musical notation—even bar codes. Much of this capability is gratuitous and can gobble endless office hours as you or your hirelings piddle with fonts or unusual characters. But should your sales report require an umlaut, if your project proposal needs an omicron or a treble clef, the ability is there. Ah, civilization.

Graphics, however, are another matter. Lasers render simple graphs and charts, line drawings (typical of comic strips, for example), logos, technical illustrations, and borders magnificently. Continuous tone graphics such as photographs come out ify. The results are grainy and unprofessional—but often passable. You certainly won't get any better results from a dot matrix printer.

Before you reach for your wallet, however, consider a few draw-backs to laser technology. For example, lasers use primarily letter- or legal-sized paper and transparencies. With some aggravation and trouble you can make a laser print an address on an enve-lope. But forget trying to print mailing labels (which can stick to the printer's heated drum and can cost hundreds of dollars in re-pairs), oversized spreadsheets or charts, thick, multipart forms, or other nonstandard media.

Also, per-page costs of laser toner cartridges are typically much higher than the price of dot matrix ribbons: two- to four-cents per page (laser) versus four pages to the penny (dot matrix). Over the life of a printer, that pennies' difference adds up to $4,000 or more. You can minimize toner costs by refilling old car-tridges (see "Recharge!"), but you'll never whittle their price down to the equivalent in dot matrix consumables.

Recharge!

The purchase price of a printer is only its initiation fee. The real dues come in the form of consumables.

Toner cartridges for laser printers fitted with Canon engines (which account for more than half of laser printers in the world) are particularly exorbitant. Purchased new, they cost $80 to $125 each—about $900 to $1,500 a year, conservatively. You can cut your outlays for toner by one-third to one-half by refilling used cartridges. In the bargain, you'll help the environment by salvaging the metal and plastic print drums and casings (dusted with toxic toner) that otherwise wind up in landfills.

Laser printers with Canon engines use a single cartridge that contains both the print drum and the black toner powder. (Printers with separate print drum and toner car-tridges are just as expensive to buy and won't save you money when you refill them.) A small guild of toner cartridge refillers has emerged in recent years. They take apart spent cartridges, refill them, and sell them at a fraction of the original price, typically $40 to $60 each.

To the chagrin of printer makers and dealers who profit handsomely from selling new cartridges, refilled units deliver the same clean, sharp pages as new ones. Better still, refilled cartridges typically contain as much as 20% more toner, up to 1,000 more printed pages per cartridge. →

Dealers Lie

All this refilling is bad business for your local computer retailer, of course. Greasier proprietors have even been known to suggest that refilled cartridges will damage your printer's works and thus void your warranty. This is poop. Refilled cartridges will not void your warranty.

When entrepreneurs first discovered that spent cartridges still had life in them, Canon and Hewlett-Packard threatened to void customers' warranties if they used refilled cartridges. Counterthreats of litigation over issues of free trade prompted the two printer giants to back down. Both bullies now claim that they'll only void the warranty if the damage is directly attributable to using refilled cartridges, an idle threat issued to save face. No printer maker has ever voided a warranty on that excuse.

Choosing a Refiller

When searching for a refiller, first ask how it replenishes toner. There are two essential methods. The cheapest and clumsiest is commonly called "drill, fill, and spill." The refiller drills a hole in the side of the cartridge, pours in the toner, and seals the hole. As the printer heats up, the seal over the hole can loosen, however, turning the innards of your printer into a coal mine. Few refillers still use this method, but don't take chances. Ask beforehand.

Better refillers first test the spent cartridge to be sure it can take a refill. Then they disassemble it and inspect the print drum for damage. Next, they clean the cartridge, lubricate it, refill it with fresh toner, and reassemble it. Good refillers also test their handiwork on a printer and send you a copy of the results. The cartridge should be sealed in a protective bag securely packed and should include a clean wiper blade.

Test a refiller by sending it a spent cartridge. Ask that the same cartridge be returned to you. Use the packing materials that the cartridge originally came with or ask the remanufacturer for packing instructions. Remember to include your wiper blade so that the remanufacturer can clean or replace the felt pad. Write down the serial number of the cartridge or make a small scratch on its plastic side so that you can verify that you've received your original back.

This method also lets you keep tabs on how many times the cartridge has been refilled. A good remanufacturer will refill cartridges no more than two or three times unless the photosensitive print drum is recoated or replaced. Recoating the print drum or replacing it makes the cartridge good for several more refills. →

Insist on a 100% unconditional money-back guarantee on the cartridge. If the refiller balks, go elsewhere. You should also get a written warranty against damage to your printer caused by the cartridge. Of course, cartridges can't damage the printer, and a good refiller will confidently extend such a guarantee. Finally, ask about discounts for high-volume repeat business.

There are more than 3,000 refillers in this country. You can usually find their ads in the classified section of local papers or in computer magazines. The International Cartridge Recycling Association (202-857-1154) in Washington, D.C., can also match you up with a refiller.

Reinking Dot Matrix Ribbons

Depending on how miserly you are, you can replenish the ink on your dot matrix printer ribbon as well. It's time consuming and messy, but penny-pinchers can get some satisfaction from the savings.

In the back of computer magazines you'll find ads for primitive contraptions called "ribbon reinkers." These artless devices apply a fresh layer of ink onto the fabric of a worn printer ribbon (and your fingers). They run $40 to $90 or more, depending on the width of the ribbons you use and whether it's an electric or manual reinker. Printer ribbons use a special kind of ink, a goopy substance that can be difficult to find. A 4-ounce bottle of ink, which is good for about 30 reinkings, will cost you $4 or more.

Ads for reinkers may falsely claim you'll never need to buy another ribbon. Don't believe this; ribbons wear out. Use 10 to 12 reinkings as a rule of thumb, even though a ribbon may hold up for as many as 75. A better solution to reinking is to reap the discount from buying new ribbons in bulk. After all, how cheap are you? ❏

Finally, lasers die. Unlike dot matrix printers (which last forever), four to five years of heavy use—about 100 pages a day—turns a laser printer into junk. The diodes go kaput; the printer engine is cheaper to replace than repair. This is true for lasers that cost $800—and for those that cost $10,000. Few printers work that hard, of course, but you should keep real depreciation values in mind when you buy.

Drawbacks notwithstanding, get one anyway. Laser technology is quick, competent, and civilized. But which model to choose? First sort out the variables.

Speed

Measured in pages per minute (PPM), the advertised print speed of a laser printer is typically a fib told by its manufacturer. It reflects how fast the printer produces a page of straight text. Graphics take longer—sometimes much longer. Even as a measure of text pages, advertised print speeds are often fudged by a half page or so per minute. No matter; you will not go gray waiting for any laser to produce your document. The hype surrounding printer speed is perpetuated by bored computer journalists. Ignore it.

This is why four- to six-page-per-minute lasers deliver the best value. You can pick one up for $700 to $1,000. Jump up a notch in speed to 8- to 10-PPM printers, and you'll typically pay at least one-third more. The extra hustle in an 8- to 10-PPM printer can be worth the added cost in any of the following situations:

1. Several PCs must share that printer.

2. You print pages and pages of graphics all the day long.

3. It's the company's money...who cares?

Memory

Use the following four rules of thumb to size up the memory your laser will need:

1. The printer should come with at least 512 kilobytes of memory in it as standard equipment (insist on this).

2. If you print full-page graphics, get 1 megabyte of memory for your printer.

3. If you make heavy use of soft fonts or if you use PostScript, buy 2 to 4 megabytes.

4. Don't let anyone talk you into buying more than 4 megabytes of memory. You won't need it.

Even if you buy a printer with only 512K, make sure you can add up to 2 megabytes later should your needs change. Also, ask whether the printer accepts the industry-standard "Single In-line Memory Modules" (SIMMs). Because you can buy this kind of memory from a variety of manufacturers, the price is typically cheaper (that is, about $80 per megabyte). Some printer makers force you to buy their own proprietary memory on circuit boards or chips—for up to $500 per megabyte. It's robbery.

Fonts

Another little deception that pops up in printer ads is the number of resident fonts (fonts hard-wired into the printer) a machine includes. Print your text in 14-point Times Roman, and it's one font. Print it in 10-point Times Roman, it's another. Print it in 10-point Times Roman underlined, it's yet a third. And so on. Thus the fourteen resident fonts that come with your laser printer might make up only two families of typefaces. When shopping for a printer, simply make sure it includes at least six resident fonts, then embarrass your dealer by asking for a list of the actual typefaces.

You can always add fonts of your own choosing as you need them. Nonresident fonts come in three varieties: bitmapped fonts on cartridges, bitmapped fonts as software (called soft fonts), and scalable fonts. All three can be tyrannically difficult to use with your word processor or other software. All three are almost always overused.

Font cartridges pop conveniently into a slot on the printer. They're faster than software-based fonts and don't require hard disk space or extra printer memory. Unfortunately they're more expensive and less versatile than soft fonts. But because you never know when you might inherit a font cartridge or find a seductive price on one, make sure your laser printer accepts HP LaserJet II cartridges, the de facto standard.

Soft fonts reside on your hard disk and must be loaded into printer memory each time you use them. They give you more fonts for the dollar than cartridges (though the extra hard disk space and memory they require are their hidden costs) and allow you to mix and match typefaces on a page with greater ease and sophistication. They improve greatly on cartridge fonts, but they can't match the versatility you'll get from scalable fonts.

Both cartridge and soft fonts are bitmapped, which means they're fixed in size. A scalable font, as the name implies, can be rendered in any point size (see "PostScript and SanSkrit"). You can get scalable fonts cheaply through font generators and on-the-fly font-scaling programs, but don't. They're complex, fussy, slow, and they hog hard disk space. If you truly need scalable fonts, get PostScript (or its equivalent, TrueImage). The extra costs are worth it.

Consumables

Even though printer makers routinely lie about how many pages their toner cartridges produce, they lie with fair consistency: expect *any* laser to produce 14% to 23% fewer pages per toner cartridge than what the manufacturer claims. Also, keep in mind that graphics use more toner than text uses.

There are a half-dozen designs for getting toner into a laser printer. None of them is pleasant; none of them is cheap. All fall generally into the following two categories, each with its tradeoffs:

1. Drum and toner as single unit: the most expensive, most convenient arrangement. Three minutes for installation, no mess.

2. Drum and toner as separate units (as many as five pieces): You needn't replace some parts as often as you replace others, which can save you money. However, independent toner canisters tend to spill over the innards of your printer during installation, creating a toxic mess.

When you buy your printer, ask whether a toner cartridge is included in the purchase price. Since cartridges cost as much as $130 a pop, this is worth quibbling over.

Nits

Finally, there are a few details, tricks, and shams to sniff out before buying a laser printer. One galling ruse many printer manufacturers pull is to provide a paper tray that holds only 50 sheets of paper. This keeps you scurrying to refill it every couple of hours like a trained hamster. Why so small a tray? Because the maker can then charge as much as $200 for a larger capacity "optional" tray—which is nothing more than a deeper-dish piece of molded plastic.

Likewise, ask about the warranty. Parts and labor should be covered for at least a full year; ask for two. Also, find out if you can get your machine repaired locally. Laser printers are heavy—between 25 and 40 pounds. Shipping costs to and fro mount quickly, especially if repairs require multiple trips to an office park in Sioux City or Singapore.

One final note: laser printers take up more desktop real estate than you might imagine. The dimensions cited in ads and brochures don't include paper trays that jut outward or unfolded racks for printed pages. Even if you're buying by mail-order, try to see the physical unit in a showroom before unsheathing your credit card.

PostScript and SanSkrit: Speaking in Tongues

When your PC hands your printer the words in a document or lines in a graphic, the printer must then dictate instructions for getting ink onto the paper in all the right places. Most lasers bark these directives in one of two tongues: Printer Command Language (PCL) and PostScript (or its clone called TrueImage). Most proletariat lasers speak a dialect of PCL, usually PCL 4; affluent printers speak PostScript or both languages.

The difference is considerable. PostScript can render complex graphics or contorted type (type wrapped around a photograph, for example, or rotated sideways on the page) in ways that make a conventional laser gag. PostScript lets you play with any number of special effects such as shading and shadowing text and graphics or bending and twirling your words and images at every conceivable angle.

PostScript can also scale fonts. Unlike the bitmapped fonts that PCL 4 printers use (in which each point size of each font is a separate and unchangeable file), scalable fonts contain all the instructions the printer needs to generate any size of a given typeface. You don't have to buy a separate font when you want 20-point Times Roman instead of your customary 12-point Times Roman. (PCL 5, the newest brogue in the PCL language can scale fonts, too, and it incorporates many of PostScript's graphics talents as well. However, your software must be able to take advantage of its capability, and few programs as yet do. Even fewer printers speak this language.)

PostScript has a third and important distinction: Files created in its format are printer independent. That is, the type will have the same shape, regardless of the printer, →

but its sharpness depends on the resolution of the printer. Publish your bowling team newsletter—bedecked with fancy PostScript fonts and radiant PostScript graphics—on a 300 dpi PostScript printer, and you'll get handsome, homespun output. Hand a floppy with that same file on it to a professional printer who will produce it at a 2,500 dpi resolution, and it will look like a page out of a magazine.

Do you need all this resplendent capability? If you have to ask, the answer is probably no. Base your decision on how much graphics design work you do and how much you spend on out-of-house professional printing. PostScript printers cost roughly double their tongue-tied PCL 4 counterparts (though there are ways to get them cheaper—read on). Ultimately they can pay for themselves many times over by publishing project proposals, reports, or presentation materials that would ordinarily go to an out-of-house printer. They're indispensable for sophisticated desktop publishing and for previewing materials destined for the print shop.

Unfortunately PostScript requires acres of expensive memory, your applications must support it to use it, and as with desktop publishing itself, you need serious graphics art talent driving it. Although these facts may seem self-evident, they are almost universally ignored.

The principles for choosing a PostScript printer are the same as those for choosing a laser printer, except that the model you buy should include at least 1.5 megabytes of RAM (2 megabytes is preferable, 4 for graphics) and anywhere from 11 to 39 built-in fonts. PostScript printers typically range in speed from 4 to 8 PPM. If some of your applications can't produce PostScript files (and many DOS applications can't), consider a printer that can switch between printing PostScript and PCL. DOS applications print faster in PCL.

One final caution before you buy: Computer salespeople who lord the "Adobe" moniker over a PostScript printer as if selling you pottery from the Ming Dynasty are trying to pick your wallet. Early PostScript clones had compatibility problems, which helped buttress Adobe's designer label, but the printers on the market today are fully compatible with Adobe PostScript. There's no reason to pay extra for a name.

Getting It on the Cheap

If it's PostScript you need, PostScript you'll get. Upgrading your current laser printer to PostScript costs less money than buying a PostScript printer outright—but that's not saying much. PostScript printers cost as little as $1,500 on the street these days (though with little effort at all, you can also pay $10,000 for one). Upgrades, on the →

other hand, cost between $90 and $1,000, depending on your printer, your PC, and the aggravation you're willing to subsume.

Upgrades take one of three forms:

1. Plug a PostScript cartridge into the font cartridge slot (if your laser has one).

2. Add an expansion card to your PC (if your printer supports one).

3. Buy software that translates PostScript files into the printer's native language.

None of these is particularly economical or efficient. Generally speaking, you're better off springing for a new PostScript printer.

PostScript Cartridges: They cost $400 to $700 and are the easiest way to add PostScript to your existing printer. Unfortunately the costs don't stop there. You'll also need at least 2 megabytes of printer memory (4 megabytes for printing on both sides of a sheet of paper).

PostScript Add-In Boards: Surely you have better things to do with an afternoon than install an add-in board. PostScript boards are expensive ($800 to $1,000), complicated to install, and require you to load software into your PC's memory to use them. They're also becoming obsolete, so don't bother. A better idea is to sell your current laser and buy an inexpensive PostScript printer.

Software PostScript Emulators: The cheapest way to go ($90 to $500), software-based emulators are difficult to fine tune and they gobble both system and printer memory. Results are also inconsistent—you don't always get true PostScript compatibility. Graphics you design on your PC may come out distorted, and the results will vary from printer to printer. ❐

Dot Matrix: When Ugly Will Do

They're cheaper than lasers, cost less than a penny per page in consumables, and will outlive your worst relatives. But dot matrix printers aren't entirely the bargain they seem. They're ponderously slow, they wail like banshees, and unless you shell out $500 or more for a 24-pin model, your documents will look as though they have a hangover. Add to that the cost of a tractor feed, and you're within tickling distance of a laser printer.

Nevertheless, these clattering workhorses can be terrifically useful. For churning out carbon-copy forms or sticky mailing labels, dot matrix printers perform where snobby lasers refuse. Ditto for printing large spreadsheets and charts on wide, 16-inch paper. If you need an impact printer, there's simply no substitute for dot matrix. But before you buy, hone in on your exact needs.

9-Pin or 24-Pin

Dot matrix printers come in only two flavors worth bothering with: 9-pin and 24-pin. For printing mailing labels, filling in forms, invoices, or printing checks, a blue-collar 9-pin printer will serve you well. They cost as little as $150. For business letters, charts, graphics, and diagrams, get a middle-management 24-pin printer ($400 to $1,400). It will do everything a 9-pin printer does and give you cleaner contrasts, darker characters, and crisper images. It's got everything but class.

Carriage Width

You have two printer widths from which to choose: 80-column and 132-column for pages that are 8.5 inches wide and 16 inches wide, respectively.

Speed

Printer makers and computer magazines measure dot matrix printer speeds in "characters per second" (CPS) as if you were reporting a Ferrari's lap times at Le Mans. Never mind that CPS is an inscrutable and useless measure for judging how fast you'll get paragraphs, charts, or pages—or that it's usually a lie.

Actual dot matrix printer speeds depend on the PC the printer is connected to, the pitch (that is, size) of characters it's printing, the print mode (italic or boldface, for example), and a host of other factors too complex to bother with. Most printers average between 180 and 360 CPS, with 240 CPS equaling about one page per minute in draft mode. Print speed in near-letter-quality mode will be about half that, and graphics print even slower. However, no one buys a dot matrix printer for speed. If speed is an issue for some reason, visit your local computer dealer with a stopwatch to judge lap times for yourself.

Memory

All dot matrix printers come with 8 kilobytes of memory, enough for your PC to shovel about four pages of text to the printer, thereby freeing itself for other uses while the printer prints. The more memory your printer has, the sooner your PC is liberated from printing chores. Expensive dot matrix printers accept additional memory—typically up to 64 kilobytes. Be forewarned, however, that such memory is usually proprietary—that is, expensive—as much as $400 for a few kilobytes.

Fonts

All dot matrix printers claim to have at least two or three fonts that are, in fact, just print modes (draft, near-letter-quality, and letter-quality). A few pricier models now come with resident fonts that print seasick approximations of a Courier or Times Roman typeface. Some very expensive dot matrix printers even have slots for plugging in font cartridges—all of which are proprietary (read: expensive and difficult to find). Buying a font library for a dot matrix printer is absurd. If you need to futz with fonts, get a laser printer.

Consumables

Although dot matrix ribbons cost far less than laser toner cartridges, you can still get gouged by proprietary ribbon designs. Before you buy a printer, call around to office-supply stores in your area to inquire about ribbons produced by third-party manufacturers for your particular machine. Compare these prices to the manufacturer's prices, and ask about discounts for buying in quantity. Keep in mind that cloth ribbons are a better value for your dollar than plastic ribbons, which produce a darker imprint but don't last nearly as long.

Paper Handling

Because you'll typically use a dot matrix printer to produce overnight courier air bills, mailing labels, bank checks, and a host of other odd-sized forms, you should be able to feed paper to your monster in a variety of ways. To help you evaluate which printer to buy, consider these six paper handling methods:

1. **Bottom Feed:** Handy for continuous forms or sheets of mailing labels, bottom-fed printers let you stow the paper in foot-high stacks on the floor. Forms and labels are less likely to get mangled because the paper doesn't have to curl around the paper roller.

2. **Tractor Feed:** If not included, these gadgets cost an extra $60 to $100 (though try to knuckle your dealer into discounting it by 30% to 50% when you buy your printer). They pull continuous form sheets past the printhead evenly to prevent jamming. They're useful for printing thick forms of four parts or more.

3. **Front Feed:** These let you feed single sheets of paper and envelopes to the printer by hand without rolling it around the paper roller.

4. **Cut-Sheet and Envelope Feeder:** If you don't want to feed single-sheet pages to your printer by hand, your dealer will gleefully relieve your wallet of $200 or more for a cut-sheet feeder that does it automatically. Cut-sheet feeders are not interchangeable among printer makers—you're at the printer maker's pricing mercy here.

5. **Paper Parking:** This feature allows you to zip a single sheet of paper through the printer without removing the tractor feed or unloading the continuous form paper connected to the tractor feed.

6. **Quick-tear or Zero Tear-Off:** The printer advances the paper so you can tear off a sheet from a continuous form. Then the printer backs the page up to start printing again without requiring you to realign the paper.

Warranty

The first component to perish on a dot matrix printer will be the printhead—which can cost as much to replace as the price of the printer. Insist on at least a one-year warranty and look for two years. Make sure the warranty covers the printhead, too.

Noise

The clamor produced by a typical dot matrix printer will chase your cats up a tree. It will rain ceiling plaster on your head. It will incite marital spats and office arguments. It is not good for the nerves, at all.

You can subdue your printer's din with a sound-proofing cowl that costs $80 or more, but you'll lose four square feet of office real estate in the bargain. Carpet and curtains can help somewhat. Also, many models now come with a "quiet mode" that lowers print quality and slows the printer (thus prolonging the racket), but that does very little to reduce the actual blare.

Your best bet is to isolate the printer in a room that can be closed off (or to locate it in any office except your own). When shopping for a printer, listen to it print *in all modes* to judge for yourself. If this is impossible, look for a noise rating of 52 decibels (dB) or lower. It will save you a fortune in aspirin.

Color Me Poor

One other temptation printers present is color. As prices on inkjet, thermal transfer, and thermal wax printers continue to spiral downward, color printing has become seductive to a broad range of businesspeople. As with many PC technologies, however, color printers too often get pressed into service for jobs at which they're not competent—at least, not yet.

Scientists and engineers have long used color for strictly utilitarian purposes: to highlight a circuit in the printout of a complex wiring diagram, for example, or to emphasize mechanical stress in a schematic. Color dot matrix ($300 and up) or inkjet printers ($600 and up) serve these purposes quite well. Both deliver grainy graphics in washed-out hues, but both get the job done. If you simply need an occasional dab of color, get an inkjet.

Businesspeople, on the other hand, typically want color for presentation graphics, slick overhead transparencies, and vivid flipcharts. They want colored props to sell ideas, to sell themselves.

Some evidence suggests that people who sit through business presentations are less likely to throw away color handouts than the black-and-white variety. Other evidence suggests that attendees are less likely to scribble notes on colorful graphics, and that gorgeous handouts get filed and forgotten. Almost all evidence suggests that business meetings everywhere are getting longer and less productive. On this score, multi-volume flip-charts and interminable slide presentations—whether in color or in drab monochrome—aren't helping. Has a flip-chart presentation ever sold *you* on anything?

Still, if business presentations for small groups of people are central to your job or if you make lots of last-minute changes to your presentations, a color printer might help you reduce out-of-house printing costs. In those instances, consider a thermal (hot) wax printer. They cost as little as $5,000, offer excellent 300 dpi resolution, and produce brighter, more consistent colors (with less bleeding) than any other color technology. Unlike thermal-transfer printers (which cost just as much) and many inkjets, thermal wax printers also let you print on plain paper.

But are they bargains? Hardly. You'll pay between 45 and 75 cents per page in consumables, and you'll be very lucky to find a third-party supplier for them. A page of color graphics takes at least two minutes to print on a hot-wax technology and as much as six minutes. For printing 50 or so handouts at a time, you'll burn out your printer and grow old waiting for your documents to bear. And guess what? They'll cost a lot more to produce than sending the job to a professional printer.

If you're not yet discouraged, consider that printheads on hot-wax printers are cantankerous and tend to fail often and without notice. A replacement will set you back $800 or more—about the price of a good monochrome laser printer. Indeed, you'll pay steeply for colorful graphics.

For the daring, however, use the same criteria for buying a thermal wax printer as you would for a monochrome laser printer—except that *all* color printers should include PostScript and all the razzle-dazzle that PostScript provides. Make sure your graphics software can print to a color PostScript printer. If your program won't print to your printer and its publisher can't help, call the printer manufacturer and explain your dilemma. At $6,000 per printer, you should expect a solution.

ALPHABET SOUP

Bitmapped Fonts: A typeface in which each character is composed of a pattern of dots.

The Lowdown: Unlike scalable fonts, you can't change the point size of a bitmapped font. You have to buy a separate font for each size of type.

CPS (characters per second): A widespread, but remarkably useless way to measure dot matrix speed except for purposes of comparison. Most dot matrix printers range in speed from 180 to 360 CPS in draft mode.

The Lowdown: In very broad terms, 240 CPS equals about 1 page per minute in draft mode, but dozens of variables affect actual printer speed.

Daisy Wheel Printer: A letter-quality impact printer that makes its imprint in a manner similar to a typewriter's.

The Lowdown: It's yesterday's technology—loud, slow, and limited. Don't bite.

Dot Matrix Printer: An impact printer that forms characters and graphics as a pattern of dots by hammering 9 or 24 pins against a ribbon.

The Lowdown: It's your best bet if you need an impact printer.

DPI (dots per inch): A measure of print resolution that counts the dots that the printer can produce per linear inch.

The Lowdown: Look for 300 dpi in laser and thermal wax printers.

Font: A complete set of letters, numbers, punctuation marks, and other special characters from a single typeface. A font represents only one point size and mode (10-point Courier italic, for example) of a typeface, whereas a typeface represents an entire family of fonts.

The Lowdown: After you find out how many *fonts* are included, find out how many *typefaces* they represent. The number for typefaces determines how many typestyles you get.

Font Cartridge: A cartridge that plugs into some printers enabling them to print fonts in several styles and sizes.

The Lowdown: Font cartridges are expensive and often proprietary. Consider soft fonts as an alternative.

Inkjet Printer: A printer that prints text and graphics by squirting minuscule droplets of ink on paper.

The Lowdown: A slow and anemic printer technology that produces wan color output. Black-and-white inkjets are dead; color inkjets are tolerable if you need inexpensive color.

PCL (Printer Command Language): The internal instructions used by Hewlett-Packard laser printers and laser printers that emulate Hewlett-Packard's models. Several generations of PCL are now available: →

- *PCL 5* debuted with the Hewlett-Packard LaserJet Series III printer and includes many PostScript-like features such as scalable fonts that can be mixed and rotated on the page.
- *PCL 4* uses bitmapped fonts. PCL 4 can handle simple graphics and some fonts.
- PCL 3 is the language in HP's original LaserJet printer. It can manage cartridge-based fonts but not down-loadable soft fonts.

The Lowdown: PCL 5 is so new that few software applications can take advantage of its advanced features and mere mortals can't afford it. At minimum a printer should support PCL 4 (unless it's a PostScript printer).

Point Size: The way of measuring the size of a printed character.

The Lowdown: Standard text in business documents is typically printed in 10- or 12-point type (72 points = 1 inch).

PostScript: A printer language that tells a printer how to produce a page that combines text and graphics.

The Lowdown: To use PostScript, your software has to be able to create PostScript-compatible files.

PPM (pages per minute): A very rough way to measure the speed at which a printer produces documents.

The Lowdown: Actual printer speeds are typically 20% to 30% slower than advertised speeds—across the board.

Scalable Fonts: A typeface that PostScript and PCL 5 printers or your PC can reduce or enlarge to any size.

The Lowdown: Theoretically you get more fonts for the money since you don't have to buy a separate font for each point size of a typeface. Scalable fonts are indispensable for serious desktop publishing.

Soft Font: Fonts that are stored on your computer's hard disk, then downloaded to printer memory when needed for printing a document.

The Lowdown: They're cheaper and more malleable than cartridge fonts. If, however, you really need a large library of fonts, get PostScript capability, not soft fonts.

Thermal Transfer Printer: A printer that uses heat to alter the color of a chemically treated sheet of paper.

The Lowdown: For color printing, thermal transfer technology is quickly fading now that hot-wax printers cost about the same, use plain paper, and deliver richer hues.

Thermal (Hot) Wax Printer: A color printer that uses a crayonlike wax-based ink, which is melted by a heated printhead and jetted onto plain paper. The ink then resolidifies instantly.

The Lowdown: Hot-wax printers produce the highest quality (and most expensive) color documents from a PC possible.

TrueImage: A reliable PostScript clone. →

The Lowdown: TrueImage printers read PostScript fonts or their own variety, called "TrueType" fonts just fine.

Typeface: The design of a family of characters (for example, Times Roman or Helvetica) that includes all point sizes and text modes (such as bold, italic) for printing that character design.

The Lowdown: Although printer makers typically list the number of *fonts* a printer comes with, it's really the number of *typefaces* that matters. ❐

Shopper's Checklist

Compare and grill a salesperson about the following features when selecting a laser or dot matrix printer.

Laser Printers

Essential Features:
- ❏ Supports PCL 4 Emulation
- ❏ Prints at least 4 PPM (by manufacturer's claim)
- ❏ Includes at least six resident (built-in) fonts
- ❏ Toner costs less than 4 cents per page (use manufacturer's claim)
- ❏ Toner cartridges available from third-party supplier
- ❏ Includes at least 512K memory for text, 1MB for graphics
- ❏ Dark, consistent print quality (no streaking)
- ❏ Includes a darkness control knob
- ❏ Dealer authorized to sell and service brand
- ❏ At least a one-year warranty for parts and labor

Other Considerations:
- ❏ Extra memory costs less than $100 per megabyte
- ❏ Includes a PostScript upgrade option
- ❏ Includes Hewlett-Packard–compatible font cartridge slot
- ❏ Can expand memory to at least 2MB (preferably 4MB)
- ❏ First toner cartridge included in purchase price

❏ Legal-sized paper tray included in purchase price
❏ Includes 300,000-page duty cycle
❏ Parallel cable included
❏ Power cord at least 5 feet long

Dot Matrix Printers

Essential Features:

❏ Includes at least 8K memory
❏ Includes at least three resident fonts
❏ Clean, legible printed output
❏ Print speed acceptable in all modes
❏ Ribbons cost less than a penny per page
❏ At least a one-year warranty for parts and labor
❏ Printhead covered by warranty
❏ Acceptable noise level (in all modes)
❏ Dealer authorized to sell and service brand

Other Considerations:

❏ Form part rating (4- to 7-part forms)
❏ Ribbons available from third-party supplier
❏ Paper handling (ask about costs as well):
  Forms: Tractor feed, bottom feed, quick tear-off
  Correspondence: Cut-sheet feeder, front feed,
  Forms and Correspondence: Paper parking, envelope tray
❏ Parallel/serial cable included in purchase price
❏ Power cord at least 5 feet long

A term that can describe virtually any computer component. Try dialing into your company's network, however, and you may find that your "intelligent" modem is only half as smart as a day-old glazed doughnut.

If you can't sell one poorly designed, half fashioned gizmo, you can usually sell three. Just package them together. Also, "Ultimate Productivity Bundle?" Not.

Tally up one obsolete $50 modem, one $200 hand scanner, and one defunct $250 CD-ROM drive. Such a deal!

The Ultimate Productivity Bundle!!

Get a fax/modem, scanner, and CD-ROM drive—a $2,000 value—all for only $800!!

Hayes-compatible 2,400 bps Fax/Modem
This "intelligent" internal fax/modem comes with MNP 5 data compression, and automatic adaptive equalization. The 4,800 bps SendFax works with most fax software.

Hand Scanner
Scan your favorite photos with this grayscale scanner that supports 16 shades of gray (256 with image enhancement) and 100–400-dpi resolution. Powerful Windows-compatible image-editing software included.

CD-ROM Drive
Bring an entire library's worth of data to your PC with this external 800 msec CD-ROM drive or listen to your music CDs while you work. Interface card included.

PLUS: Free computer cleaning kit and keyboard skin!!! A $50 value is yours free.

CompMatic
1-500-YOU-SAVE

A bottle of Windex and a keyboard condom.

That's one way to put it. Another is to say that it smudges images to look less grainy, but hardly sharper. It's called "dithering," a process akin to smearing Vaseline on a camera lens.

Whoop-Whoop-Whoop! Do you hear sirens? You should. 4,800 bps is a tip-off to obsolescence; "works with" is a code for "software not included."

Listening to music CDs while you work is about all you'll be able to do with a drive this slow. You'll want at least a 500ms (or faster) drive if you actually plan to use it.

This is technoguff. It means only that the modem drops to a slower speed to compensate for bad phone lines or to match the speed of a slower modem. All modems do this.

A Compendium of PC Add-Ons and Peripherals

One reason that chipheads find the PC so blissfully engrossing is its expandability. You can hitch to it modems and scanners, fax boards and sound cards, CD-ROM drives and trackballs—an endless chain of devices. Suddenly your computer becomes a cathedral of high technology (or a digital pimp-mobile).

There's no question that many of these *chatchkas* are technical marvels. Drag a hand scanner across Dagwood in your morning comics, then pop his vacant glaze into wedding anniversary invitations. Type in the word "tamale" and your CD-ROM encyclopedia will serve up every spicy detail about the husked comestible. Write a note to Aunt Clare on your word processor thanking her for the tie she knitted you, then fax it to her directly from your PC.

The possibilities are interminable. However, for every problem a PC peripheral solves, for every new capability it delivers, it also adds complexity to your system and to your work. Peripheral compatibility problems abound. Peripherals frequently cause memory and system interrupt conflicts. They teem with hidden costs for cables, software, and sub-peripherals. They require you to learn new software. They're often poorly constructed and poorly supported. Their manuals tend to be impenetrable.

Occasionally a peripheral makes terrific sense. Before you plunk down for one, however, consider these five maxims about peripherals and add-ons:

1. **Whatever the gadget, it will require software.** Craftier merchandisers will charge extra for the program that makes

the device operable, but you can almost always find it elsewhere at the same price, software included.

2. **The price should include all of the pieces.** Many of these gizmos require expansion cards, cables, adapters, and the like. These can be a sneaky way for a dealer to tack on extra costs.

3. **Get "scuzzy."** If your toy uses an expansion card (also called controller cards), look for one that conforms to the SCSI (Small Computer System Interface, pronounced "scuzzy") standard. Gadgets that use SCSI controllers may be a tad more expensive than ones that use proprietary cards, but they're faster and don't tie you to a single manufacturer. You may also be able to hook up more than one toy to the same adapter and save an expansion slot.

4. **Don't go parallel.** Many devices run either from an adapter card or from a parallel port. Opt for the adapter card variety (unless you shuttle the device between several PCs). Devices that attach to an external parallel port are easier to install, but you'll pay a heavy price in speed.

5. **Ease of installation is key.** Peripherals vie with your PC's internal components and other peripherals for your processor's attention (interrupts) and for space in memory. Conflicts can arise, which you can solve typically through dip switches or software. Look up "interrupts" and "memory address" in the add-on manual's index, then read how easy it is to change these settings. Highly complex instructions indicate either a bad board design or a poorly written manual. You decide.

What follows is a compendium of the most common PC add-ons (in alphabetical order) with a quick sketch of what each is about, what everyone needs to know about it, and how it can take you to the cleaners if you're not careful. Each of these gadgets brings a *new* capability to the PC. Devices that goose system performance or otherwise expand on existing capabilities (memory chips, video cards, and hard drives, for example) can be found in Chapter 7.

CD-ROM Drive

Essentially the same thing as a stereo compact disc player, a CD-ROM drive for a PC reads text, graphics, and sound from compact discs and transfers them to your computer (some can even play your music CDs). Because compact discs can hold 540 to 680 megabytes (or more) of computer data—enough to put the entire *Encyclopedia Britannica* on a single CD—they're used primarily for references and highly animated games.

The "ROM" in "CD-ROM" stands for Read-Only Memory, which means that, like compact discs for your stereo, they can read the data from a CD, but they can't record to them. Computer CD applications cost between $45 and $600. Several hundred titles are now available, and their leagues proliferate.

What Matters

CD-ROM drives are slugs. They creep along at a torpid rate—many magnitudes slower than even the most ancient hard drives. CD-ROM drive speed is measured by its access time and transfer rate. Access times range from 275 milliseconds (msec) to 1500 msec (the *lower* the number, the faster the drive). Look for a drive with at least a 500-millisecond access time—anything slower, and you'll find yourself finger-drumming grooves into your desk.

Transfer rate matters only if you plan to use multimedia CDs, which shimmy and sing with sound and video. They'll need at least 150-kilobyte-per-second transfer speeds (in this case, the *higher* the number, the faster the transfer rate) so that animation and video don't stutter with frame-by-frame transitions. Also, make sure your drive has a 32K or 64K buffer. For simple database text search and retrieval, a buffer isn't necessary.

Interface. To connect to a computer, CD-ROM drives need a "controller" card that fits into one of your PC's expansion slots. Most newer CD-ROM drives use a controller card designed around the Small Computer System Interface (SCSI) standard, although a few use nonstandard interfaces. Stick with SCSI; proprietary drives are doomed. Make sure the controller card and cables are included in the price of the drive; they can add several hundred dollars to the cost. Finally, be aware that a few CD-ROM manufacturers peddle drives that attach to your PC's serial or parallel ports. These don't require controller cards— and the fuss of installing one—but you'll pay for the convenience in speed. They're dogs.

Internal vs. External. Internal drives sit in a standard-sized drive bay just like your PC's floppy drive. You have to install them. There's little difference in price between external and internal drives, but keep in mind that you can shuttle an external drive between PCs. Also, "carousel players," CD-ROM drives that hold several discs at once, are all of the external variety. Finally, so-called portable CD-ROM drives typically lack batteries. You have to run them from an electrical outlet. As with all portable PC toys, you'll pay a premium for their diminutive proportions.

Software. To make it go, a CD-ROM drive needs software called "device drivers," which put your PC and the CD-ROM's controller card on speaking terms. You'll also need Microsoft's CD-ROM extension drivers (these files usually come on a floppy diskette and are labeled "MSCDX"). They ensure that DOS can talk to the manufacturer's drivers. Look for the newest version of MSCDX (currently Release 2.2). Also, browse through the installation instructions in the manual before you buy a drive. Getting all this junk to work together can be trickier than you think.

Audio. Most CD-ROM drives can play musical CDs. Look for a drive with a headphone jack on it and insist that your dealer include audio software and headphones in the price.

Discs. Use the purchase of a CD-ROM drive as an occasion to ply free CDs from your dealer. Manufacturers sometimes throw in as many as ten CD titles to charm you into buying the drive. As you might expect, most bundled CDs are junk. Ask your dealer to replace them with titles of your own choosing (even one decent title is better than ten weird references you'll never use). Don't get too hopeful about this. Also, make sure that the CDs you're buying are fully functional. Some free titles turn out to be demo discs intended to tease money from your wallet.

What to Watch Out For

CD-ROM drives start below $400, and their prices move upward with faster speeds, larger buffers, and dumber consumers. While avoiding high-priced drives, also beware of those advertised at very low prices; they often augur a model destined to be discontinued. The latest software drivers may not work on them, or they may lumber along at a near unusable pace.

Fax Boards and Fax/Modems

A fax board turns your PC into a fax machine, sort of. It enables you to send a document, report, or graphic from within your PC to any fax machine. Better fax boards can receive faxes from fax machines (or from other fax boards), store them in your PC, and print them on your printer. Some fax boards also include a data modem so that two computers can exchange information in a digital format over a phone line.

What Matters

Yes, fax/modem cards are whizzies. They're also a terrific way to get a fax machine cheap. Widely available for under $200, they're less expensive to feed than standalone machines since they don't require special fax paper (which can cost up to five cents per page received). Incoming faxes are received as an image file and saved to your hard disk. You can view them on your screen with your fax software, delete them, or print them on plain paper.

Unlike standalone fax machines, fax cards have the intelligence of your PC at their disposal. This endows them with several key conveniences (which is what fax is all about, isn't it?). They transmit faxes faster, for example. Also, you can schedule faxes to be sent when phone rates are cheaper—say, 3:00 AM, when no one is around to feed the fax machine. Because the data they receive is in digital form, a PC can pipe the data over a network or phone line, save it to a floppy, and let you edit or retouch it. Finally, fax cards take up little space, if any.

Speed. Look for a fax card that transmits at 9,600 bits per second (bps)—it's the speed any fax machine built after 1986 uses. Anything slower will monopolize your PC and raise your phone bills. Fax cards should also support a standard called Group III, the international standard for fax transmissions. Avoid modems that support only the Group II standard; they're obsolete.

Internal vs. External. Fax boards disappear into an expansion slot inside your PC or sit outside it in a case the size of a cigarette pack (and connect to your PC through a serial port). Neither design is superior, though external models can be easily shuttled between PCs.

Software. The software bundled with most fax boards is abysmal—a pity, given how important it is. If possible, try to judge the software for yourself in your dealer's showroom or on a colleague's PC. If you hate it, spend the extra $80 to $100 for a separate fax software package. It will make the process far more agreeable.

Essential to fax software is how it converts a file to the proper fax format. Better packages allow you to fax anything you can print, using a simple key combination command. Cruder programs force you to save the file, manually convert it to fax format, and then send it.

A good fax package also generates cover sheets automatically (some even let you add company logos or your signature to a cover sheet). They log both incoming and outgoing faxes. They'll "broadcast" faxes to everyone on a telephone list you create. They'll even redial a number automatically when there's a busy signal.

Background Operation. Many fax cards claim the ability to send and receive faxes "in the background," meaning they send and receive as you tootle away in your word processor or spreadsheet. But only those with an onboard processor can truly manage this. Fax boards *without* a processor slow your computer to a near or complete halt when sending or receiving. For frequent faxing, spend the extra $100 to $150 for a fax board with a processor. It's the difference between turning your computer into an $1,800 fax machine or getting both a PC and fax machine for about $300 more.

Modem. A fax card with a built-in modem can save you $100 or more if you're also in the market for a modem since they typically cost only slightly more than fax-only boards. The modem should transmit data at at least 2,400 bps, though you may find good deals on modems that run at 9,600 bps as well. (See the "What to Watch Out For" section under "Modem.")

Scanner Support. Because fax boards can only send documents created in your computer, they can't entirely replace a fax machine. To fax a friend a magazine article, for example, you'll have to type it into your computer or scan it in—if you own a scanner. Some fax boards even come with ports to which you can connect a scanner. The scanner costs extra, of course, and fax boards typically support only a few scanner models. For heavy fax traffic, a standalone fax machine is cheaper and far more convenient than a scanner/fax board combination.

What to Watch Out For

The words "sendfax," "broadcast fax," or similar advertising blither mean the card can send faxes but not receive them. For the same money you can get a fax board that does both. Make sure the board can both *send and receive* at 9,600 bps; a few send at the higher speed but only receive at a slower speed (or vice versa).

Beware that fax programs are greedy for system memory; they can gobble as much as 65K of RAM—enough to bump elbows with software running concurrently. Better fax packages take up 15K of memory or less.

Also, faxes you receive hog hard disk space. A simple one-page fax can engulf half a megabyte of precious storage space. This is because your PC reads and stores faxes as bitmapped images, not as text.

For this same reason you can't load faxes you receive into a word processor without first converting them to text files with optical character recognition (OCR) software, which changes the images of text into a format your word processor can understand. A few fax programs now include OCR features (and many similar packages are heading to market soon). However, their accuracy depends largely on the quality of the received fax, a highly erratic factor. In general, expect 90 to 95 percent accuracy with OCR: about one typo in every ten words.

Finally, installing a fax board can be a twenty-minute cinch or a week-long enterprise. Make sure you can return the board, software included, for a full refund if you're not satisfied.

Joystick

Resembling a tiny gearshift, a joystick controls the action in video arcade-style computer games.

What Matters

Most games let you get by with using cursor controls rather than a joystick, but hard-core gamers will tell you that a joystick makes games far more enjoyable.

Joysticks usually connect to a special game port on your PC—many newer PCs have one built in. If not, you'll need to buy a game port controller card that fits in an expansion slot.

What to Watch Out For

Don't pay a lot for a controller card: they're widely available for under $15 and commonly include extra serial ports as well.

Math Coprocessor

A chip that plugs into your PC's main system board to speed up some math and graphics calculations. It's used primarily for engineering software, sophisticated mathematical and graphics software, programming, and compiling.

What Matters

Simple addition and subtraction generally won't benefit from a math chip. Only in complex math or graphical computations does a coprocessor start to make a difference. To use a math chip, your software must be specifically designed to take advantage of it. Some spreadsheets, for example, support math chips. Others don't. Check your program manuals.

The specific math chip you need depends on your PC's CPU and its clock speed. A 286-based PC, for example, only works with a 287 math coprocessor. A 386 computer works with a 387 math coprocessor. (Some older 386s can accept either a 287 or 387 chip. In such cases, opt for the 387—it's faster). Incidentally, the 486DX chip has a math coprocessor built into its circuitry; you don't need to buy one. However, the 486SX chip doesn't (see Chapter 3).

Once you've matched the coprocessor number to your PC's processor chip, the only other thing you need to do is match the speed of the coprocessor chip with the clock speed on your PC (25MHz, 33MHz, 40MHz, and so forth).

What to Watch Out For

Anyone who needs a math chip is probably a good candidate for a 486DX-based PC. Adding a coprocessor to anything slower than a 20-MHz, 386-based PC is largely a waste of time and money.

Installing a math coprocessor is simple—it plugs directly into a socket on the motherboard. Whoever sells you the chip should be able to walk you through the installation. If you decide to let a service shop install it, don't pay for more than 10 or 15 minutes of labor.

Modem

The equivalent of a telephone for your PC, a modem allows a computer to send and receive computer files or messages over the phone lines.

What Matters

Perhaps more than any other technology, modems are steeped in a haze of standards, protocols, and acronyms. Don't get hoodwinked by them; only a few factors really matter:

Speed. A modem's speed is rated by the amount of information (bits) it can send or receive per second. Common speeds for modems are 300, 1,200, 2,400 and 9,600 bits per second ("bps" is often referred to incorrectly in ads as "baud"). A few modems even send and receive information at speeds of 14,400 bps or faster, although the higher speeds are useless unless you're sending or receiving from another equally fast modem that uses the same data compression schemes. Incidentally high-speed modems can cost as much as a PC.

If you need a modem for electronic mail, sending and receiving a few files a day (or less), or for dropping in on an information service such as CompuServe or Prodigy, you'll find the best deals in 2,400-bps models—the speed supported by most electronic mail and online information services. You can generally find one for under $200 and often for as little as $50.

9,600-bps modems are still a luxury—and a gamble. Although their prices are dropping, they still hover over 2,400-bps varieties often by hundreds of dollars. Also, with faster modems, the soup of standards gets thicker and less certain. But high-speed modems begin to make sense if you send and receive lots of large files every day from another high-speed modem. They'll pay for themselves in what they save you in long-distance phone bills. Also keep in mind that any 9,600 bps modem can communicate with slower speed modems—at the slower speed. If you find a 9,600-bps modem priced comparably to a 2,400-bps variety, spring for the higher speed.

Hayes Compatibility. Look for the phrase "Hayes-compatible" on the modem's packaging. This means the modem recognizes some or all of the AT command set developed by the modem maker Hayes Microcomputer Products. This ensures that all communications software and other modems speak the same language as yours.

Standards. The free-floating standards that govern how a modem compresses data and checks it for errors are unbearably hard to pin down. They provide endless ways for a salesperson to pick your pocket. However, a slow consensus has begun to emerge. These guidelines will protect your investment.

A 2,400-bps modem should support a standard called "V.22bis"— and fortunately you can take it for granted that most do. In addition, look for a modem that supports "MNP 5," a protocol for compressing data before it is transmitted. Compressed data travels across phone lines faster and more efficiently than non-compressed data. It saves you money in phone bills. Newer 2,400-bps modems support two other protocols called "V.42" and "V.42bis." The V.42 protocol is an error-correction routine that protects against garbled data due to static on the phone line; the V.42bis is for data compression. A few modems only support either the MNP protocols or V.42 and V.42bis; better modems support both.

A 9,600-bps modem should support a standard called "V.32," as well as V.42, V.42bis, and occasionally MNP 5. The V.32 standard enables a high-speed modem to communicate with a slower modem; without it, your modem can transmit only to other 9,600-bps modems.

A 9,600-bps modem that supports both V.42 and V.42bis can achieve speeds of up to 38,400 bps when talking to another 9,600-bps modem. Some inexpensive 9,600-bps modems don't truly support V.42 and V.42bis. Make sure you can return the modem for a refund if you want this capability and discover it's not there.

Internal versus External. Internal modems are slightly cheaper than the external variety and don't junk up your desk. External models, however, attach to a standard serial port on the back of your PC and are easily moved to another computer. If you're struck with panic at the prospect of opening the case on your PC, get the external variety.

The exception here is with high-speed (9,600 bps or faster) modems. The serial ports on many older PCs can't handle these high speeds. In these cases, get an internal modem.

What to Watch Out For

To use a modem, you need communications software, which tells your modem what to do. It's not uncommon for modem makers to bundle their modem with some kind of communications software, although it's usually pretty chintzy. If you like the software, great. If not, spend another $100–$200 for a good communications software program.

Mouse

A screen pointing or drawing device slightly larger than the fuzzy little creature it's named after.

What Matters

Mice come in a menagerie of sizes and designs, costing between $30 and $350. A serial mouse plugs into the standard serial port on any PC. A bus mouse connects to a special mouse port. There are also wireless mice that signal your PC with infrared technologies, optical mice that bounce light off a mirror, left-handed mice, three-button mice, crazy-colored mice, and so forth.

Many PCs come with a built-in mouse port. If yours doesn't, you can install one in an expansion slot. However, you're better off with a serial mouse—it's cheaper and easier to install.

Design. Choosing a mouse you can live with is highly subjective; test drive a few models before settling on one.

All mice have at least one button; some have several. Of course, the number of buttons is irrelevant if your software doesn't support them. Most programs use just one or two mouse buttons.

Protocols. To ensure that your mouse will work with the widest selection of software programs, make sure it supports the Microsoft mouse protocol. Look for the phrase "Microsoft-compatible mouse" on the box.

What to Watch Out For

Mice often come bundled with software, video cards, or an entire PC. When bought separately, however, they can cost as much as $100 to $150. Whenever possible, try to get your dealer to bundle a mouse into a larger purchase. (For example, consider requesting a free mouse when you are buying Microsoft Windows, a hand scanner and imaging software, a drawing program, a portable PC, or a desktop computer.)

Optical Drives

Optical drives, which include magneto-optical; WORM (Write-Once Read Many—lovely acronym, no?) drives and rewriteable optical drives all read data with lasers, which are far more precise than drive heads on a disk drive. Data can be packed onto their media far more compactly—per square inch, a CD holds many magnitudes more data than a hard drive. However, prices start at $2,000 and rise sharply.

What Matters

Nothing, yet.

What to Watch Out For

These technologies buy you into a highly fickle future. They'll need several years for their standards—and prices—to come down to earth.

Removable/Portable Disk Drives

Like big floppy diskettes, removable hard drives read cartridges that hold between 20 megabytes and 1 gigabyte of data. Portable hard drives are simply external hard drives that you can move from one PC to another. Both are useful if you shuttle between several computers, working with the same body of data on each.

What Matters

Yank a removable hard disk from its drive in the middle of a disk write, and quite often, you'll lose your data. Drop or lose the disk, and unfathomable hours of work vanish. Removable drives are fragile and expensive but they can make sense if you need to shuttle 20MB or more of data between two PCs. Just be prepared to pay dearly for the privilege. They're a technology to watch, not buy.

Ditto for portable drives, which slap between $500 and $2,400 onto the cost of an ordinary hard drive and are just as prone to damage, theft, and loss as removables.

What to Watch Out For

The price for a removable disk inevitably includes only one drive. To shuttle a disk between home and office PCs, say, you'll need two drives. When you ask about the price of the second drive, be prepared to burst out in laughter. Also, the disks themselves cost $100 or more.

Some portable drives have optional battery packs (to use with laptops) which deliver three to seven hours of battery life. Don't pay more than $60 for one.

Scanners

A scanner is like a photocopier for your computer. Pass a scanner over this page, for example, and it sends the image to your computer. You can then edit, print, or drop this page into another document. Scanners hold a wealth of promise but seldom deliver as much as expected.

What Matters

Scanners come in three essential flavors: handheld, flatbed, and sheet-feed. Handheld scanners are toys. They're fine for scanning logos, doodles, family photos, or images no wider than 4 to 6 inches, especially if you don't mind spending an afternoon tinkering with it. They're widely available for under $200, but the results are hardly professional. To scan an image, you have to drag the scanner head (which resembles a small, hand vacuum cleaner) across an image, taking care to move it in a straight line and at a constant speed. It requires patience, good motor skills, and *lots* of free time.

Flatbed scanners are easier to use and can create images that are passably professional—suitable for dropping into a newsletter or business presentation. They also start at $800 and work upward. Flatbed scanners (also called "full-page scanners" because they can scan a full 8.5" × 11" page) work like photocopiers. Place a page face down on its glass window, close the cover, and the scanner reads the image into a digital file.

Sheet-feed scanners are used primarily for optical character recognition: scanning in text, not images, then converting them to a format that your word processor can read. Sheet-feed scanners can only scan unbound sheets of paper; they can't read a page bound in a book.

Most scanners require a controller card that fits in one of your PC's expansion slots. Make sure it's included in the price of the scanner—shifty dealers have been known to advertise a scanner at a very low price, neglecting to mention that the controller card costs several hundred dollars extra.

Black-and-White, Grayscale, or Color. A scanner's sophistication is determined by the contrasts and hues it can render. Accordingly, scanners fall into three categories: black-and-white, grayscale, and color. Black-and-white scanners, the crudest technology, are adequate for line art, logos, and for reading text.

Grayscale scanners (which cost about the same as black-and-white scanners) also allow you to scan in images with grays and "continuous tones" typical of a black-and-white photograph. Grayscale scanners will discern between 16 and 256 shades of gray—the more shades of gray there are in your image, the greater the detail it picks up.

Color scanners are expensive, fun to use, and largely useless. Unless you have a color printer, there's not much you can do with scanned color images. They're still five years away from practical use.

Resolution. The clarity or fineness with which a scanner renders an image is its resolution. Most scanners provide a resolution of 100–800 dots per inch (dpi). A typical laser printer only prints at 300 dpi, so you needn't bother to pay extra for a scanner that offers higher resolution unless you're having a professional printing house reproduce the image.

Scanner Software. As important as the actual scanner is, its software is even more important. Good imaging software lets you to shrink, enlarge, crop, rotate, and flip graphics. You should look for the ability to adjust image contrast and brightness and to save images in several key file formats: TIFF, PCX, BMP, and PIC, at a minimum. You'll also want the software to include a few basic drawing tools for touching up scanned images.

There is no such thing as great OCR software. Passable OCR uses omnifont technology, which can read a wide variety of typefaces without requiring you to "train" the software beforehand. It's the most accurate OCR you'll find.

What to Watch Out For

Test drive a scanner before buying it. Bring a photo from a magazine and a simple cartoon from a newspaper to test resolution and image quality. Try to spend at least half an hour with the imaging software; many programs are atrociously awkward.

Bear in mind that scanners are finicky, sometimes hard to install, and often conflict with other hardware in your computer. Before you buy, make sure you can return the whole arrangement, scanner and software, for a full refund. If you want both imaging and OCR software, buy them together and try to negotiate a discount. Some scanner makers still sell their scanners *sans* software. This is unacceptable. Let them know it.

Sound Card

A sound card is a relatively inexpensive way ($75–$200) to give your PC a voice. It fits in an expansion slot and brings stereo-quality sound to your PC (depending on the speakers hooked to it). Great for games and crucial to multimedia, sound cards have little practical value. They're good for grins.

What Matters

All sound cards use a different method for recording and storing audio data. To be able to use a sound card, your software must support your particular brand of sound card. Also, fidelity and general sound quality vary widely. Listen to several before you buy.

The sound quality of a board depends on its sampling (recording) speed and the bit size of the sampling. The bare minimum requirements for multimedia are a sampling speed of at least 22 kilohertz and a sampling size of 8 bits. This is fine for games. You'll get better sound from a board that samples at a rate of 44.1 kilohertz with a sampling size of either 12 or 16 bits, though you'll pay more for it too.

Also, look for a sound card that is stereophonic rather than monophonic—monophonic cards make everything sound as if it's coming out of a kazoo. The quality of a board's stereo capability depends on the number of stereophonic voices it supports. Look for a board with at least 20 voices.

To take full advantage of a sound card, you'll need to hook speakers to it. A few manufacturers sell mini PC speakers—boombox style—with their boards (for the benefit of your neighbors).

As more software comes equipped to make noises at you, sound cards are proliferating. Video card makers are beginning to add sound capability to their boards as well. Myriad ways to get sophisticated sound without paying for it lurk on the horizon. All you need is a little patience.

What to Watch Out For

Audio data devours scads of hard disk space. Although most sound boards compress sound before storing it, expect to devote between half a megabyte to a full megabyte of storage *per minute* of sound.

Surge Protector

Sometimes called a "surge suppressor," a surge protector sits between the plug on your PC and an electrical outlet. It intercepts electrical line power surges (including those caused by lightning) that might otherwise fricassee your computer.

What Matters

Look for a UL (Underwriter's Laboratory) rating on the unit. This ensures that it passes basic fire, shock, and electrical hazard safety tests (so it doesn't intercept a surge, burst into flames, and burn your house down).

Lightning surges can also come in across the phone line to zap your modem or fax board. Many surge protectors include a jack to intercept phone line surges as well.

What to Watch Out For

Don't open your wallet too wide for these devices. Although it's a good idea to have a surge suppressor (an ounce of prevention and all that), there's typically little difference between a $25 model and the $250 variety.

Tape Drive

A tape drive is a device for backing up your data to magnetic tape cartridges. It's a slow, somewhat expensive solution.

What Matters

Tape drives are a smart idea caught in a snarl of nonstandard standards. Cartridges cost $20 to $100 each—about $2 to $3 per megabyte. It's a relatively cheap and reliable way to archive data, except that you must also buy the drive they go in, which can cost between $250 and $5,000, depending on its capacity.

The woeful lack of standards among drives means that your brand of drive most likely won't read cartridges created in other brands—this, despite your salesperson's solemn oaths to the contrary. It means that every computer you ever buy will have to include that same brand of tape drive—and possibly the same model—in order to read your archived data. It's a shotgun marriage between you and a rather clumsy piece of technology.

Tape drives begin to make sense when backing up large hard disks (350 MB or more) found primarily on networks. For PCs with fewer than 120 MB of data, there are better solutions. Several excellent backup software packages expedite the dreary process of backing up to diskettes or to a network drive. Most cost well under $150. For that matter, a second hard drive costs roughly the same as a tape drive and you get much faster performance. Let the two drives mirror each other; it will protect your data against most any disaster, save for your computer catching fire.

Capacity. The two most common types of tape drive are DC-2000 and DC-6000. DC-2000 drives use cartridges that hold between 40 and 640 MB of data, and sell for $250 or more. For a single PC, this is the type you want. DC-6000 drives hold tapes with 150 MB to 1 gigabyte of data or more, cost $600 to $2,000 (and up), and are best suited for network hard drives.

Standards. A salesperson may evangelize about one tape-drive standard over another, but you should presume from the beginning that your drive will not read another drive's cartridges. The only standard to worry about is QIC (quarter-inch cartridge), which ensures only that you'll be able to buy cartridges long after your drive maker has filed for Chapter 11. QIC cartridges are described in terms of capacity: QIC-40, QIC-80, QIC-150, and so forth.

Speed. DC-2000 systems back up data at 2.5 MB to 12.75 MB per minute. DC-6000 systems are slightly faster, at 5 to 30 MB per minute. The faster the drive, the more it costs. Advertised speeds tend to be...shall we say...embellished. Use the numbers only for comparison. Actual speeds are typically 0.5 to 5 MB slower than manufacturers' claims.

Internal/External. Internal drives are typically several hundred dollars cheaper than external drives. However, an external drive lets several PCs (in close proximity) share it. Most tape drives require an expansion slot, though a few can plug into your PC's floppy drive controller. These drives are typically less expensive than those drives that have their own controller, but they're also slower.

Software. Good tape drive software performs unattended, automatic backups. It can back up and restore both individual files or entire directories. Look for software that does file-by-file backups rather than an "image" backup; this makes it easier to find and restore individual files later.

Some software compresses data while backing it up, thereby squeezing more information onto a single tape cassette. Back-ups take longer with compression, though, and they raise the likelihood that no other drive can read your tapes. Tape cartridges also must be formatted, which can take up to an hour. Look for software that formats the cassettes as it saves data to them.

What to Watch Out For
Make sure the advertised capacity of the tape drive indicates the capacity *without* data compression.

Uninterruptible Power Supply (UPS)

Think of a UPS as an emergency backup battery for your computer. It supplies a constant supply of electricity to your PC should the electricity in your house or building go off.

What Matters

UPSs aren't meant to be an alternate power source for your PC for very long. They supply five or ten minutes worth of electricity—just long enough to save your work and shut down your PC. Look for a UL rating or seal on the unit guaranteeing that it passes basic fire, shock, and safety standards.

UPSs come in both internal and external varieties—the external ones are easier to install.

What to Watch Out For

UPSs are not inexpensive; prices start at roughly $250 and work their way up to over $1,000. Unless you live in an area with frequent power blackouts, you don't need one.

Trackball

A variation on a mouse, a trackball is a stationary pointing device. Instead of rolling the entire mouse around the desk, you manipulate a ball on rollers. Because they're stationary, trackballs save space on a crowded desk. Controlled by a finger rather than the entire hand, a trackball gives you finer control over the cursor (for graphics and artwork, for example) than a mouse.

What Matters

Like mice, trackballs come with either serial connectors or a connector for the dedicated mouse port on your system. Also like mice, they come in several shapes and sizes. Test one before buying.

Compatibility. Make sure the trackball supports the Microsoft protocol (look for the phrase "Microsoft-mouse compatible") to ensure that it will work with most software applications.

What to Watch Out For

Make sure the trackball comes with an adapter that turns a 9-pin serial connector into the 25-pin serial port found on most newer PCs. Bought separately, the adapter costs $15 to $25.

Six Totally Weenie PC Add-Ons and Peripherals

Paper Partner: Put this $70 doodad in your printer's paper tray and it bleets at you when the printer runs out of paper. Why would you pay for anything this annoying?

Post Code Controller Card: A $100 add-in card that translates your PC's Power On System Test (POST) into near English. Whatever happened to reading the manual?

Dongle: (Yes, you read that right.) This $50 serial port attachment stores information about your PC's system configuration so you can recover from a virus. A fifty cent floppy diskette does the same thing.

TV-Video Windows: A $1,200 add-in card for displaying broadcast television in a window on your PC. How bored are you?

PocketPost Diagnostic Test Card: This $250 add-in card plugs into any computer's expansion slot. Switch on the power and it tells you why your PC won't boot. Of course, you should also know that the average PC repair costs under $250—and fixes the problem.

Pocket Logger: This $600 pocket-sized temperature recorder saves up to 32,256 temperature readings and then graphs them on your PC.

Spend three grand on a notebook, and the maker throws in a $2 carrying case? How generous.

No one makes 20MB hard drives any longer. Nothing wrong with an old drive—except that this computer costs $1,400 more than it should.

A 386DX chip slurps battery charge far faster than 386SL or 386SXL chips. What's the 386DX's performance advantage for spreadsheets, word processing, or communications? Zip.

Only 8.5 pounds!

Buy before March 16, and we'll throw in the carrying case for free!

Powerful enough for the office but small enough for the road... Don't let the slim notebook size fool you—our LightLoad 386 notebook PC with a 20MB hard drive packs full desktop PC power. The LightLoad 386 features cutting-edge processing muscle with all the deluxe features and add-ins you'll ever need!

- Full-powered 386DX CPU
- 17 power-management features
- 640K RAM expandable to 2MB
- Large, backlit, triple super-twist VGA display (with 32 shades of gray!)
- Up to 6 hours of life with rechargeable internal battery
- Modem/fax communications slot
- 80-key high-quality tactile keyboard
- 3.5" 1.44 MB floppy drive
- Port for optional docking station
- Math coprocessor slot

Only $2,800!!!

LapIt INC
1-500-TOO-GOOD

Ouch!

Ugh. Imagine lugging a frozen turkey from one airport terminal to another as you change planes. The ad fails to mention whether a battery is included in the weight. A notebook should weigh 5.5 to 6.5 pounds—batteries, cables, and stuffing included.

Sounds sophisticated, doesn't it? You're being conned. When judging a screen, trust your eyes, not the techno-babble.

It's a proprietary slot, of course. Expect to pay $250 or more for your maker's version of a $99 fax/modem.

The word "expandable" invites extortion. Almost all notebooks use proprietary memory. You'll pay through the wazoo for extra RAM.

Sheesh! Most makers stopped telling this fib two years ago. Expect 2.5 to 3.5 hours of charge, max.

Portable Computing

Five years from now the computer on your desk will probably be a laptop. The hulking PC you use today will resemble the electronic equivalent of a 1976 Pontiac Bonneville: immense, primitive, astonishingly ugly. Given the marvelous advances in portable computing in recent years, it's tempting to nudge the future, to junk the monster on your desk today in favor of a portable PC as your sole machine.

There's even good argument behind this arrangement. Why not get two PCs for the price of one and save the aggravation of shuffling files between desktop machine and portable? Many computer journalists even recommend using a portable as your only PC (almost none of whom would actually live with this arrangement, of course).

Except for the traveling salesperson who lives out of motels or the foreign correspondent still burning with ambition (and peptic ulcers), few people would truly be happy shelling out for a portable PC to serve double duty. For the price of a full-featured laptop and its requisite baubles, you can buy a solid desktop machine and a serviceable portable as well (see "Ten Reasons Not to Spend $3,500 on a Notebook PC"). Your dual systems are cheaper and easier to repair or upgrade; your data is safer, and when one computer fails, you have a spare.

Use a portable computer for travel. If travel is your business, perhaps a portable is all you need. But think twice about that before you buy. →

Ouch! Ooops! Bof!
Ten Reasons Not to Spend $3,500 on a Notebook PC

1. The sound that a $3,500 notebook PC makes when it falls from an overhead luggage bin is very depressing. The same applies when fellow passengers or big-footed flight attendants step on a notebook that peeks into a cabin aisle.

2. A notebook PC (with all your data) is easily forgotten in a conference room, hotel suite, restaurant, taxi cab, or lover's boudoir.

3. Slosh your daiquiri on a notebook keyboard, and you'll typically have to buy a new computer, not a new keyboard.

4. Thirty-five hundred dollars will buy one pair of silk underwear, one case of Gevrey Chambertin (1981), four steel-belted radial tires, six pounds of smoked Norwegian salmon, a Bugs Bunny tattoo, a fax machine, two Adirondack lawn chairs, new running shoes, a decent electric guitar, one-year's subscription to the *New York Times,* not a bad mountain bike, *and* a ten-day canoeing expedition (for two) down the Mackenzie River in Canada's Northwest Territories.

5. Batteries for fancy notebooks deliver less than three hours of charge; from either coast, you'll get no farther than Kansas City.

6. Even a pampered $3,500 notebook will die from overheated components within two to three years.

7. A notebook PC will fly freely from your arms as you race down a jetway; it will slip sadly from your shoulder as you fish for change to buy a newspaper.

8. Notebook PCs steal away from their owners in briefcases or shopping bags, under overcoats, or in open arms. A $3,500 notebook fetches $500—easy—at almost any pawn shop in America, no questions asked.

9. To civilize a notebook for day-to-day office work, you'll need an external monitor, an external keyboard, an expansion chassis (or an external floppy drive), and a well-padded carrying case. Suddenly $3,500 becomes $5,000.

10. Almost anything a $3,500 notebook PC can do a $1,200 notebook PC can do.

Portable computers fall along a continuum with high *usability* on one end and high *portability* on the other. Highly usable portables, optimistically called "luggables," are little more than desktop PCs with carrying handles. A typical model weighs as much as a German shepherd and will bang your shins bloody as you schlep it around an airport. Before you buy one, examine the thickness of the steel and leather on the handle. It will give you an idea of how much shoulder, back, and shin pain to anticipate.

At the other extreme of the continuum—high portability—are electronic organizers. These palmtop devices function like spiral-bound appointment books—except that they cost five times as much, break easily when dropped, require batteries, force you to learn a new software program (from a 200-page manual), are easily stolen, take twice as long to enter data into or retrieve information from, are impossible to read in dim light, and communicate with your office PC only at great expense and trouble. But they cut a sophisticated image (geek chic), and lots of business-people, especially in Japan, now use them. Heaven knows why.

If this sounds discouraging, understand that between high portability and high usability you'll find hundreds of splendid portable computers. Settling on a model with compromises you can live with rests on two criteria: touch and feel, and actual road work.

Touch and Feel

Despite the computer industry's obsessive preoccupation with notebook power, memory, and speed, it's the layout of the machine's keyboard and the snap and throw of its keys that more realistically determine how much work you'll accomplish on the road. Likewise, the brightness and clarity of its screen matters more than the size of its hard disk. To be happy with a portable, you've got to do more than dance your fingers across its keyboard and glance wistfully at its display. Try to *live* with a notebook before you buy it.

But how? This can be tricky, especially if you're shopping by mail-order. Consider a couple of tactics:

- Borrow one from a colleague or friend. Even if you know beforehand that it's not the model you plan to buy, a borrowed portable can help you recognize what you like—and don't like—in a keyboard and display.

- Rent one. Better still, get your company to rent one for you. A weekend rental should cost no more than $100. (Hint: Avoid outfits that are strictly in the PC rental business; look for computer retail shops that rent machines on the side. You'll find less selection, but better prices.)

- Buy one on a trial basis. Whether from a showroom or a mail-order house, your computer should come with a 30-day, money-back guarantee (never buy a computer, portable or otherwise, that doesn't). Use this grace period to get intimate with it. But be prepared for your salesperson's sarcasm when you explain that you're returning the machine "because it just doesn't feel right." It is an unfortunate consequence of selling complex technology over the counter. It is not your problem.

As you scout around for a suitable machine, also consider how much work you expect to accomplish on the road—and be fiercely honest with yourself on this score. It's easy to believe that, with portable PC in tow, you can use work to mortar over the delays, snags, and endless empty hours that pock business travel. But only the dreariest grind makes every traveling moment miraculously productive. Because most of us tend to pack more work than we'll ever accomplish, we buy portables with more gadgets, features, and Ho-Hos than we'll ever use.

Contrary to the images portrayed in laptop advertisements, engineers do not design human heart valves in hotel bars. Accountants do not reconcile corporate receivables on the 8:40 Delta to Denver. Wayfaring businesspeople who attempt elaborate PC projects have forgotten about howling babies, droning in-flight announcements, endless queues, jet lag, delayed meetings, missed appointments, banquet-food nausea, and the thousand other interruptions and distractions that make business travel so dreadful.

Our advice? On that next 16-hour flight to Taipei, tap out a memo on your $1,200 notebook PC, tweak your spreadsheet sales forecast, then sink into a long, cheesy sci-fi novel. It'll make you more productive than you ever imagined.

Heft

Portable PCs come roughly in four categories of size and weight: luggables, laptops, notebooks, and palmtops. Bear in mind three maxims about size:

- The smaller the PC, the more fragile it is.
- Powerful, feature-crammed notebooks have proportionally shorter lifespans than rudimentary models.
- Many manufacturers neglect to include the battery and/or recharger in the weight they cite. These can add 2 to 4 pounds to your load.

Seasoned travelers will also tell you that, despite your better instincts, size is often more important than weight. Notebook-sized PCs drop nimbly into briefcases, poise primly on airplane tray tables, and slip snugly under the seat in front of you. Laptops and luggables require overhead luggage bins, sky caps, and wheelbarrows.

There's almost no reason to buy a luggable these days, unless you need it for presentations in which great processing muscle, immense storage capacity, expansion slots, or detailed color graphics drive the show. Instead of paying the premium that luggables command, consider renting a desktop PC in the cities you visit (most rental outfits will deliver and configure a machine to your liking). Or, send one of your company's desktop systems to your host's office via overnight courier. Not only does this save the nuisance and peril of transporting a computer by hand, but your machine is insured during transit as well.

Traditional laptops, which weigh 8 to 18 pounds, are receding almost as quickly as luggables. Before you dismiss them, however, consider that many come with gas plasma screens, which are far easier on the eyes than most notebook LCD displays. Many laptops also feature larger screens and snappier, fuller sized keyboards than notebooks.

If your portable travels only between your home and a weekend retreat, say, a dowdy 12-pound laptop might prevent you from going walleyed. The key is to ensure that both offices lie no more than two hundred paces from your car and that each has an available AC outlet (completely ignore what the laptop manufacturer claims about battery life). A better, though pricier solution is to buy a full-sized monitor for each location and shuttle a feathery notebook PC between them.

In fact, notebook PCs make sense for almost any arrangement. Weighing less than 8 pounds, they pack as much computing capability as most full-sized desktop systems. Consolidation of support chips, miniaturization of components, and vastly improved shock-mounting techniques have made them engineering marvels. They should be your first consideration.

This is not to say they are without compromise, of course. Cramped cases and the lack of a fan cause components to overheat and fail. Plan on two to three years of life for a 386 notebook; simpler models will last four or more. Also, notebook screens, port covers, hinges, and hard drives are still terribly fragile. Treat your machine gingerly.

Processor

As recently as a year ago, selecting a notebook by its processor was relatively easy. However, a flood of new chips from Intel and Advanced Micro Devices has spread splendorous hype and merchandising murk across the portable market. Let computer magazines fret over the 25-megahertz 386SL notebook that delivers 12.6 more minutes of battery life than the 20-megahertz 386SXL, which consumes 14% less power than the 386DX, which costs $800 more than...et cetera, et cetera. The practical issues behind processors have changed very little in the past year. Deal with the practical issues.

The most economical, dependable, and durable notebook you can buy has either an 8088 or its equivalent, the V20 processor, a non-backlit screen, and no hard drive. You can pick one up for less than $600, its battery will last six hours or more between charges, and the machine will endure the ages. Unfortunately you must entrust software and data to frail floppies (that are easily forgotten, scrambled, or lost), and three hours of work with a non-backlit screen will give you hallucinations and spasmodic tics. But for receiving and answering electronic mail, dashing out a letter or memo, or patching a spreadsheet model on an afternoon commuter train, an 8088 delivers tremendous value.

Step up a generation of processors, to an 80286 notebook, and you get enough processing brawn to run any software that your desk machine runs (including Windows, though we advise against it). You also get a backlit or sidelit screen, which vastly improves on the shadowy blips of a nonilluminated LCD. Best of all, you can buy a 80286 notebook—with a hard drive—for less than $1,000. This is the price of civilized computing, and if you spend more than two hours at a time pecking on a portable, an 80286 is the processor you want.

That is, unless you use Windows, which singlehandedly justifies an 80386 notebook. Windows is slow, its applications slower. An 80386 processor will churn Windows' programming code fast enough to keep you from nodding off as you wait for a program to load or a file to save. Also, 80386 notebooks are more likely than 80286 varieties to accommodate the acres of memory and miles of hard disk space that Windows requires. If you use Windows on the road, however, you'll have to sort through a dozen or so hybrids of the 80386 chip. In so doing, keep four guidelines in mind:

- There is no such thing as a designer label for a microprocessor. The name of the chip's manufacturer matters not a whit.

- A 16-MHz 80386SX (SX) processor gives you the best value for the dollar; 20-MHz versions of the SX chip cost more, devour battery charge faster, and deliver proportionately less performance than their speed suggests (due to video and hard disk bottlenecks). Other, high-powered incarnations of the 80386 chip are power pigs that raise the price of a notebook by a full magnitude.

- Three exceptions to this last claim are the 80386SL (SL), the AM386SXLV (SXL), and the AM386DXLV (DXL), which allegedly save up to 50% more battery charge than other 80386 chips (and were designed specifically for portables). This claim is mostly gas; battery life depends on the design of the machine, the design of its components, and its power-management features. These low-power chips generally aren't worth the premium they slap onto the price of a notebook (as much as $1,500). But, if you find an SL, SXL, or DXL notebook priced comparably to an SX model, forego the SX. The other chips are faster, and they'll save at least marginally more battery life.

- If you think you'd be happier with an 80486 notebook for travel, you need a reality check. It's gross overkill.

Display

Great promotional hoopla will be made about your notebook's screen technology, whichever technology that might be—super-twist, double super-twist, or any of a dozen other designs. But no display technology is inherently superior. After a weekend of work, your eyes will report back on the quality and long-term usability of a notebook screen. Trust your eyes. Leave the brochures with your salesperson.

Aside from addressing any obvious visual clues, you should investigate several key questions about the display:

- Is the screen backlit or sidelit (sometimes called "edgelit")? Backlit screens are typically brighter than sidelit screens, but they consume battery charge faster. Is battery or brightness more important to you?

- Does the screen display 16 or 32 shades of gray? Do not pay extra for a 32–gray-scale display; 16 gray scales are usually more than adequate. In fact, a shoddy 32–gray-scale notebook display is often murkier than a run-of-the-mill 16–gray-scale variety. Examine gray scales by using a graphics file (the logo on the opening screen of many software programs will suffice). Look for evenness of shading across the display. Also, scrutinize graphical details for clarity. Can you discern a tool icon in a Windows toolbar from a glance, for example?

- Is the display area at least 8 inches × 6 inches? Does the image on the screen fill the entire display area? Even automated teller machines offer larger viewing areas these days.

- Does the notebook come with an adapter to which you can hook an external monitor? Even if you use your portable primarily on airplanes, occasions will arise (during a visit to a client's office, for example) when the availability of an external monitor will bring blissful relief to your eyes. VGA is the de facto graphics standard today.

- Does the machine include a reverse-screen mode so that you can switch from black letters on a white screen to white letters on a black screen? Not only does this help when working under dubious light, but the white-letters-on-black mode saves up to 25% of your battery charge.

- Does the display provide adequate brightness and contrast? A good notebook has independent knobs for adjusting these. Set them for the clearest image you can, then look for flicker—a telltale sign of a bad display. Also, scroll through some text on the screen to see if a faint trail of letters lingers. This is called "ghosting," and it is the stuff of headaches.

Color displays are a fetish. Resist them. Color is coming to portables, yes, but it hasn't arrived. The current crop of "passive-matrix" color notebooks costs in the $3,500 to $5,000 range. They offer dim screens, washed-out hues, and murky tones. They're awful. "Active-matrix" color notebooks, on the other hand, look fabulous, but you should expect to pay $4,000 to $11,000 to get one out of a dealer's showroom. Try not to drop it on the way out.

Memory

Most notebook memory is proprietary, plain and simple. Prices per megabyte range from a steep $99 to an appalling $945. Even when one model of notebook wears different labels (as many imported notebooks do), prices for memory between the same machines can differ by as much as $470 per megabyte. It's criminal.

All notebooks should come with at least 1 megabyte of memory as standard equipment, which is adequate for most road work under DOS. If you use Windows—or if you think you might use Windows in the future—you'll want at least 2, but more likely 3 or 4 megabytes.

To keep memory costs down, buy all the memory you'll ever need at the time you purchase your notebook. Negotiate a discount on the price of the extra memory by 20% to 40% as part of the whole package. This not only gets you a better deal, but it saves future installation costs and hassles. Be aware that many notebooks promise to save you said installation costs by letting you add memory yourself through a latched opening on the machine. But such memory tends to be pricier than other varieties. Besides, dust and moisture collect and corrode the innards of your notebook when the latch breaks off—which it inevitably will do.

Storage

Most of the loonier schemes for storing data on portable PCs have died fitful, overdue deaths. Of the practical survivors, stick to conventional hard and floppy disks.

Advances in hard drive design have been absolutely staggering. Today it is possible to buy a 6-pound notebook PC with a 200-megabyte hard drive—an unthinkable feat even three years ago. Of course, you'll pay steeply for such storage capacity, and any boob who entrusts 200-megabytes of data to a computer that gets bandied about in everyday travel has an unhappy surprise lurking in the future. However, because so many businesspeople now demand notebooks with large-capacity hard drives, prices on humble 40- and 60-megabyte models have plummeted.

Therein lies a bargain. A notebook with a 40-megabyte hard drive can cost 35% less than the same notebook with an 80-megabyte hard drive. For most any road-bound businesspeople, even if they use Windows, 40 megabytes is more than adequate. If you work more hours at your portable PC than at your desktop PC, you might look for bargains in notebooks with 60-megabyte hard drives; sales will proliferate in the coming year. But, whichever capacity you settle on, make sure the drive's advertised "seek time" is 25 milliseconds (msec) or less. Slower drives often use a moribund technology that has proven less reliable and less shock resistant.

Don't even consider buying a notebook that doesn't include a 1.44-megabyte internal floppy drive. It's the quickest way for shuffling files between desktop and portable PCs. Floppies are also handy for backing up data—critical for road work since notebooks get stolen and hard drives crash, especially when they travel.

The alternative for shuttling data between notebook and desktop PCs is a fussy file-transfer program or an external floppy drive. These require cables and manuals and forethought. They add complexity and bulk to your travels. They're a pain.

Power

Most notebooks run on rechargeable nickel cadmium batteries (NiCads). Though notebook manufacturers routinely exaggerate the charge life of their batteries, the preposterous claims that the industry issued just two years ago have largely stopped. An occasional salesperson might report straight-faced that your portable will hold six hours of battery charge. Tell him that his nose is growing. Notebook batteries last, at most, two to three hours between charges, regardless of the machine.

A few notebooks come with nickel metal hydride batteries, which hold a longer charge than NiCads (though claims that they'll provide 33% more charge are ridiculous). Also, nickel metal hydrides don't suffer the "memory effect" of NiCads. To get a full three hours of power from a NiCad, you must drain the battery completely before recharging it. If you drain it only half way before recharging, you'll get only half the charge. It's a nuisance. Although nickel metal hydrides don't have this problem, they remain an expensive alternative, as you'll quickly glean from the sticker price of the notebooks that use them—and from replacement batteries when the originals finally die. Generally the convenience of nickel metal hydrides isn't worth their cost.

Battery life also depends on your notebook's power-management features, though their importance is often grotesquely overstated both by salespeople and by the computer press. At best, power-management features extend battery charge by minutes, not hours. On many models, they deliver not even a gasp of extra battery life. Windows users beware: power-management features that operate under DOS won't necessarily work under Windows, despite your salesperson's vague, sincere promises. You'll have to investigate these firsthand. In any case, here are the key power-management features to look for (in order of importance):

- Deep-sleep and stand-by modes: Stop typing for a few (specified) minutes, and the computer automatically dims the display and spins down the hard disk.

- Instant resume mode: Stop work for a longer period of time, and your machine shuts down automatically. Tap a key, and the computer springs back to life exactly where you left off, without going through a power-consuming cold boot.

- Slow clock speed: The computer automatically switches to a slower speed when the processor isn't being used to prolong battery life.
- Battery gauge: Punch a special key combination, and a gauge pops onto the display to show how much battery charge is left. Unlike low-battery warning lights (or obnoxious beeps), battery gauges let you plan your work around remaining battery charge.

Don't get too hopeful, however. Batteries are a fuss, not only for their short lives, but because they add bulk and weight to your travels. Notebook makers should instinctively provide two batteries with each portable they sell, so that you can recharge one battery while you're using the other. But, of course, they don't. You'll have to pay for the extra battery—and for an external recharger in many cases (most notebooks recharge their batteries internally). Negotiate these items when you purchase your notebook—and demand that your dealer discount their prices.

Ports

For all the bother that batteries present, your notebook should keep other nuisances to a minimum by connecting to the civilized world wherever possible. In addition to a VGA port that lets you hook a desktop monitor to your notebook, for example, a good portable should come with a serial port (to connect a modem, a fax, a serial printer, or a pointing device) and a parallel port (to connect a parallel printer or a device that hooks you to a computer network). Also, look for a port that lets you attach a full-sized keyboard to the machine, and for a "PS/2 Mouse" port that lets you connect a bus mouse, leaving your serial port free.

Many notebooks also feature ports that connect to an expansion chassis, sometimes called a "docking station" or "expansion bus." These boxy devices look like—and purport to function as—full-blown desktop PCs, minus the processor. Dock your mothership notebook to one and, presto, your portable PC becomes space-age desktop computer. At least that's how the ads portray them. In reality, docking stations are expensive ($300 to $3,500), fragile, and limited.

Nits

Though personal preferences and travel experience will guide you to a notebook you can live with, design details can haunt you months after your purchase. These few secrets should keep regrets at bay:

- Better notebooks position cursor keys in an inverted "T" shape. Cursor keys positioned horizontally or as a backwards "L" will drive you to profanity after an hour's work.

- The *best* notebooks offer independent Page Up and Page Down keys.

- Middle-hinged notebooks are easier to use on airplanes than "clamshell" designs with the hinge on the back of the unit. When the person in front of you lowers his or her seat back, a clamshell unit folds.

- Look between the keys of your notebook for a rubber or plastic lining beneath the keyboard. This helps protect circuit boards from dust and spills.

- Port covers that slide open are less likely to break off than the hinged kind that flip open. Also, some makers design port covers that pop off. These are easier to lose, but less likely to break.

- If your notebook manufacturer seems obscure, check for an FCC Class B Certification on the bottom of the unit. If there's no FCC label or if the label looks suspicious, call the Federal Communications Commission (check the blue pages in your phone book for the FCC office in your area). FCC certifications are often counterfeited and sold to back-alley manufacturers.

- If you're buying a notebook to run Windows, insist that the dealer throw in a pointing device such as a portable trackball mouse. You'll need it to run Windows, and it'll cost you as much as $100 if you have to buy it separately.

- Notebooks absorb life's knocks as gracefully as overripened cantaloupe. Your portable should come with a carrying case; if the case is just thinly lined with foam, consider getting a thicker one.

Warranty/Service

Unlike desktop PCs, there's almost nothing inside a notebook you can repair or replace yourself (and prying open a notebook case invites catastrophe). Repair shops charge $100 or more per hour, which makes even minor maintenance expensive. Thus your notebook should come with at least a one-year warranty that covers every wire and screw.

You should also find out if you can service your notebook locally—and how long repairs take. Many notebook problems result simply from wire connections that have jostled loose, which is a five-minute repair that can take weeks if you have to box up your portable, ship it across the country, and then have it shipped back. Better shops will even provide a loaner notebook while yours is in surgery (ask about this).

Excess Baggage

A raft of sleek, miniature notebook add-ons and peripherals now promise to put your entire office on an airplane tray table. Portable printers, modems, hard drives, fax cards, and CD-ROM drives increasingly squeeze out galoshes and extra underwear for space in the traveling businessperson's luggage. "They are practical accessories," computer magazines assure us. Unfortunately these gadgets travel with baggage of their own.

With your portable modem, for example, you'll probably want to bring along a spare battery and an AC adapter (in addition to the one you carry for your notebook). Add a portable printer to your load (don't forget the cable), and you'll need a third AC adapter, a battery, spare ribbons, and paper. Besides the bulk, weight, complexity, and arguments with airport security that these toys incite, they're almost always underused.

If a specific chore turns up frequently in your journeys, a traveling gizmo might make life easier. More likely, it will just get stolen, lost, or damaged. Apply even a little imagination, and you can almost always find a safer, cheaper, more convenient arrangement. If you're not sure you will need a traveling peripheral, you probably won't. The peripherals most likely to make themselves useful are printers, faxes, and modems (see Chapter 5 for more on portable CD-ROM and hard drives).

Portable Printers

Portable printers suffer all the shortcomings of early portable PCs. They're heavy, slow (one to two pages per minute), costly (both in price and in consumables), finicky, and short-lived. Also, their print quality tends to be primitive when compared with the documents that a full-sized desktop printer produces. But, for printing copies of contracts or legal documents to be signed on the spot, a portable printer can make sense. Models that produce near-professional-quality pages cost less than $500.

Printers come in three flavors: thermal transfer or thermal fusion, inkjet, and dot matrix. Thermal transfer and thermal fusion printers produce pages that approximate laser-quality documents if you don't look too closely. Inkjets cost anywhere from $50 to $150 less, but the type is generally fuzzier than what thermal printers churn out (and most models use an ink that isn't waterproof). But for simple charts and documents that don't need to endure, they'll suffice.

Portable dot-matrix printers are...loud. Churlish and crude, they cost as much or more than their full-sized counterparts—and as much as portable thermal printers. You won't save much on consumables, either, since their ribbons are proprietary.

Because no portable printer delivers the quality of a desktop laser, the technology driving the machine matters less than its convenience. Keep several key criteria in mind.

Portability

The best portable printers slip into a briefcase alongside your notebook—cables and AC adapter included. Portable printers weigh between 3 and 8 pounds, with most falling in the 5- to 6-pound range. Keep in mind that when traveling with both an 8-pound notebook and a 6-pound printer, you'll want curb-to-curb taxi service wherever you go. (Try to avoid changing airplanes in Chicago, Atlanta, or Dallas.) Make sure you have very well-padded shoulder straps on your carrying case, and think about buying the type of luggage dolly that's popular with flight attendants.

Battery

The battery, AC adapter, and necessary cables should be included in the price of your printer—this can be a shifty way for a dealer to lift an extra $40 to $350 from your wallet. Battery life generally isn't too important. You'll run out of cartridge ink first.

Consumables

Portable printers are expensive to feed. Their cartridges are, of course, proprietary and, hence, expensive (figure $15 for a cartridge that prints 20 to 50 pages). They're also hard to find. Make sure you can get cartridges from a variety of sources.

Compatibility

A printer is only as useful as the software applications that can print to it. Make sure your portable printer emulates Hewlett-Packard's DeskJet printer (the standard for inkjet printers) or that it has IBM ProPrinter or Epson emulation.

Modems and Fax/Modems

Most notebooks now come with proprietary slots that hold an optional internal (built-in) modem. This cuts traveling bulk and weight and ensures you won't forget or lose your modem (unless you forget or lose your notebook). However, because each modem design is proprietary, it's typically overpriced—as much as three times the cost of an external portable modem. Internal modems also draw on a notebook's battery power, shortening an already fleeting workspan.

An emerging standard in the industry, called PCMCIA, will eventually junk the proprietary designs of today's internal notebook modems. When enough notebooks come with PCMCIA slots, third-party modems will begin to appear. These will drive prices down. Unfortunately this is a year, probably two, down the road.

Instead, stick with an external portable modem or fax/modem. Widely available, they cost roughly the same as a full-sized modem. Also, an external portable modem can serve double-duty for home and office—and save space in the process.

When buying one, apply the same rules you would for choosing a desktop modem (see Chapter 5), but take size and weight into consideration. Few portable modems have LED lights (blinking lights that tell you what the modem is doing), though most

people don't need these anyway. There are a few other considerations to keep in mind as you buy.

Battery and Power

Portable modems draw their power either from batteries, an AC
adapter, or from the phone line. Older portable modems are
smaller than desktop models, but they rely on a bulky AC adapter
for their power. Toting both modem and AC adapter is a hassle;
if possible, go with a battery-powered model. Your best bet is one
that uses standard AA alkaline batteries, which are inexpensive
and are available everywhere.

Sleeker portable modems draw their power from the phone
line—a terrific convenience that raises the cost of the modem by
$100 or so. Bear in mind that faster (9,600 bps) modems require
too much power to run off a phone line. They need batteries.

Make sure an AC adapter for your modem is included in the purchase price. An "optional" AC adapter means you pay extra for it.

Heft

Modems vary between a few ounces to as much as 5 pounds. The
lighter (and smaller) the modem, generally, the more it costs. It's
like nouvelle cuisine.

Warranty/Service

Most modem problems are software, not hardware, related. Modems typically fail the first time you use them—or never. Don't
be seduced by extended warranties. Just make sure you can get
a full refund should the thing fail in the first few weeks.

Fax/Modems

If you truly expect to send faxes on the road, consider a portable
fax/modem—but don't pay more than $100 extra for the faxing
capability. (As an alternative to buying a fax card, some electronic mail services such as MCI allow you to send messages as
faxes—a far better solution for infrequent faxing.)

Beware of fax/modems that seem too inexpensive; they may only
allow you to *send* faxes, not receive them. Fax/modems should
come with some kind of fax software (if you have to buy software
separately, it'll cost another $75–$150 and may not support your

particular fax/modem). Also, make sure it can fax files created with your word processor. Fax software can be fiercely annoying to navigate, so try to test drive the software first or get a fax/modem you can return, software and all. If you can't bear the fax software, at least you can return the whole package for a refund.

ALPHABET SOUP

Backlit Display: Unlike the nonlit LCD display typical of a calculator or a digital watch, a backlit display illuminates text and graphics from a light source directly behind the screen. It enables you to read your screen in dim light.

The Lowdown: Brighter than sidelit displays, backlit screens use battery charge faster. Make sure your notebook comes with a reverse screen mode, which saves battery life when power is more important than brightness.

Expansion Chassis: Also called "docking stations" or "expansion buses," these devices typically come with extra disk drives (for floppies and/or hard disks), expansion slots, and communications ports. Plug your notebook into an expansion chassis, and it becomes a full-powered desktop PC...sort of.

The Lowdown: An expensive and quirky compromise between true desktop and portable computing, most expansion chassis are fragile, limited, and lack a fan to prolong your notebook's life. They'll also cost you $800 or more, even though their components

cost less than $200. This price rarely includes the full-sized keyboard and external monitor you'll want for working extended hours at your computer.

File Transfer Program: A software program that copies files to/from your portable PC from/to your desktop PC via a special ("null modem") cable that connects to the communications port in each machine.

The Lowdown: Despite several excellent file-transfer packages available, the technology is still a hassle. Instead, get a notebook with an internal floppy drive.

Gas Plasma: A type of laptop display that renders finer resolution and higher contrast than standard LCD displays.

The Lowdown: Gas plasma displays devour battery charge faster than sidelit displays, but slower than backlit varieties. Although they offer much better contrast than other kinds of displays, they're nearly impossible to read in bright light. Also, they cost more, typically adding $300 or more to the price of your notebook.

Laptop: Briefcase-sized portable PC that weighs roughly 8 to 18 pounds. →

The Lowdown: Walk five city blocks with an 11-pound computer on your shoulder, and you'll realize how nonportable a portable can be. Brighter screens and fuller sized keyboards than you'll find on notebooks make laptops handy if you travel only between car and office. Otherwise, look for something svelter.

LCD (liquid crystal display): Most laptop and notebook PCs use a display that is flatter and dimmer than a conventional desktop monitor. A few of the many variations on LCD technology are super-twist neumatic (STN), triple super-twist neumatic (TSTN), and thin film transistor (TFT).

The Lowdown: Don't concern yourself with a display's underlying technology. Judge a screen with your eyes.

Luggable: A portable PC that weighs 18 pounds or more.

The Lowdown: Used mostly for traveling business presentations, luggables are onerous to tote—even with their requisite luggage dollies. Simpler, more agreeable solutions abound.

NiCad (Nickel Cadmium) Batteries: The most common type of rechargeable battery used in portable PCs.

The Lowdown: To get a full three hours of power from a NiCad, you must drain the battery completely before recharging it. Also, NiCads eventually lose their ability to hold a charge. Find out about prices for replacement batteries before you buy your portable.

Nickel Metal Hydride Batteries: A type of rechargeable battery used in some portable PCs.

The Lowdown: Unlike NiCads, nickel metal hydride batteries don't require you to deplete the charge completely before recharging. They also hold their charge longer, but they're more expensive—often twice the price.

Notebook PC: A portable PC weighing between 4 and 8 pounds, and measuring 9 in. × 12 in. × 3 in. or smaller.

The Lowdown: For most computing chores, notebooks offer the least portability/usability tradeoffs possible.

Palmtop PC: A portable PC that weighs two pounds or less and that slips daintily into a jacket pocket.

The Lowdown: An overpriced, overcomplex, highly fragile "DayTimer." Though eminently portable, palmtops aren't even remotely as useful as notebook PCs.

Personal Computer Memory Card International Association (PCMCIA): An emerging industry standard that allows credit-card-sized peripherals such as modems, network cards, or fax boards to fit into notebooks with PCMCIA-compliant slots.

The Lowdown: Because all manufacturers can build peripherals to this standard, prices for notebook add-ons will drop. But don't hold your breath; significant price drops are at least two years away. →

Power-Management Features: Software utilities that come with a notebook to conserve battery life by powering down the hard disk when it's not in use or dimming the display, among other tricks.

The Lowdown: At best, they'll extend battery charge by 50 minutes or so. At worst, they'll do nothing at all. Unfortunately you can only determine their effectiveness with first-hand experience.

Sidelit Screen: Also called edgelit screens, sidelit displays are typically dimmer, with less evenness of illumination than backlit screens.

The Lowdown: Sidelighting conserves battery life better than backlighting—and costs less as reflected in the sticker price of the notebook. ❏

Shopper's Checklist

There's no substitute for living with your notebook before you tie the knot. The quality of its display and keyboard are highly subjective matters. An extra pound of weight can mean everything... or nothing. Personal work styles and travel habits notwithstanding, any decent notebook should include the following features:

❏ Acceptable keyboard layout and feel

❏ Legible 8" × 6" display

❏ Reverse screen mode

❏ Weighs less than 8 pounds—battery and cables included

❏ Battery and recharger included in price

❏ 1.44 MB, 3 ½-inch floppy drive

❏ Acceptable size (think notebook, not encyclopedia)

❏ 1MB of memory (2–4MB for running Windows on a 386)

❏ At least one serial and one parallel port

❏ Connector for external keyboard and VGA monitor

❏ 30-day return period

❏ One-year parts/labor warranty on all components

❏ Repairs available locally

For a 286 or 386 notebook, also insist on the following:

❏ 40MB hard drive with 25 msec seek time (or less)

❏ Backlit or edgelit display

❏ Power-management features:

    ❏ Deep-sleep, stand-by, and reverse screen modes

    ❏ Instant resume

    ❏ Slow clock speed

    ❏ Battery gauge

This more likely describes the manufacturer. Notice there's no mention of warranty and support.

Fh?! Noise is not exactly a burning issue with any hard drive. Besides, your PC's fan will easily drown out a groaning hard drive.

A manufacturer shouting in a tin can; this means nothing.

Luger Technologies' Carbine MX80

Low-profile, 80-megabyte 3.5-inch form factor drive with embedded AT or SCSI controller and 15-msec access time

Unsurpassed performance and design are the Luger trademark and the Carbine MX80 delivers both. Our 64K FlintLock Cache, a 1:1 interleave, straight-arm actuator with patented magnetic lock, embedded servo controller, and high-performance rotary voice coil add up to the fastest 80-MB drive you can buy. Our low-acoustic, 150,000-hour MTBF Carbine MX80 is also one of the most reliable drives available.

Key Features	
Internal transfer rate	up to 24.0 Mbits/sec
External transfer rate	6.0 MBytes/sec
Track-to-track seek	under 4 msec
Average seek	12 msec
Maximum seek	35 msec
Average latency	6.67 msec
Recording method	RLL 2,7

The mention of seek times is a sleight of hand to divert you from the numbers that matter: transfer rate and access time. Notice the latter isn't included.

Find out if mounting rails are included. If not, add $10 to $100 for brackets or rails that hold the drive in place.

An abbreviation for "Mean Time Between Failure," MTBF is the manufacturer's guess at how long the drive will chug along before it dies. Operating eight hours a day, seven days a week, this drive should last more than 51 years. Do you believe that?

Triths dwethmun aslpikftm dokszfaq. Got that?

Upgrades
and
Repairs

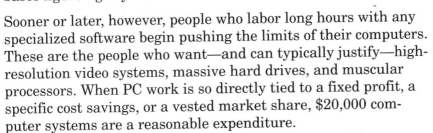

To a privy cast of professionals, the computer doesn't augment work so much as define it: the self-employed graphics designer who owes his livelihood to desktop publishing, the engineer whose career rides on the blips of light she chases around a screen all day, the accountant whose software maintains lordly corporate order. Their ranks are smaller than computer marketeers would have you believe, and whatever it is that they do with their PCs, word processing, spreadsheets, and databases figure lightly into their work if at all.

Sooner or later, however, people who labor long hours with any specialized software begin pushing the limits of their computers. These are the people who want—and can typically justify—high-resolution video systems, massive hard drives, and muscular processors. When PC work is so directly tied to a fixed profit, a specific cost savings, or a vested market share, $20,000 computer systems are a reasonable expenditure.

Of course, the vast majority of people who buy such high-end gear don't need it at all. They're PC hot rodders, people for whom the computer is a source of amusement, a science project, a media center, a hobby, and perhaps, reluctantly, a tool. Usually considered the office experts in PCs, hot rodders wheedle extravagant equipment from their bosses under the fatuous guise of "need." ("But sir, with a larger monitor, I'd spend less time scrolling through my spreadsheet. I could get that report out faster.")

Egged on by computer magazines, hot rodders tend to infect whole organizations with possessive longings for new gadgetry, slicker components. Eventually office electronics become status symbols, dreary desk ornaments that signify an employee's worth to the organization. Many companies even reward diligent workers with new computer toys. It is only mildly ironic that the corporate overlords outfitted with the most expensive computer equipment generally accomplish less with it than do their underlings.

PC hot rodders bleed money from an organization in countless unnecessary ways. They also ruin it for everyone else. When a non-nerd has a legitimate need for upgrading components, he or she must surmount bureaucratic skepticism and scowls to get it. The operative term there is "legitimate need," which is admittedly treacherous terrain. By and large, you'll have to conclude for yourself when an upgrade merits the cost. Some general symptoms, however, will tell you when your system is hitting a wall and how to upgrade it without selling your children into slavery.

Your Software Throws Tantrums

The signs can be subtle: occasional "Out of Memory" error messages; a glib refusal to open help screens or spelling checkers; prolonged memory-to-disk swapping as manifested by frequent, short flashes of the hard drive light; and general foot-dragging as a program loads or saves a file, changes fonts, or scrolls through pages. When one program exhibits these traits, it may indicate nothing more than poor software design. When two programs show these signs, you probably need more memory. Adding memory is the cheapest way to pacify cranky software.

You're Growing Old

No one likes waiting for a computer to do its job, but speed is a complex problem, only sometimes solved with one-stop solutions such as adding more memory or by installing a video board with a graphics coprocessor. More often a slow computer results from several bottlenecks. Try software solutions first; any good book on DOS or Windows will entreat you to try tricks for hot rodding your operating environment without spending a penny. Then consider adding memory. Keep in mind that if your word processing software, your database manager, and Windows all run slowly, you'll likely want to upgrade your CPU, your hard drive, and your video card. A better solution? Buy a new computer.

There's No Place to Stash

Hard drives fill woefully fast, especially if you use Windows. When you run out of room, take an hour to clear off old files you no longer need. Then consider compressing old "archive" files that you seldom (or never) use, but want to keep. Both hardware and software compression utilities will do this. Software solutions are cheaper; hardware/software solutions are faster, but cost as much as a hard drive. A second hard drive that works alongside your current drive is the most painless solution. They're expensive, yes, but like household closet space, you can almost always use more. You won't regret buying one.

You're Going Blind

Upgrading your PC's video system often requires two pricey purchases since the monitor you buy is only as good as the video card supporting it. The pair can set you back $500 to $2,500 or more—but it may save your eyes. Headaches and dizziness often result from vision problems (exacerbated by sitting in front of a monitor day in and day out).

R.I.P.

A defunct hard drive, monitor, system board, or other component provides a timely excuse to replace it with a faster, spiffier version. The key is to decide when replacing the whole computer makes better sense.

CPUs

Computer makers love to crow about their "upgradeable CPUs" as a sign of their continuing commitment to protecting your technology investment. However, the fact is that *all* PCs have upgradeable CPUs, and the "upgradeable" designation so fashionable in computer advertisements these days guarantees neither cost savings nor convenience. Worse, it tells you nothing about how long the PC will remain upgradeable into the future (in fact some companies sell upgradeable PCs even though the upgrades don't exist).

Brain Transplant

There are scores of ways to switch out an older CPU for a more advanced processor. Besides cost and convenience tradeoffs, most solutions inflict some kind of technical compromise, some performance hit.

At the very least, you can switch out your system's motherboard. Not only does this give you a more sophisticated processor, but it ensures that the basic input/output system (BIOS), the chips that control the underlying instructions between your PC and its peripherals, are compatible with the new CPU. Also, it allows your system to accept memory fast enough to keep from dogging your CPU. Moreover, motherboards quite often cost less than the upgrade cards on upgradeable PCs: $350 for a 33-MHz 386 motherboard, compared to as much as $1,100 for some upgrade cards.

Replacing a motherboard is not for technical sissies, however. It can devour a day or more of your time. Installation instructions tend to be scant, if they exist at all. Furthermore, most board makers sell to PC manufacturers—not to consumers. You might not be able to get technical support of any sort. Check this out well in advance, and look for an illustrated book on building your own PC before you begin. Better yet, let a dealer swap boards for you. If the $100 to $150 fee isn't worth the time it saves you, the warranty on workmanship is.

When shopping for a motherboard, you'll want to know not only the number of expansion slots and the amount of memory it can hold (for technical specifics about these and any other components discussed here, see Chapter 3), but also whether such extras as a memory cache, integrated video or drive controllers, and serial and parallel ports come with it. Otherwise, you may have to buy these. Make sure the motherboard can fit inside your old computer case; new cases cost $50 to $250. Check to see that your old power supply is compatible with the new board; power supplies cost $50 to $200. Find out if your old memory chips are both fast enough to work in the new board and come in the right configuration; memory will set you back about $50 a megabyte.

Indeed, it's frighteningly easy to wind up wrapping a new PC around an old hard drive without noticing you've done it. Swapping motherboards will often cost more in cash, time, and trouble than buying a new computer outright. You'll have to fight with several vendors for warranty and technical support. It drives the resale value of your system down, not up. It's rarely a good idea. Look carefully before you leap.

Accelerators

Another moribund technology, accelerator cards, places the barebones components of a motherboard on a card that fits in an expansion slot. They're far easier to install than motherboards, but they cost almost as much and don't offer nearly as complete a solution.

Use an accelerator to transform a 286-based PC into a 386 system, for example, and you'll get a noticeable increase in performance. However, because the 386 chip still traffics data along the 286's narrow 16-bit bus, your applications don't run nearly as fast as they could. A good CPU upgrade should deliver either a startling increase in performance at a high price or a noticeable increase at a reasonable price. Accelerator cards do neither. May they rest in peace.

Let your software help you find the price/performance tradeoff that best suits your needs; a specific program that won't fly on your current system should lead you to a CPU upgrade. Don't swap processors merely to satisfy vague yearnings for faster system performance. There are cheaper ways to get speed; more memory, a disk cache, and a faster video card are good places to start.

286 to 386

Windows makes the best case for turning an 80286-based PC into an 80386 (don't even contemplate upgrading an 8086-based PC; see "Diminishing Returns"). The 386 provides "virtual 8086 mode," which enables Windows to run more than one program concurrently—something it can't do on the 286 chip. The 386 also accommodates the memory manager that comes with Windows (or any memory manager, for that matter), which provides as much free RAM to your programs as DOS will let them use.

Unfortunately you can't simply yank the 286 processor and insert a 386 CPU in its place. The 386 requires support chips; it comes mounted on a circuit board that you install. If your PC is "upgradeable" by design, you'll have to get the upgrade board from your manufacturer, though several third-party companies make 386 upgrade boards for "non-upgradeable" PCs as well. These must be designed specifically for your system's make and model. Installing them can be tricky, and they sometimes →

Diminishing Returns:
The 10 Commandments of Upgrading

Upgrades don't always pay off. A new video card, extra memory, or a fast hard drive can revitalize an old clunker—or simply hang off it like a dashboard ornament. The trick is knowing when to upgrade, and when to sell your heap for money that can help buy a better machine. It's never a clear issue, but several tenets may help lead you to the promised land:

1. **Don't upgrade an 8088 PC—ever.** They're antiques. More memory, a faster video card, or a bigger, speedier hard drive won't make an iota of difference in performance. Besides, most 8088 upgrades cost as much or more than the value of the PC.

2. **A PC is only as fast as its slowest component.** Dress up a sluggish 10-MHz, 286-based system with an ultra-fast hard drive, 6 megabytes of memory, and a high-end video card, and it still plods along at 10 MHz.

3. **Upgrades don't always improve the resale value of your PC.** Chic add-ons and snazzy extras lose 50 percent to 90 percent of their original value as soon as you drop them in your PC. Buy them to add value to your work; they add little to your investment.

4. **Add to a system rather than replace core components.** Adding more memory or a second hard drive is generally a better upgrade than replacing the motherboard or the original hard drive. If replacing core components is an issue, consider buying a better PC. →

5. **The best upgrades are those you can do yourself**. Installing your own components saves you the bother (and hazards) of packing up your PC and taking it to a shop—where technicians will fleece you for upwards of $50 to $75 an hour even for routine installations. Besides, repair shops charge top dollar for replacement parts; buy them yourself and you can shop around.

6. **Don't spend more than $1,000 on an upgrade**. Ideally you want to spend no more than $200 to $300 on an upgrade, and considerably less than the cost of buying a new system. After all, for $1,000, you can buy a decent 386-based computer.

7. **Everything costs extra**. Add a $600 hard drive, and you may discover that you also need a new BIOS ($75–$300), not to mention the mounting kit, cables, and host card it may require. Pretty soon your upgrade costs more than replacing the entire PC. Incidentally, don't forget installation costs.

8. **Proprietary parts will plunder your credit card**. A PC that only accepts one manufacturer's memory chips or an unusual size power supply is by definition expensive to upgrade and repair. If you discover this too late, sell your designer PC and put the money toward a new machine. Get out while you can.

9. **Don't run Windows on a 286 PC**. A 286 with 4 MB of memory can *load* Windows, but it can't take advantage of its multitasking or memory management features. Upgrade the processor or sell the machine for a 386-based PC.

10. **Multimedia is a very expensive science project**. Multimedia upgrade kits are the best way to turn your system into a singing, dancing distraction. They're widely available for $1,000 or less. As far as we can tell, however, there's no compelling evidence that multimedia has sufficient practical applications to offset its exorbitant costs. ❑

render an expansion slot unusable in the bargain. Even so, making them work is nothing like the open-heart surgery required in replacing a motherboard.

It makes little sense to upgrade a 286-based PC with anything more powerful than a 386SX chip. The SX delivers the functionality and speed Windows desires, and it matches the relatively narrow 16-bit data bus built into all 286-based PCs. More sophisticated incarnations of the 386 CPU cost more and can't run at full throttle without a wide 32-bit data bus. Also, they might require you to upgrade BIOS chips, which adds cost and complexity to your upgrade.

You'll get the best price/performance tradeoff on boards that run their SX chips at 25 MHz; they cost as little as $175. At those speeds you'll want your board to include at least 128K memory cache (256K is better) to compensate for lackadaisical RAM. Slower, 16-MHz and 20-MHz SX boards cost as little as $100 and don't really need a memory cache. The prices cited here are a bargain-basement variety. Owners of proprietary "upgradeable" PCs should expect to pay more—sometimes much more. Just be aware that the manufacturer that charges more than $500 for an SX upgrade board is swindling you. You're better off buying a new PC.

386 to 486

Turning a 386-based PC into a 486 machine requires more money, but it constitutes less of a technical leap since the guts of the 386 chip are what spawned the 486. Practically speaking, the 486 *is* a 386, a very fast one with a math coprocessor attached. (The exception is the 486SX chip, which has no math chip. Consequently there is no reason in the world to upgrade to a 486SX.) The 486 also includes an 8K internal cache, which allows the processor to work with slower memory in an old 386 without too much of a performance penalty.

Graphics, publishing, engineering, financial and mathematical modeling programs—any software that requires a math coprocessor—will probably benefit from the 486's brawn. However, standalone math chips cost less than $200, compared to the $450 to $900 price tag on a proprietary 486 upgrade board. Generally you're better off upgrading your 386 PC with a math coprocessor. The cost of the CPU upgrade isn't worth the price or compromise.

486 to Fast 486

The clock-doubling technology introduced recently by Intel (and soon to appear in other CPUs) lets you switch a 25-MHz or 33-MHz 486 for a CPU that runs at twice these internal clock speeds. You can make the switch yourself in minutes simply by installing the 486DX2 CPU in the "overdrive socket" in your PC (directions that come with the DX2 chip explain how). Removing the original 486 chip isn't necessary, though it could probably fetch $150 if you knew a willing buyer.

Be aware that the DX2 doesn't deliver full 50-MHz or 66-MHz 486 performance since the chip communicates with the PC's other components at the old speed. Also, to make the CPU sing, you'll want 128K to 256K memory cache and a very fast video card that features either a graphics coprocessor or local bus architecture. These can add $200 to $600 to the $400 to $800 price of a DX2 chip. Given the long-term reliability questions surrounding the DX2 and the performance tradeoffs, it's a dicey upgrade. (For more on clock-doubling systems, cache, and local bus, see Chapter 3.)

> **"It** rarely makes sense to add memory to an 8088 (it rarely makes sense to add *anything* to an 8088)."

Memory

Today's software programs crave memory. They'll take you for all you've got. Adding more RAM is also a quick and easy way to goose PC performance. The more memory your PC has, the less time you'll spend waiting for your system to swap information to and from the hard disk. Also, memory is cheap. Already widely available for less than $50 per megabyte, memory is getting cheaper all the time.

Of course, you can quickly reach the point of diminishing returns. It rarely makes sense to add memory to an 8088 (it rarely makes sense to add *anything* to an 8088). Tacking 16MB onto a 10-MHz 286 PC will do you no good at all. Upgrading a 286 with 1 or 2 megabytes, however, can give your system the horsepower to run nearly any DOS-based spreadsheet, word processing software, or database with ease. Stock a 386- or 486-based PC with

6 to 8 MB of RAM for running Windows, and you won't feel like taking up knitting as you wait for an application to load.

Beware that some memory upgrades require additional hardware, however. Motherboards on older PCs often accept only 1, 2, or 4 megabytes, max. Beyond that, you'll have to purchase a memory board—an add-in card that fits into an expansion slot. It will typically add several hundred dollars to the cost of a memory upgrade. Expansion board memory is also slower than memory you add to the motherboard.

Memory chips come in various shapes, sizes, and speeds. When upgrading, you'll have to match new chips to those already in your PC. Older PCs (circa 1986 or earlier) require memory chips called DIPs (dual in-line packages) or SIPPs (single in-line pin packages; see Chapter 3). If your PC uses DIPs or SIPPs, be forewarned that upgrading them can be a grueling process. Both have small, easily breakable wire pins that plug into sockets on your PC's motherboard. Generally, DIPs come in sets of nine chips which add between 512K and 1 MB.

If your PC is only a few years old, upgrading memory is much easier; it uses single in-line memory modules (SIMMs), which combine the nine DIPs onto a wafer that snaps onto the motherboard. (For more on system memory, see Chapter 4.) You can order these by mail and pop them into place in no time. SIMMs come in a variety of capacities, most commonly in 512K, 1-MB, 2-MB, and 4-MB sizes, though 16-MB SIMMs and larger are also starting to turn up. Not all sizes work on all systems; and even if your PC accepts more than one size, you generally won't be able to mix and match. In most PC designs, all of the memory chips in your system must be of the same capacity.

When adding memory to your system, you must match the speed of the chips to those already in your system. You can determine the speed of the chips in your system by examining the chips themselves (if it shows "-7" it's 70 nsec, for example; "-10" means 100 nsec), by checking your original sales invoice, or by calling your PC dealer or manufacturer.

Depending on the PC, you may have to add memory in increments of 1, 2, or 4 megabytes at a time. You can only tell by checking your PC's manual, by calling the manufacturer, or by trial and error. Avoid doing the latter. When buying SIMMs, keep in mind that there's no guarantee that they'll work in your system. Always make sure that the dealer guarantees compatibility or a full refund.

One final consideration: Not all PCs accept standard SIMMs. Older Compaq, AST, NEC, and IBM machines, for example, use proprietary SIMMs. These easily cost more than $50 per megabyte, often three to six times more. Several third-party companies clone this memory, however, and sell it for a fraction of the price. It's worth shopping around.

Drives

By universal nature, people strive—but fail—to hold onto more information than they lose. This axiom about computing (about humanity) levies a high cost in personal anxiety, social discord, human progress, and hard disk space. If we could clear our minds and hard drives of the trash that both receptacles hold, we'd be happier, wiser, and richer. Unfortunately it runs counter to our nature.

Compression

When a hard drive reports less than 60K of free disk space, it risks losing or corrupting any new data you plan to store on it. Dozens of techniques for nickel-and-diming free space from a packed drive abound, the best of which is simply to clear off files you no longer use. Inexpensive software compression utilities can squash files down to half or less their normal size. However, they rely on your CPU to do the compressing and decompressing, which interrupts or slows down your work. Compression utilities work best on a weekly or monthly basis for archiving data that will be seldom used.

Working in conjunction with a new generation of add-in boards, compression software can relieve your CPU of compression chores. The duo provides a fast, safe, and reliable way to cram more data per square inch onto an existing drive, even on a day-to-day basis. Hardware/software solutions are pricey, in the $250 to $350 range—about the price of a fast 80-MB hard drive. Also, many require you to disable disk cache utilities that help boost drive performance. Use a compression board only with very fast, very large (250 MB or bigger) hard drives, or when no alternative exists.

The Second Hard Drive

Sometimes the obvious solution makes the most sense. Consider the advantages of a PC with two hard drives:

- There's no compromise in drive performance.
- The second drive is covered by warranty.
- Data divided between two mechanical devices is only half as vulnerable.
- There are no conflicts, incompatibilities, or fuss (after installation, at least).
- The resale value of the PC rises.
- The extra capacity will almost certainly get used.

Once data on your PC's hard drive begins bumping elbows, it's hard to argue against adding a second drive.

This solution isn't fool-proof, however. Your first choice for *any* hard drive should be the IDE variety. However, if the primary drive in your system is an MFM, ESDI, or SCSI drive, an IDE drive won't cooperate with it. Junk your MFM drive for an IDE drive with twice the capacity. Though this is a very expensive solution, you can recoup some of the cost when you sell the system; also, you'll keenly appreciate the faster performance. Augment a primary ESDI drive with another ESDI drive *only if you can find a bargain on one*; otherwise, replace it with IDE as well.

SCSI clouds the picture considerably. A second SCSI drive will deliver fast performance and support your system's resale value, but you'll typically pay through the nose for one. Also, installing any SCSI device will send you reeling. Is it worth the expense and trouble? Let your decision ride on price and personal patience. Shop around.

Don't be suckered by the advertised prices of hard drives; they can teem with hidden costs. Most prices don't include the mounting kit you'll need to hold the thing in place inside your PC's case. The kit is a $2 set of metal rails and screws that will probably cost you $10 to $100. Likewise, you may have to buy a ribbon cable if the one that connects your primary hard drive to the host card or motherboard doesn't include a second 40-pin "head." Don't pay more than $10 for one.

Finally, the BIOSs in some older PCs won't officially support IDE. Write down the drive's manufacturer, the drive type (found in your system's manual and recorded in its setup routine), and its total capacity. When shopping for a second hard drive, ask your dealer whether the new drive will work in a "master-slave" configuration with the old one. Make sure the drive comes with a 30-day, no-questions-asked return policy in case your dealer knows not of what he or she speaks.

Once you settle on a drive, check out the documentation and technical support. You'll have to reset the jumpers on your original drive to make it work as the "slave" drive in your system. (Because the newer drive will likely be faster, designate it as the "master" drive so that your system boots from it. Also, store your applications on the faster drive; put your data files on the slower one.) The documentation should show how to set these. Otherwise, consult your system's manual, your PC maker's technical support center, or the drive manufacturer.

Hard-Disk Cards

The very idea of setting jumpers and attaching cables can give some people a rash. The alternative is a hard-disk card, literally an add-in card with a hard drive mounted on it, which sits snugly in an expansion slot. Installation is mercifully painless— a twenty-minute process. Owners of small "slimline" PCs that often lack extra drive bays may have no alternative for adding a second hard drive. The cost for this convenience is a 20 percent to 40 percent premium over the price of a standard drive. Also, some hard-disk cards don't perform as quickly as conventional disks, but they're every bit as reliable.

Repair or Replace

Even if you've got adequate storage capacity, hard drives sometimes bite the big one. If this happens after the warranty expires, your drive must be repaired or replaced. Many drive manufacturers will repair drives they've manufactured, but this generally costs at least several hundred dollars. Some third-party shops will do it as well, though they'll charge even more.

Repairing a hard drive doesn't bring your data back—such services cost more, usually *a lot* more. Outfits that specialize in resurrecting data from dead drives charge $200 just to examine the cadaver; the costs for actually recovering data start upward from there and don't include the price for repairs.

Depending on the capacity of the drive, it might be cheaper to replace it. Two-year-old (or older) drives with 20 MB to 60 MB of data cost more to repair than replace. They use older technology, and replacement parts are often not readily available. A 40-MB drive that costs $150 to repair may only cost $200 new. The new drive will be faster and more reliable.

As drive capacity increases, it becomes less clear whether you should repair or replace the drive. A 350-MB hard drive that costs $250 to repair may cost $1,000 new. Repair/replace decisions should ride on costs. A difference of $200 or less makes a good case for replacement. Whether you repair or replace, make sure you get a one-year warranty on the drive.

Floppy Drives

High-density floppy drives can read low-density diskettes, but low-density drives can't read high-density diskettes—a good reason for replacing a 360K, 720K, or a 1.2-MB floppy drive with one that reads 1.44-MB diskettes (which hold five times as much data but use diskettes that cost only pennies more). Also, many PCs come with either a 3½" or a 5¼" floppy drive, but not both. Sixty bucks will get you whichever one you don't have, though you should beware that higher density drives may require a new floppy controller. Don't pay more than $30 for one.

Incidentally, when a floppy drive gives you trouble (common signs of distress are problems reading from and writing to diskettes), scotch the drive for a new one. Repairing it typically costs more than replacing it.

Video Adapters and Monitors

Your PC's monitor and video card are like a window that allows you to peer at the inner workings of your PC. Whether you see 16.7 million or just 16 colors, whether you have high- or low-resolution graphics, and whether refreshing a screen takes 0.0002 seconds or 20 seconds have no effect whatsoever on the work the computer does. Monitors and video cards merely let you see it. The main reason to upgrade your PC's video equipment, therefore, is to improve your view.

That's not to say that an upgrade isn't warranted. Staring at a computer screen for long hours can make you painfully aware of even the smallest flaws in any display. Monitors, after all, age. Color guns can shift out of alignment, circles start to look like ovals, color begins to fade in and out, and controls may break over time.

Not all monitor problems are serious. If the image merely needs adjusting, a quick tuneup may suffice. Misaligned color guns, loss of focus, or skewed images can sometimes be easily corrected. Many older monitors have only contrast and brightness knobs in front, but other image controls are hidden in back that can help fix your problem. If not, a generic computer repair shop often has the tools to tweak an old monitor and may charge only a few dollars to do so. Just make sure to package the monitor securely when transporting it so it doesn't incur even more damage in transit.

Image problems are one thing, but problems with electronics are more serious. If a control knob breaks, if the monitor makes snapping noises when you turn it on, or if the image wobbles as you work, for example, a simple tuneup probably won't suffice. In such cases, monitors are a lot like televisions: they're cheaper to replace than repair, particularly if they're already several years old.

Even a monitor that forestalls the insults of age can still suffer from flicker, glare, and other annoying qualities that become more pronounced when you spend long hours staring at them. Headaches, eyestrain, and fatigue are all common side effects of spending too much time in front of a cheesy monitor. An upgrade can help.

Keep in mind that the quality of a monitor depends on the quality of the video card. If you buy a higher resolution video card, you'll also need a monitor that supports these resolutions. If you get a monitor with higher refresh rates to avoid flicker, the video card must support the higher rates.

Windows users can boost their applications' performance with video cards called graphics accelerators, or more specifically, Windows accelerators, which rev the lethargic speeds at which Windows redraws screens. Accelerator cards include their own processor chips designed to take over graphics functions that might otherwise mire your PC's CPU. They cost a bit more than non-coprocessed video cards, but they can often single-handedly improve Windows' performance. After investing thousands of dollars in memory and CPU upgrades to raise the sluggish pace at which Windows scrolls through text or resizes screens, many users find out too late that a simple accelerator would have solved the problem nicely.

Few applications justify a high-end video card and monitor. Desktop publishers who need to view the layout of two full pages simultaneously can do so with a 19-, 20-, or 21-inch monitor and a video card that supports resolutions of 1024 by 768 or higher. Illustrators who need to view their work in true color as they're designing it or artists who retouch photographic quality images on the PC can truly use a 24-bit video card capable of displaying up to 16.7 million colors. The $2,000 to $4,000 price tag for such gear should scare most everyone else away. If you're shelling out for such dazzling capability, get your dealer to install it and make sure it works with your software.

Most people, however, just want pretty colors, clear images, and a monitor and video card that won't make them go blind. When selecting your PC's video, consider these points to keep your choices in perspective:

- Higher resolutions are only worthwhile if your software supports them.
- More colors are not always better (anything over 16 or 256 colors slows your system down).
- A monitor is only as good as the video card driving it, and vice versa.

Finally, make sure that any monitor or video card comes with all the cables and documentation you need to configure and install it. A video card should include the necessary software drivers for all the resolutions and colors you want. Both video card and monitor should be backed by a full one-year warranty and an unconditional money-back guarantee. You may not like what you see after all.

Power Supply

The gentle whirring noise that rises each time you switch on your computer is produced by your power supply. Quite simply, it regulates the power that surges through your computer to each of its components and spins the fan that prevents your PC's components from overheating.

Small wonder then that with so many mechanical parts, the power supply is also the component most likely to fail over the life of your PC. Should you turn on your PC one day to sad silence, there's a high probability that you've got a defunct power supply on your hands. Fortunately they're relatively inexpensive ($50 to $200) and easy to replace.

Power supplies produce anywhere between 60 watts (used in the original IBM PC, for example) to 350 watts or more for jumbo-sized network servers housed in tower cases. The capacity you need depends on the number of drives and add-ins your PC houses.

In general, a 200- to 250-watt power supply is adequate for most desktop PCs. Some PCs with so-called slimline cases that aren't much larger than a pizza box can often get by with a lower capacity power supply since they have fewer expansion options than their full-sized cousins. Large tower cases with several add-in cards, a high-capacity hard disk, and lots of memory (memory, by the way, is a real power hog) may require a 300- to 350-watt power supply.

Short of adding up all the power requirements of each component in your PC (which varies widely), there's no way to determine exactly how much wattage you need. Take it on faith that the power supply that came with your PC is adequate; when swapping out a dead one, replace it with one of the same capacity.

Depending on the size and design of your PC's case, you can generally replace your dead unit with an inexpensive generic model. An unusual size PC, however, may force you to buy the manufacturer's replacement power supply—typically at a higher price. A discontinued PC design (or a defunct manufacturer), will force you to comb through mail-order ads looking for a power supply that will fit inside your PC's case. Custom power supplies are, of course, overpriced.

Almost anyone who's comfortable opening a PC's case can replace a power supply. Read the instructions. The procedure is basically to turn off and unplug the PC before starting, disconnect all the cables leading from the power supply to other components, undo the screws, and lift out the power supply. Then reverse the process. If you opt to have a repair shop make the switch for you, don't let the technician charge for more than 20 minutes of labor.

I/O Ports

Serial and parallel ports sometimes die. If the ports are integrated on your motherboard, a repair typically means days—sometimes weeks—of lost work as your system gathers dust in a repair shop. A better solution? Replace it with a $30 I/O add-in card, many of which will provide two serial ports and a parallel port in a single package. Just make sure the serial port supports the "UART 16550," which is necessary for high-speed (9,600 bps) communication, should you need it in the future. This arrangement also lets you add more ports than your computer originally came with (most PCs logically accommodate as many as three parallel ports and four serial ports).

Beware the Warranty

When installing new components in your PC, you should consider two warranties: that of the new part and that of your PC. Depending on the PC's manufacturer, opening the case to replace or install new add-in cards can officially void the machine's warranty—at least that's what many manufacturer's claim. Don't believe it for a minute.

The same manufacturers typically disavow all responsibility for their machines unless an "authorized technician" handles (and gouges you for) repairs. The truth is, there's seldom a way for a manufacturer or dealer to tell if you've installed your own components. Dealers replace expensive name-brand components with cheaper varieties all the time. A dealer may buy a bare case with a bare-bones motherboard, floppy drive, and power supply in it, and then install a Brand X hard drive and Brand Y video card du jour to cut costs. (That, incidentally, should tell you what's *really* in a brand-name PC). Unless the problem is related to the new component, your manufacturer doesn't have a leg to stand on in claiming it voids your warranty.

A more important warranty to worry about is that of the new component. Many add-in cards come with generous four- and five-year warranties. Shop with dealers who honor the manufacturer's warranty for you, instead of forcing you to deal with the manufacturer directly. Also opt for dealers who replace rather than repair defective parts. Repairing a dead hard drive or video card can cost you months of waiting.

In any case, *never* buy a component unless the dealer offers a full 30-day money-back guarantee. This is when most problems rear their heads. With luck, you'll never have to look at your dealer again.

How to Kickstart a Dead Add-In Board

You just bought a slick new fax board. You installed it precisely as the manual instructed. You typed a fax in the program's editor, pressed the send command, and ... nothing. Not a flicker of fax life. Chances are the board suffers from an input/output address (I/O) conflict, an interrupt conflict, or a direct memory access (DMA) conflict—all very common contentions between the many components in your PC. Nothing tells you this, however, and after several blind stabs, you turn despondently to the trouble-shooting section of the fax board's manual. →

The trouble with trouble-shooting sections is their propensity to ramble endlessly about how interrupts or DMA conflicts occur (not fascinating subjects) before instructing you to call your PC manufacturer for real help. Worse, they'll simply slap a chart of hieroglyphic memory addresses on a page, assuming that you're up to speed on your hexadecimal notation. Manuals translated from other languages are particularly entertaining.

Unfortunately, manuals rarely solve your problem. If you'd like to learn more about the spellbinding world of PC interrupt conflicts, a good book on upgrades or on building your own computer can help. If you'd just like to get your add-in cards working, follow these steps:

1. Jot down some essentials about your system, in case you zap the setup information that the machine uses to remember how it's configured. Run your PC's setup routine (check your PC manual if you're not sure how this is done) and record all the information there. If you have a printer attached to your PC, hit the Print Screen key and it'll send everything on screen to the printer. Also, print copies of your AUTOEXEC.BAT and CONFIG.SYS files. (At the C: prompt, type "type autoexec.bat" to display the contents of the file, which you should scribble onto paper or print using the Print Screen key. Then type "type config.sys" and do the same).

2. Keep a DOS diskette on hand to boot the system in the unlikely case that you wipe out your system information. If you don't have one, create one by simply inserting a blank diskette in Drive A:. Then type "format A: /S" at the C: prompt. This reformats the diskette and puts the system files on it so that you can boot from drive A:.

3. Start your PC with the add-in card installed. If you hear the power supply's fan whirring, but nothing appears on the screen, check the system's video setup. You may have knocked something loose while poking around inside your system. Make sure the video card is seated securely in its slot, that it's properly connected to the monitor, and that the monitor is turned on. Try rebooting again. →

4. If that doesn't cinch it, remove the new add-in card from its slot and turn the computer back on. If your PC runs through its normal startup routine and flashes its jaunty C: prompt, the add-in card is the culprit. Go to Step 7.

5. Still no C: prompt? Make sure all other add-in cards are properly seated in their respective slots. Also, if your system has a circuit breaker (typically a red switch on the back of the case), flip it and then flip it back to normal.

6. If that doesn't do it, boot your system from a DOS diskette. If this works, go back to Step 3. If it doesn't work, you're hosed. Call your PC's technical support line for help.

7. Interrupts for the add-in board are set either through tiny switches or jumpers on the board itself (the manual should illustrate what they look like and where they're located) or through software. Experiment by resetting them; it won't hurt your computer. Each time you try a new setting, write down the configuration of the switches, start the computer, and try the board. Through the process of elimination, you can often find a setting that lets the board work peacefully with your PC.

8. If not, reset the add-in card's interrupts to the manufacturer's original settings. Pull out all other boards in your PC (except the video card, you'll need that one to drive the monitor). Now start the machine by booting from a DOS diskette. Try to use the add-in card. If it still doesn't work, it's probably dead. Call the board maker's technical support line before you go through the trouble of returning it.

9. If the board works, shut off the PC, and reinstall one of the original add-in cards. Reboot and try to use the card. Turn the machine off, reinstall another card, then boot again. Keep doing this until the conflict reemerges. When you find the card that conflicts with your new add-in board, try resetting *its* interrupts. Eventually you should find mutual settings that work. It's a painstaking process, but it beats learning hex. ❏

Offer $40; go as high as $80. Otherwise, buy a brand-new 24-pin printer for $300, and get a warranty to boot.

Tip: The last 10-MB hard drive rolled off an assembly line circa 1986—which should tell you about the age of this machine. Also, an "XT" PC means only that it's powered by an 8088 processor. Offer $150.

This whisper-weight "laptop" weighs a portly 18 lbs. Better your lap than ours.

"Must see" is right. This is either a great deal or a mirage.

mo... ...reat ...ware ...nter, coprocessor. $900

Leading Edge XT 10-MHz, 640K, mono, 10MB HD 360K FD, mouse. Great software. $500

Printer, 24-pin, industrial strength. $300

386SX-16, 1MB RAM, 40MB HD, 1.2 and 1.44MB floppies, math co-processor, mini case. $900

Genuine IBM 14" EGA color monitor. Excellent cond. $125

IBM 286-16 hard drive and 1.2 floppy, printer/game port, 101 keyboard, lots of sware, $400

External 1200 bps modem, manuals avail. $150

HP Vectra 386/20, Tower case, 144MB HD, 1.2 FD, 1MB memory, 32K cache, Super VGA. $2,050 or best offer.

286, 65MB Hard drive, 1.2MB floppy, 1MB RAM, SVGA monitor, 24-pin printer. $950

...MB ... ...ase. $1,...

Toshiba 5100, 4MB memory, 40MB hard drive, math coprocessor. $2,400

16-MHz 386 complete system with 40MB fast hard drive, fully loaded. Must see! $600

386/16; 1.44MB floppy; color VGA; 1 parallel 1 game port; 65MB HD 1 keyboard. $1,299

Toshiba laptop 386SX 40MB hard drive. Excellent condition. $1,900 or best offer.

Laptop, color, NEC 386/20, 100MB. Month old! $2,400

386SX Computer, 8MB of memory, 80MB hard drive, plus software. Extras! $3,000

SHARP brand laptop, 286, 5MB RAM, 2400 bps modem, case. $1,000

14" VGA color monitor; .31 dot pitch. $175

386SX, 40MB HD, VGA color, 3.5 inch drive, Extras! $800

Take the zero off this price, and make an offer. Go as high as $25, but don't waste time dickering.

Good price, but way too much memory. Also, no mention of a hard drive ... it may not include one.

Gads! It's been years since "Genuine IBM" meant anything. Also, it's one thing to inherit an EGA monitor; actually paying for one is nuts.

This poor ding-dong paid five grand for a faded color screen, then realized he didn't need color on the road after all—especially when he must worry constantly about dropping or losing the thing.

This seller supposes that the brand name will support this lofty price. Toshibas get battered around as badly as any other notebook, and $1,900 will buy a new portable with comparable features.

CHAPTER 8

How to Tire-Kick a Used Computer or Peripheral

New computers cost too much. Cut the tape on the box, and suddenly they're worth 15 to 50 percent less than their value moments earlier. Laser printers, modems, video cards and other peripherals fare even worse—they lose 70 to 90 percent of their resale value the minute you attach them to your PC. Moreover, for each year you own them, both systems and add-ins shed at least another 10 to 15 percent per year.

Though you'd never suspect it from the rate at which they depreciate, computers age quite gracefully. With the exception of the power supply and hard drive (both of which can succumb at any time without warning—even in new PCs), few computer components are likely to give you trouble, even after several years of heavy use. If it's going to fail, it will usually do so within the first few months of its life. Otherwise, expect your PC to hum along happily for years, no worse for the wear.

Which is exactly why used computers make excellent bargains. Buy a new PC today for several thousand dollars; turn around tomorrow, and you'll often find the same machine second-hand for half the price—with a printer, extra memory, and software thrown in to sweeten the deal.

Contrary to popular perception, the used PC market is *not* a repository for technological relics, either. It teems with one- and two-year-old 286-, 386-, and 486-based computers that typically cost less than half the price they fetched when new. Buying a used computer is a splendid way to let someone else absorb the shock of depreciation.

157

Of course, it's not for everyone. It's hardly convenient, for example. Shopping for a used machine requires time and patience. Faced with limited selection, you may have to compromise on the exact configuration of the PC you buy. Also, depending on where you buy it, you may forfeit warranty and technical support. Unlike new PCs, a used computer requires testing before you buy; don't take it on faith that all its components work. Manuals might be missing, or the keyboard a little worn. Also, you may have to visit strange people's houses to see the machine.

When you consider the savings, however, a second-hand machine makes a lot of sense, particularly if it's going to serve as a general-purpose home PC, a tool for churning out term papers and letters, or for playing games.

When scouting for a second-hand computer, a few rules will help steer you clear of junk:

1. **Don't buy cadavers**. There's no telling how much a dead component will cost to repair or replace, and you don't want to find out. It's someone else's headache. No matter how good the deal, if all the parts don't work, pass.

2. **Prices are arbitrary**. The advertised price of a second-hand machine typically reflects the owner's inflated estimate of its worth, based on its original cost. Learn the PC's fair market value before you enter a deal.

3. **Take it for a spin**. However sweet the machine may seem from the ad or the owner's praises, never buy used computer equipment sight unseen. The exception is buying it from a computer broker or mail-order dealer; these merchants allow you to return a lousy system.

4. **Software, add-ins, and other frills shouldn't cost extra**. Calculate the value of the PC you want without extras, then ask the seller to throw them in for free. A spreadsheet program, word processing software, a mouse, a dot matrix printer, or even games all improve a deal, but shouldn't inflate the price. Insist that manuals and original diskettes come with these extras as well.

5. **You call the shots**. The person selling a used PC typically wants to recoup any part of his or her original investment

possible. Few sellers seriously anticipate turning a large profit; those who do quickly smell the coffee. Even when the ad claims the price is firm, it's not. Always offer less.

6. **Beware of obsolescence**. It's less common than you think, but don't get stuck with a PC for which there's no longer any software being written. Watch out for names like Commodore, Osborne, and PC Junior; they're roadkill.

Yes, Price Is Still Everything

The biggest snare to avoid when buying a second-hand computer is paying too much for it. This is particularly true when buying from original owners who tend to base resale values on some combination of the machine's original price (too much) and what they hope to apply toward a replacement PC (also too much). Disabuse the owner of this idea early in negotiations.

A quick way to estimate any used PC's worth is to find out what you'd pay for the same system new. Divide that number in half, and work your way down from there. (All new PCs lose 50 percent of their sticker price in the first few years of life. Always.)

Also, determine fair market value by comparing prices among used PCs. Classified ads in local computer publications and even your morning paper can help. So can a call to a used PC store and to a computer broker, an organization that matches buyers and sellers of used equipment. (If none of these exist in your area, place a call to the National Computer Exchange in New York City at 800-622-6639 or the Boston Computer Exchange in Boston at 617-542-4414.) Use these quotes to leverage your seller downward on a high price. When possible, bring along several classified ads. Wag them when you visit a seller to help deflate his or her exaggerated expectations.

Brand-name PCs such as Compaq and IBM fetch a higher price than generic clones (they also retain more of their original value when *you* want to unload one). However, premium brands, new or used, command more than they merit. They're usually more expensive to maintain—as you will sadly discover when you see the bill for adding extra memory to an older IBM PC or when you need to replace a power supply in an old Compaq.

Where you buy is important, too. Shopping from classified ads, for example, can waste astonishing amounts of time as you chase around town trying to meet someone else's schedule, working from bad information and idiot optimism about a machine's value. You'll have to decipher cryptic three-line blurbs that are often inaccurate, and you shouldn't attempt to do any of this in a hurry.

On the other hand, some of the best deals lurk in classifieds. Consumers who sell used PCs to other consumers generally seek a fair deal for everyone concerned; you rarely have to worry about the institutional greed that greets you in storefronts. When shopping by classified ads, try to buy locally. Knowing where your seller lives reinforces a certain honesty in negotiations. The last thing your seller wants to see is your glowering face in his doorway two weeks after the deal was supposedly done.

Used computer dealers, who trade in the second-hand market from a storefront or warehouse (by mail-order), make the process easier. You can usually look at several machines in a single trip. Most dealers test and inspect PCs before selling them and back them with 30-day to full-year warranties. Plus, you can pay with a credit card, which gives you extra protection.

But used PC dealers take a cut. Expect the prices to be 20 to 30 percent higher than what you'll find in the classifieds, with scant room for negotiation. You generally can't expect to get extras such as software, add-ins, or a printer thrown into a deal, either.

A third tier of used PC sellers, computer brokers, match buyers and sellers of used equipment over the phone. The broker holds a deposit on a used PC in escrow until the owner of the machine ships it to you. You then have 48 hours to test drive the PC and pay up the balance. If you decide you don't want it, you have to eat the cost of shipping and send the PC back to the original owner.

Brokers take a cut on transactions as well—usually 15 percent. Despite the higher cost, the equipment comes without a warranty. Still, brokers tend to see some of the best equipment available—reasonably well maintained PCs acquired from companies going out of business or upgrading to newer PCs. Unless you live in the sticks or need to buy in quantity, you can usually find better prices locally.

The Test Drive

To test drive a used PC, bring several sizes of both flat head and Phillips screwdrivers so you can open the computer's case for a glimpse inside. Also bring both a 5¼" and a 3½" bootable diskette to test the floppy drives. (You make diskettes bootable by typing at the C: prompt "format A: /S" or "format B: /S". This transfers essential system files to the floppies).

Diagnostic software will provide a quick summary of system information, including processor speed, hard drive capacity and speed, floppy drive capacities, the amount of system memory (RAM), and monitor and video card resolution. Many computer owners don't truly know how their machines are configured and often mistakenly advertise wrong information. You'll want to check it for yourself.

Diagnostic utilities also flag hard disk problems and verify that serial and parallel ports exist and are working properly. Available from any software store for $30 to $100, diagnostic programs quickly pay for themselves in the headaches and repairs they can prevent months after you buy a PC. Several software publishers offer diagnostics programs; they all reveal the same essential information. Any package will do.

Once you've got a diagnostics report, get behind the wheel. If the PC is running, turn it off. Give it a minute to cool, then turn it on and off again several times. Problems with the hard drive and controller might be intermittent (indicated by an occasional "Hard Drive Failure" or "Boot Device Failure" error message on the screen). Make sure the machine boots properly each time. In warming up, a healthy PC tests its memory, then reports how much is installed. The hard drive and floppy lights should come on briefly before the trusty C: prompt appears.

During the warm-up ("self-test") process, look for a message about the PC's BIOS, the chip that ensures the computer's compatibility with other hardware and software. BIOS compatibility problems are very rare today, but when buying a PC that's three years old or older, look for the name "Phoenix," "Award," or "AMI," the companies that make BIOSs for more than 90 percent of all PCs. It's your best guarantee for compatibility.

Next to (or directly below) the name of the BIOS maker on the warm-up screen, you'll find the date the BIOS was released; it should be no more than three years old. The "fresher" the BIOS, the more likely that it will run the latest hardware peripherals and software quickly and accurately. If the PC fails any of these tests, thank the owner and keep looking. If it passes, move on to testing the drives.

From the C: prompt, type "CHKDSK/F". It should report no more than 30,000 bytes of "bad sectors," which can suggest manufacturing flaws, bad read/write heads, or that the computer has fallen off a desk or otherwise taken a low blow. It could spell trouble down the road.

Next, insert one of your bootable diskettes in drive A: and make sure the system can start from it. Also, make sure the floppy drives can read *and* write to diskettes, by copying a file from the hard drive to the diskette, then back again. If possible, open a file from a diskette using any application on the hard drive.

If the machine has two floppy drives, check their ability to read and write to one another by typing "diskcopy a: b:" and then "diskcopy b: a:". This copies the entire contents of one diskette to another. Also try formatting a blank diskette with the Format A:/S command to create a system disk. Restart the computer with the newly formatted diskette in drive A:. If the A: prompt appears, the drive checks out fine. To use *any* capacity DOS diskette in your machine, the 3½" floppy drive should have a 1.44-MB capacity and the 5¼" drive a 1.2-MB capacity (the diagnostics software will report their capacities).

Now listen to all the drives for strange noises. Whirring from the hard drive is natural, but grinding and clicking noises should scare you away. Noisy floppy drives are relatively normal. While you're at it, listen to the other noises the PC makes. The fan should hum, not rattle. The monitor should give off only a barely perceptible hum, if any; squealing noises could mean trouble.

Check the monitor for flickering, discoloration, or shadows on the screen. Test all the knobs, and turn up the contrast and brightness all the way to make sure the monitor suits various lighting conditions. Turn the monitor off, then face it toward a light; if you can see the faint image of an old document etched in the glass tube, the monitor has a "burned screen." A ghost of that image will linger in the phosphors forever.

A monitor suffering any of these problems may need to be replaced—expect to pay $100 to $400 for a new one. During negotiations for the PC, you should point out these signs of wear to the seller and demand that he or she knock $200 off the price.

Next, run your fingers across all the keys on the keyboard to see than they all work without sticking. Keyboard lights (NumLock, CapsLock, and Scroll Lock) should work. Turn the keyboard upside down and shake it—hard. If any of the keys pop off, the keyboard needs replacing.

An ailing keyboard isn't grounds for rejecting a PC outright. Replacement keyboards cost as little as $50. However, as with any other aging component, make the seller aware that you'll have to shoulder the cost of replacement, then insist that the system price come down.

Innards

If a PC passes inspection from the outside, remove the case and have a look inside. A thick layer of dust under the hood could mean years of neglect. It might also indicate that dust has settled in the floppy drives—you'll want to test them carefully.

Look for signs of sloppy home repairs such as a broken seal on the power supply or loose connections from slipshod soldering. Also check the chips on the motherboard and make sure they're firmly mounted. Examining the chips will also help you surmise the computer's actual age (not to mention the owner's candor). Look for a four-digit number on the chips' labels—the first two digits indicate the year they were manufactured.

Your diagnostic software will give you the vitals about the amount of memory and hard disk capacity, but double check the labels on the processor, modem, and video card to make sure the system features everything the seller claims. Try to get documentation for all components.

While you're under the hood, check for the number of available expansion slots and the amount of memory you can add to the motherboard (see Chapter 3 on buying systems). You shouldn't compromise on these essentials just because you're buying a used system.

Once you're satisfied that everything works and you've whittled the price to an acceptable figure, press the seller for as much of the original packaging and components as possible—especially cables and manuals for all the hardware and software.

If software comes with the system as part of the bargain, ask whether the original diskettes are available. Without them, you may not be able to use the software. Games, for example, frequently use copy protection schemes that require you to type a word from the manual to run the program. Other programs require you to enter the serial number from the diskettes to reinstall them or change the system settings. Most companies refuse to offer technical support if you can't provide the serial numbers on the diskettes.

Flea Market

Just when the seller thinks he's got a deal, negotiate for other extras as well. If he's also selling a printer, for example, suggest that he throw it in for free. Modems, hand scanners, mice, joysticks—even dust covers—enhance a bundle.

You may also consider buying any of these used components separately. A second-hand 1,200-bps modem might seem laughably obsolete to the computer whiz down the hall, but pick up one up for $20, and you'll get the last grin. Even if it turns out to be too slow, you can recoup your investment by selling it. Modems last forever.

Dot matrix printers, which also survive the ages, can cost as little as $30 to $40 used. Just make sure you can buy replacement ribbons for it before you bite. Also, check out its print quality for yourself.

Laser printers and monitors, on the other hand, are dicier purchases when buying them used. Steer clear of laser printers that are more than three years old (make the seller produce the original receipt) and examine the print quality carefully. Inspect a used monitor by examining an image that fills its screen (to check for overall focus and color quality).

Finally, wherever you buy, avoid paying in cash. Use a simple bank check when buying from a private citizen. This gives you several days to stop payment on it should anything go awry. If you're purchasing from a computer shop that refurbishes used PCs, pay with a credit card and make sure the machine comes with at least three months of warranty.

Selling Your Heap

Because PCs last longer than hair dryers but cost a lot more, odds are you'll one day find yourself on the other side of the classified ad—your turn to let strangers paw your PC. When it's time to put your heap on the block, keep a few issues in perspective:

1. **You will never recover your original investment**. Don't even try. Find out what an equivalent system (same processor, memory, and hard disk) sells for today, then have a good weep.

2. **It's worth less than you think**. Yes, a machine that cost $4,000 just two years ago may be worth just $400 today. Sad but true, it's a good reason to reconsider selling an old PC. There are dozens of good uses you can find for one; begin by thinking of an impoverished student you know and care about.

3. **Dead components turn a PC into trash**. A few computer shops will buy derelict machines for parts, but not many. Calculate the resale value of the PC as if it worked, and then get an estimate on the repair needed to get it running. This will help you decide whether to repair and sell it—or to donate it to your nine-year-old neighbor as a science project.

4. **Esoterica doesn't sell**. Complete systems, printers, and other mainstream items sell readily. High-end 24-bit coprocessed video cards, tape drives, and other unusual add-ins and peripherals don't.

5. **Premium-brand PCs hold their resale value better**. An IBM, Compaq, NEC, or other premium-brand system commands a better price than a Blipo Speedster that you assembled a la carte. Keep this in mind when pricing your machine.

6. The more time you can spend hawking your heap, the better your returns. Selling a PC yourself cuts out the middleman. You pay for this higher return in the time and hassle of peddling the thing.

As with *buying* a used PC, find out what your old heap is worth. Prices can vary hundreds of dollars from week to week, but you can place your PC in the right ball park by halving the price of similarly configured new systems. Also, phone calls to a computer broker and a few used computer stores to learn what your system might sell for will help you hone your price. Then you'll have to decide whether you care more about recouping a bigger fraction of your original investment or unloading a bomb.

Selling through the classified ads will generally give you the best returns. Try to limit your ads to computer weeklies or newsletters, which typically offer cheaper ad rates. They tend to filter out casual buyers (who will waste vast amounts of your time) and novices (who will turn you into their technical support center once they've bought your machine).

The most effective classified ads are boring—forget jazz, wit, and hype. Merely state the machine's vitals: processor type and speed, hard drive capacity, amount of memory, type of display, and the available extras such as printers, mice, dust covers, software, or a joy stick. Also, if it's a premium brand, state that as well. Indicate that the machine comes with all manuals and documentation (only if true, of course). Include a price, a phone number (no address), and the hours to call.

Used PC stores, another option, tend to trade mostly in recognized brand-name PCs and later generation computers with only a year or two of wear. Few will hawk your 8088- or 286-based machine. Also, some stores sell their wares on a 50-50 basis; you get half of the price a customer ultimately pays, the store gets the other half. There's no guarantee of a sale, however; if the store can't find a buyer, you're back at square one.

Computer brokers present the same problem. They take a 15 percent bite from every sale. You must also pick up the cost of shipping the PC (about $50–$100) to the buyer. Brokers also prefer to deal primarily in name-brand and high-end PCs. If your PC isn't worth more than $1,000, it's hardly worth it.

Trading in an old PC on a newer machine reaps the worst returns of all. It's quick and painless, however, and if desk and closet space are more precious than recouping an old investment, it's a good way to dump old technology. Remove high-end video cards, sound boards, tape drives—any extras that won't diminish the trade-in value of the computer. You can use these in your new machine.

However you plan to sell, take a few moments to improve its chances. First try to erase the signs of age. Wipe any fingerprints off the monitor and case, clean up the keyboard, and blow out the dust that has accumulated inside the case. Try to offer as complete a deal as possible. It's tough to sell a PC without a monitor, for example. An inexpensive VGA monitor will improve its prospects—and resale value—immensely. Also, a dot matrix printer or a modem tossed into a deal attracts lookers quickly.

Depending on how old your PC is, you may also have to do a little upgrading to find a buyer. Bring your computer's memory up to a standard configuration. Spending $50 to $100 to upgrade an 8088 to at least 512K or ideally 640K can make the difference between finding a buyer and no sale. A 286 PC should have at least 1 MB of RAM. A 386-based machine should have at least 1 MB, ideally 2 to 4 MB. Money for extra RAM is easily recoverable in the selling price and makes your machine more competitive—especially if it's an unknown brand.

Don't push the point of diminishing returns on upgrades, however. For example, 6 MB of RAM won't enhance the value of an 8088—and 16 MB of RAM is more than most people ever want, even on a 386. If your system already comes outfitted with overdoses of memory, remove some of it and sell it separately for about $25 per megabyte. Buyers will flock to your door.

Keep in mind that mainstream computer equipment sells better than esoterica. A high-end monitor, a 24-bit video card, or an internal CD-ROM drive, for example, add value to a system only if you find a buyer who wants them—which screens out many, many prospective customers. If you've tricked your computer out with snazzy high-tech extras, be prepared to remove them and sell them separately. (Computer clubs and computer user groups are terrific places to hawk them.) High-end toys are generally a tough sale any way you approach it, but peddling them yourself enhances your prospects.

One final note: Original packaging and manuals improve a PC's resale value—something to bear in mind when you buy a *new* computer. Try to find some closet space for these things.

Road Warriors:
The Second-Hand Portable PC

Pity the poor traveling laptop. Dropped, stepped on, banged, and bruised, it still stubbornly boots. At least, some do.

Despite tremendous inroads in shock-mounting techniques and other methods of protecting delicate electronics, portable PCs eventually fall apart. The cost of repairs can be forbiddingly high. Few shops even bother to work on them since even simple problems often require replacing whole subsystems. When a serial port in desktop PC dies, for example, it's a $30 replacement. On a notebook, it can mean replacing the entire motherboard—to the tune of $1,000 or more.

The price of a second-hand portable should reflect these realities. Whenever possible, find out the cost of a new portable with the same weight, processor, memory configuration, and hard drive capacity as the second-hand model you're eyeballing. Subtract 20 percent from that price for every year the used portable has been owned. (Ask to see the original purchase receipt to verify the age and purchase price. If the owner claims to have lost it, make it clear that you're not inter-

ested in buying a portable without the original receipt. You'd be surprised how this can jog an owner's memory.)

Inspecting a portable may require some creativity. You'll certainly want to take along diagnostics software. You'll also want to verify that every knob, feature, port, key, and drive actually works. Make sure you can boot from the floppy drive, for example, that you can copy files to and from the hard drive, and that your diagnostics software recognizes the machine's serial and parallel ports.

Testing a used portable also requires some judgment calls. Cracks or fractures in a laptop's plastic molding, for example, suggest that it's been dropped, kicked, or hurled at someone. Examine the case carefully, especially at the display hinges which are prone to cracks and which cost a fortune to replace.

Look at how the communications ports and floppy drive are seated as well. If they're off-center from the openings on the case, construction was shoddy or the portable was probably dropped. Either way, it's not a machine you want to own. →

Next, latch the display down and hold the unit from its sides. Twist it slightly in opposite directions with each hand. Better notebooks actually flex somewhat (rigid cases tend to crack), but the motherboard should flex with the case; otherwise, the machine has probably taken a tumble. Also, turn the machine over several times close to your ear. Listen for rattles that suggest loose parts battering around the machine's innards.

Run DOS's CHKDSK command and your diagnostic software. They shouldn't report more than 30,000 bytes of bad sectors on the hard drive. When you jar or drop a notebook, the drive head can sometimes slam into the platter, permanently destroying a sector on the drive (not to mention the file it was reading or writing). Too many defective sectors indicate that the machine's owner bumbled around with it, or that the hard drive was built before technologies that safeguard hard drives in portable PCs were invented. Too many bad sectors presage future disaster.

Listen to the hard drive as the machine boots, then again when it's loading an application. Unusual groaning and grinding, the telltale signs of age or failing drive motors, augur disaster. Replacing a dead hard drive in a portable can easily cost you a down payment on a new machine.

In fact, any time a repair shop opens the case on a laptop, expect the meter to start ticking at about $200. Don't even *think* about doing it yourself.

Even more expensive to replace is your laptop's display. You certainly don't want to get stuck with a defective display, but you should also be on guard for aging displays, which are characterized by uneven backlighting, streaking, fuzzy characters, and poor contrast. Allow the portable to "warm up" at least four minutes before judging its display. Then look at a bare screen for evenness of backlighting. Next, fill the screen with text to examine how sharp the characters appear. Scroll through a page to see if text lingers on the display or whether it changes with crisp transitions. Finally, study a graphic image of some kind onscreen for subtleness of detail and shading.

Like laptop displays, nickel cadmium batteries, the near-universal standard for portables, lose their luster. After years of charging and recharging, they hold less juice. When shopping for a used portable, better buys feature removable batteries. Just make sure you can still purchase replacement batteries for your particular model. Replacements are exorbitant, but what good is a laptop that won't even last until the in-flight movie begins? ❑

Shopper's Checklist

Buying a used PC is a great way to get the system you want for far less than you'd pay for it new. When looking over a used system, bring along several sizes and types of screwdrivers, 5¼" and 3½" bootable DOS diskettes, your diagnostic software, and this checklist; it'll help ensure that you don't buy someone else's bomb. You should be able to check off every item listed here. Otherwise, thank the owner and keep shopping.

Price

The price should be less than half that of a comparable new system (the same processor and processor speed, same capacity hard drive, and the same amount of memory)

Diagnostic Software Confirms:

❏ Processor type and speed

❏ Total system memory

❏ Hard drive capacity and speed

❏ Serial and parallel ports work

❏ Video card and monitor resolution

❏ Floppy drive capacity (1.44 MB for 3½" drives, 1.2 MB for 5¼" drives)

Booting

❏ System boots without problems several times in row.

❏ BIOS is manufactured by Award, AMI, or Phoenix.

❏ BIOS is less than three years old.

❏ System boots from floppy drive.

Drives

❏ CHKDSK reports under 30,000 bytes of bad sectors on hard drive.

❏ System can read to and write from both floppy drives.

❏ System boots from a floppy that it formatted using the /S switch.

❏ Hard drive and power supply do not rattle or grind.

Monitor

❏ Image quality on monitor is good (consistent colors, no flicker).

❏ All monitor control knobs are in working order.

❏ Monitor doesn't emit a whine or squeal.

❏ Image does not linger on monitor.

Keyboard

❏ All the keys and lights on the keyboard work.

❏ All the keys on the keyboard are firmly mounted.

Inside the PC

❏ Seal on power supply is intact.

❏ Chips and expansion boards are firmly mounted.

❏ There are no signs of sloppy home repairs.

❏ Four-digit number on chips confirms the PC's age.

❏ Video card, processor, and memory type are confirmed.

Extras

❏ Original packaging and manuals come with the machine.

❏ Cables are included.

❏ The owner will toss in a mouse, printer, dust covers, modem, or joystick.

❏ Free software (with original disks and manuals) is included.

❏ Payment is by check (to a private owner) or credit card (to mail-order or used PC dealer).

This fine print is teeming with hidden costs: $4.00 for this, 5% for that, plus shipping and handling. On top of it all, you can't even return it.

Call once and you'll get one offer, call again and you'll get another, call yet again and you'll get …

Hard Drives

Super Stash 300MB... $CALL
Barracuda 80MB........ $CALL
StorMor 120MB.......... $CALL

CompStuff, Inc.
1-500-555-1000

For faster delivery, send cashier's check or money order. Include $4.00 for all software orders and 5% for all hardware orders. All goods include a factory warranty. We do not guarantee compatibility or version numbers. Due to our low prices, all sales are final. Defective returns must have a return authorization number and must be in as-new condition, without modifications, and include original documentation and packaging. We reserve the right to substitute equivalent items. Prices and availability are subject to change without notice. Shipping and handling are nonrefundable. Not responsible for typographical errors.

Have you ever been rolled? NEVER, EVER, EVER send cash or its equivalent. Always put it on plastic.

Whose definition of equivalent? This is bait and switch.

Which means they guarantee nothing at all. You're on your own, Jack.

Some day we'd like to find out just what "handling" means. It sounds as if you're paying to have someone grope your groceries.

Translation: We are a cash-strapped, fly-by-night operation.

CHAPTER **9**   BAZAAR . . . . **How to Buy**

You probably can't buy a PC at a jewelry store, a fruit
stand, or a muffler shop—not yet, anyway. You *can* buy
them at five-and-dimes, toy boutiques, discount merchandisers, warehouse liquidation outfits, and department
stores; from manufacturers or mail-order catalogs; and
through brokers, school programs, classified ads, and computer dealers. The variety of merchants who peddle PCs
grows larger, stranger, more motley, and less stable by the
day. Fierce competition results, which pommels computer
prices. That's good news. Unfortunately any circus that grows
this large attracts unsavory elements. That's bad news.

The marketplace for PC equipment manages to maintain a kind
of hypertensive equilibrium. Consumers burned by seedy warehouse operations will thereafter seek the security of overpriced
computer boutiques where the salespeople wear ties and proffer
fancy business cards. Likewise, consumers who discover they've
been gouged by their retailers' mark-ups will turn to mail-order
houses for future purchases. Where you buy your stuff, however,
matters less than the price, service, and support that come with it.

In the broadest terms, there are two ways to buy computers and
software: through the mail or from a storefront. Each has advantages and drawbacks that depend on where you live, how you
use your computer, what hours you keep, and a host of other issues. Shopping by mail-order, for example, can be tremendously
convenient if you live in a rural area or if you prefer to do business in pajamas on your living room floor in the wee hours of the
morning. It can be terribly inconvenient if you must repeatedly

173

box up a broken computer and fuss with shipping services—at your expense.

Generalizations about retail and mail-order tend to fall apart on inspection, and they produce terrific myths and misunderstandings about both types of merchants. Recognizing these myths is the first step to getting a good deal regardless of where you buy your hardware and software.

Myth #1: PC novices should buy from retailers. There's something comforting about looking into your salesperson's eyes as she explains the differences between various machines or software programs. There's palpable reassurance in dancing your fingers over the keyboard on the unit you're actually going to buy. Unfortunately retail salespeople tend to be some of the most technologically uninformed in the business. Their expertise more often lies in sales (in effecting that reassuring twinkle in their eyes). Their selection of machines is usually overpriced and better suited to businesses than to individuals. Also, novices too often walk out of retail shops with more equipment than they need.

Myth #2: An authorized dealer offers better service and support than a generic PC shop. Once universally true, this maxim is becoming a relic of a bygone era. A few computer manufacturers still require their authorized dealers to undergo extensive training, to maintain sizable inventories of replacement parts, and to conform to exacting standards for repairs and support. With tighter profit margins, however, most manufacturers' standards have seen some slippage. In fact, many makers require no more of a computer shop than scant evidence that the place is a legitimate business. Fax the manufacturer your federal tax number, and it then mails you a decal you can stick in your window as proof of authorization. Instant knighthood.

Myth #3: Mail-order houses offer the cheapest prices. Though often true, this assumption is highly misleading. Mail-order houses flush with success have a bizarre tendency to *raise* prices, then go belly-up. It's usually the result of greed and amateur management. In any case, compare prices at superstores, discount merchandisers, and even dealers before you settle on any type of distributor.

Myth #4: Financially, PC retailers are more stable than mail-order houses. Hah! Pick up the Yellow Pages in any medium-sized city, and call ten PC retailers. How many are still in business? The type of merchant you buy from is no guarantee of solvency whatsoever. How long the company has been doing business and what customers and computer user groups have to say about it are better barometers of stability.

Myth #5: The specific brand and model PC you want to buy is available only through a dealer. The days when PC manufacturers swore solemn allegiance to one form of merchandising over another are long gone. Even when a manufacturer claims that its products can be bought only through one type of merchant, you can almost always find evidence to the contrary. Just keep looking.

Myth #6: Retailers provide faster repairs and better support than mail-order houses. Many mail-order outfits offer onsite service and guarantee that a repair technician will ring your doorbell within 24 hours. Waiting around all day for a repair person to show is hardly convenient, of course, and if you live outside a major metropolitan area, you may not qualify for doorstep service. But it beats the two-week wait for a routine repair at some retail outfits. Speedy repairs depend on the establishment that performs them, not on how the merchant hawks its wares. Incidentally, many mail-order houses provide around-the-clock technical support lines. Good luck finding a retailer that will answer a technical question at 3:00 AM.

Myth #7: Mail-order houses offer a wider selection of merchandise. Anyone who visits a superstore will beg to differ with you. Also, even tiny computer boutiques can often put their hands on any product you like in a matter of days.

Once you've dispensed with these popular superstitions, mail-order houses and retail shops line up toe to toe. Key to shopping at either kind of establishment is an understanding of their byways and backwaters, how to find bargains, and how to flush out the snakes before they bite you.

Case the Joint

Before buying anything more sophisticated than a $15 printer cable, you'll want to find out who you're doing business with. Several clues can tip you off about the integrity of a dealer before it snatches your money.

Retail

Word of mouth is one of the best ways to find a good retail dealer. Seek recommendations from friends, co-workers, and computer user groups. Also, a quick call to the local Better Business Bureau (BBB) will shed light on a merchant's history from the peeved consumers it leaves in its wake. A company has to burn more than a few customers to earn an unsatisfactory rating from the Bureau. Likewise, if the BBB hasn't even heard of a local merchant, steer clear of it.

A dealer's reputation says a lot, but its financial solvency—and business ethics—manifest in other ways as well. A retailer that handles its own repairs, for example, typically has a larger investment in sticking around and supporting its products, not to mention its customers. It's also probably in better financial shape than the shop that merely brokers sales and relies on manufacturers for repairs. A parts inventory is expensive to maintain, whereas you can sell machines on credit from the manufacturer. Check out a dealer's commitment to service by asking about the turnaround time on a very simple repair—replacing a dead floppy drive, for example. If it takes more than 48 hours, the dealer probably must order the component, which suggests a small or nonexistent parts inventory.

Also, shop only with dealers that offer unconditional 30-day money-back guarantees on all the equipment they sell. Outfits in which all sales are final have something to hide. So are shops that only offer store credit on refunds. Both are signs of cash-strapped operations.

When you visit the shop, take a look around. A wide variety of merchandise often indicates that the merchant is in good standing with an array of manufacturers and distributors. Shops with bare shelves may be just waiting to pull up stakes. If anything makes you nervous, trust your instincts and keep shopping. After all, there's no shortage of places to buy computer toys.

Mail-Order

It's an awfully weird way to do business when you think about it: Talk to a stranger on the phone, give her your address and the number embedded on a piece of plastic, then ten days later several thousand dollars of computer equipment shows up at your doorstep. Because shopping by mail-order is such an abstract experience, the industry has taken great pains to assuage very reasonable apprehensions that consumers hold. Today it's as safe as retail. As with shopping anywhere, however, your experience depends on the particular establishment you patronize. You'll have to evaluate a mail-order house yourself. With so few visual clues to go on, this can be difficult.

Most people select an establishment based on an advertisement or a brochure. Consider this to be the merchant's showroom. It will often tell you as much or more about who you're dealing with than paying an actual visit to a retail site. Better still, you don't even have to get in the car to visit it.

The first thing to look for in the ad or brochure is a full mailing address. If none exists, turn the page. Once it has your money, the merchant may not exist either. Ditto for the outfit that lists a post office box number or just a city and state in its ads. The company's actual offices might be a telephone booth for all you know. Mail-order houses that publish their full addresses have probably signed a lease of some sort. They tend to be more forthright in all business practices. They're also easier to track down should something go awry with your order.

If possible, flip through back issues of computer magazines to look for a history of steady advertising by the merchant. A mail-order company that previously ran six-page glossy color ads produced by professional photographers but now runs a half-page of very small black and white type has probably seen better days. Also, beware of mail-order merchants for whom you can only find one ad. A company that pins its hopes on such sparse exposure is playing a dangerous game of roulette.

> **"The first thing to look for in the ad or brochure is a full mailing address. If none exists, turn the page."**

Drop to the bottom of the page and comb the fine print. Look for telltale phrases such as "All sales final," "Prices and availability subject to change without notice," and other slippery wording that can bilk you. (See "AdSpeak" for more on the fine print in mail-order ads.) These are the trademarks of nomadic merchants.

Check the fine print for a return policy. Read it carefully. Unbeatable prices save little money if the equipment is dead on arrival and the merchant refuses the return. Better mail-order dealers offer an unconditional, 100 percent, 30-day, money-back guarantee on everything they sell. They want your business. →

ADSPEAK:
A Guide to the Fine Print in Mail-Order Ads

The fine print in mail-order advertisements can reveal worlds of information about a company's solvency, its business practices, and the type of service you can expect once it has your money. Read it carefully. Here are some of the more common disclaimers you'll see, what they mean, and what you need to know.

"Specifications, terms, prices, and availability subject to change without notice." If you buy from a company with this disclaimer in its fine print, you may find that what you order is not what you receive or that your credit card is overcharged or that the merchant no longer accepts returns. These are business practices common to vendors who sell love potions from the backs of panel trucks. Don't buy electronics this way.

"All orders including D.O.A.s carry only manufacturers warranties." This means the company doesn't even prom-

ise to send something that works—D.O.A. stands for dead on arrival. Supporting it is out of the question. Don't bite.

"We reserve the right to substitute any and all items with equivalent or better parts." "Equivalent" is a snare. You pay for one item but get another. It's a timeworn tactic called "bait and switch." Unless you get the specifics in writing and can return the merchandise for a full refund, stand clear.

"Prepaid orders get up to 3% discount." Often an indication of a weak cash flow, this policy is issued by companies that encourage customers *not* to pay with a credit card. It's financial suicide.

"Shipping costs are non-refundable." This is standard practice from most mail-order outfits. You're usually expected to absorb the shipping costs of returns (which, incidentally, can run $60 or more if mailing a computer or a printer). →

Unfortunately it also means that if the company sends you the wrong goods, you'll probably have to pay shipping charges—twice. Make sure you insure anything you return for its full value.

"Money-back guarantee." This is one of the most common traps buyers fall into. Notice it doesn't say that it's an *unconditional 100% money-back guarantee*—which means it probably isn't. Shipping and handling costs, restocking fees, and other surcharges lurk in its midst. Get the details in writing if you're still tempted.

"All prices are for cash transactions." Expect to pay 3% to 10% more than the price listed in the ad for using a credit card. It's a back-handed way to raise prices.

"Defective equipment will be repaired or replaced at dealer discretion." Whether the hardware you order is defective or dead on arrival, the dealer claims the right to decide whether to repair or replace it. Waiting for a repair could take weeks or months; always insist on replacing dead components.

"Claims on defective products must be made within 7 days of receipt." This means you have 5 days from the day you receive an order to test the equipment and then contact the company if there's a problem. You'd better hope that the customer service line isn't tied up. Thirty-day returns are now standard for the industry. Don't settle for less.

"Software, chips, and other electronic components are not returnable." In other words, nothing is returnable. Turn the page.

"Some system options may be refurbished." Refurbished is a euphemism for "used." There's nothing wrong with used gear so long as you know it's used. Don't pay more than half of its original price and make sure it's fully warranted.

"Compatibility is not guaranteed." No dealer can guarantee complete compatibility. Just make sure you can return the component for a refund if necessary.

"Shipping and handling additional." Get an itemized list of these shipping and handling fees, preferably in writing. It could add several hundred dollars to your order.

"All returns are subject to our approval." This means that the merchant decides whether or not your reasons for returning merchandise are valid. Right. You should be able to return merchandise for any reason whatsoever.

"Returned items must be in resalable condition." Mail-order vendors count on being able to resell returned merchandise, and they require it to be in mint condition. Hang onto all original packing materials, warranty cards, and manuals; you may need them for returns. ❐

Don't assume anything about a company's sales policies, especially those not explicitly stated in the ad. A salesperson's earnest promises about money-back guarantees mean nothing. Get it in writing by asking the salesperson to fax or mail you the details on the merchant's letterhead.

Mail-order houses that provide an 800 number for sales, technical support, and customer service tend to care about their customers. If the company's support number doesn't appear in the ad, ask for it when you call to order. Then test it to see how long you sit on hold. Mail-order houses eager to serve you on a sales line may turn slow and surly when you need an answer to a technical question or want to return a damaged machine.

Keep an eye out for hidden fees in the ad, including credit card surcharges, restocking fees, and disclaimers such as "Refunds are for credit only." Also be wary of companies that offer incentives for payment with cash or a check instead of a credit card. These are all signs of flagging cash flow and gypsy operations. Next month the same companies will be selling Elvis portraits on velvet from the same 800 numbers.

Successful research should leave you with several candidates—whether mail-order or retail or both. You'll want to play them off each other. In any case, you're ready to negotiate.

Brass Tacks

The price tag that adorns a PC in a retail window is never the price you should actually pay. The same is true for prices in most mail-order ads. Shopping for computers is akin to browsing for oriental rugs or cabbages in an open-air market. You're supposed to haggle. Even dealers that insist that all prices are fixed expect you to barter; don't believe otherwise. Much of this is just marketplace ritual and a waste of time, but if you learn the dance well, you can save yourself a bundle. Crafting a good deal depends on timing, compromise, and attention to detail. This is true for buying a PC from the appliance department of a department store, Pierre's PC Boutique, or Bubba's Mail-Order Garage.

First, do your homework. Bone up on the true street price of the merchandise you're courting—its price in retail shop windows as well as teensy-print mail-order ads. This provides leverage for nudging a bid downward, especially if you can produce copies of the ads when your salesperson challenges the prices you quote. Also, find out *when* the product was introduced. The computer press tends to slaver over inchoate technologies with sexy (often useless) gimmicks. Demand for these products shoots skyward, and then it evaporates. Their prices follow a similar arc. Slightly older products, on the other hand, can be yours for a reasonable price.

When you're ready to negotiate, try to sound confident about what you plan to buy and give the impression that you're ready to spend your money—now. Don't wait for the salesperson to initiate a dialog on price; make it immediately clear that you plan to dicker. Keep in mind that making demands is confrontational and pleading is useless. Speak in simple declarative sentences, punctuated by questions that make the salesperson feel as if he's calling the shots: "Two thousand dollars is out of my price range. I can give you $1,800 for the whole system, but can you throw an extra megabyte of memory into the deal as well?" Also, have a counter-proposal in mind when your salesperson turns you down.

Always begin small, however. If you need a system with 4 MB of memory and 100 MB of hard disk capacity, start haggling over a system with 1 MB of memory and an 80-MB hard disk. As you barter, agree to buy more memory or hard disk capacity in return for concessions from your salesperson. As common sense should dictate, you'll also want to bid less money than you actually plan to pay, but be realistic. Dealer profit margins get slimmer by the day. A good place to start is 25 percent to 30 percent off the original price; 15 percent off the sticker price is not a bad place to end. If you aim too high, the salesperson may sense that you're not serious about buying.

In lieu of cash savings, you can try to get extras thrown into the deal. A mouse, a joystick, or a modem, for example, all sweeten a package. So do cables, printer cartridges, and paper. You're less likely to get software for reasons peculiar to how dealers have to buy it, but you should insist on getting DOS and Windows (if the system is powerful enough to run it) thrown in for free with any system you buy. If you're shopping by mail, try to get the merchant to pick up the shipping costs or send your order by overnight express rather than by standard mail. Mail-order houses can often waive the fee for onsite service if you press them. Just get it in writing.

A salesperson who won't budge on a price or a bundling arrangement might be inexperienced or may lack the authority to dicker. Ask for a sales manager; you'll almost always get better results. Whoever you deal with should know that you've shopped around. Tell your salesperson about a better price down the street, and ask her to match it. This is particularly effective when ordering by mail, though it can work anywhere. Be prepared to produce evidence of the lower price either in an advertisement or on the competitor's letterhead.

In the final stages of negotiations—when you're still bartering over price—casually pull out your wallet and begin tapping it in your hand without losing eye contact with your salesperson. If discussions stall, quickly stick your wallet back into your pocket or purse and let a glower of disappointment shine from your face. You should always be prepared to walk away from a deal—even several times. Nothing prevents you from coming back. For that matter, nothing prevents you from getting a better deal elsewhere.

Service and Support

Shopping for low prices is easy. Shopping for competent service and support, however, can stymie an otherwise sweet deal. The key is to understand the quality of these intangibles before you need them.

Technical Support

Even the nerdiest, most technically proficient computer user you know occasionally needs technical support. The sheer complexity of hardware and software ensures that problems, glitches, and technical mysteries will arise.

The only qualities that matter on this score are competence and convenience. For this reason, you'll want your dealer to be your technical support contact whenever possible. This is particularly important if you're buying an entire PC system since heaven knows which brand-of-the-week components your dealer has stuffed inside it. When you need support, you want to deal with one company, not five.

That said, better PCs manufacturers augment dealer service and support with their own support. After all, your dealer may not be an expert on the video card inside your system. Either way, test the technical support before you buy. Call at times you're likely to need help (evenings and weekends, for example) to see how easy it is to get through.

When you call, tell the technical support shaman that when you turn your system on, the message, "Hard Disk Failure" appears. The technician should tell you to boot your PC from a DOS diskette and then to try to read drive C:. Next, you should go into your system's setup screen to see if the battery is dead. Finally, you'll want to open your PC to make sure that the cables connecting your hard drive to its controllers haven't come loose and that the controller is firmly seated in its slot.

Don't worry about actually following these procedures. Just make sure that you understand the instructions, that the technician waits on the line while you purportedly try them, and that the two of you exhaust all three possibilities before you box up your machine for repairs. Some technical support centers offer fax support—terrific for zapping diagrams and instructions back and forth. Others offer electronic bulletin boards that you can tap into 24 hours a day with a modem. Even if you lack a modem or fax machine, such services show a support center's commitment to its customers.

Warranty and Repair

Whether you're buying a single memory chip, an add-in card, or a complete PC, make sure it comes with at least a one-year warranty that covers both parts and labor (watch out for those that cover only one or the other). Better warranties last two years or more and subsume the cost of shipping both to and fro.

Quite often the manufacturer's warranty extends only to the "original purchaser"—the dealer. This means that you'll have to lean on the dealer for service or go to the manufacturer on bended knee for repairs. Manufacturer repair shops tend to move at a glacial pace. Simply swapping a dead component can take months. Dealers can do it in a matter of hours.

Consider *how* the warranty is served as well. Avoid dealers who repair rather than replace faulty components. It's a crafty way to run up service charges. Also, many dealers have to farm component repairs out to manufacturers—a process that can take weeks, sometimes months. Better shops offer some kind of 24-hour service. Some mail-order houses will ship replacement parts to you by overnight delivery and then talk you through making the repair yourself. Others require you to mail in the dead component (or worse, your whole computer) at your expense and trouble.

Onsite service, now a standard offering from many mail-order houses and some retailers as well, can be terrifically convenient for small businesses and individuals who don't mind waiting around the house all day. You can usually get it for free if you press hard enough. Just remember to ask for details and get them in writing. If you live outside a metropolitan area or don't live within 50 miles of a service center, you may not qualify. Also, some services make no guarantee about when the technician will ring your doorbell. That can mean days of waiting.

Regardless of where you buy, the specifics for warranty and support need to be spelled out in writing. If you've negotiated for extra services (a two-year warranty, a 24-hour turnaround, or onsite service, for example), these need to be documented as well. Politely ask your salesperson to put the details in writing (on company letterhead) in case you need to jog his memory later.

Closing the Deal

Even with handshakes or verbal agreements in the offing, a little nervousness is natural. Purchasing anything involves risk, and computer technology is particularly complex. Three rules for buying computer equipment, however, will keep the worst risks at bay.

Rule #1: Always pay with a credit card. Credit cards give you 60 days to stop payment if a dealer refuses a return or if your technology turns out to be a lemon. Don't pay the balance on the charge until the merchandise arrives. If the mail-order house doesn't deliver, dispute the charge by notifying your bank within 60 days. (See Chapter 10 for more on protecting your rights.) Also, American Express, VISA, and MasterCard offer buyer protection plans that can as much as double your warranty if you pay with their credit card.

Rule #2: Document everything. This is particularly important when ordering by mail. Keep a copy of the ad you ordered from, the purchase receipt, the name of the salesperson, and dates and notes from your phone conversations. It makes life easier if your purchase goes awry. Also, don't forget to ask for an order number.

Rule #3: Inspect and use the equipment as soon as it arrives. A badly mangled box that arrives by mail or courier should be refused. Call the dealer and explain why. Equipment that fails to work out of the box should be returned—immediately. Don't tinker with it, and don't wait until the 29th day of a 30-day return policy to drop it on your dealer's doorstep. Move quickly with bum equipment; it'll save you tremendous grief.

> "**A**void dealers who repair rather than replace faulty components. It's a crafty way to run up service charges."

Shopper's Checklist

Retail

Buy from a local retailer and you can walk out with your hardware the same afternoon.

Background Check

- ❏ Recommendations have been received from other customers.
- ❏ Record with local Better Business Bureau is clean.
- ❏ Inventory is well-stocked.
- ❏ Full refunds (not store credits) are offered.
- ❏ 30-day unconditional money-back guarantee is stated.
- ❏ There are no restocking fees.

Service and Support

- ❏ There is a one-year (minimum) warranty.
- ❏ Warranty is honored by the dealer.
- ❏ Warranty terms are provided in writing.
- ❏ Dealer handles own repairs.
- ❏ Dealer provides technical support.
- ❏ Turnaround on basic repairs is under 48 hours.
- ❏ Terms of onsite service (if included) are clarified.

Closing the Deal

- ❏ Ask dealer to install software and peripheral components.
- ❏ Final price includes necessary cables, mounting rails, etc.
- ❏ Pay with a credit card.
- ❏ Get salesperson's name.
- ❏ Keep records of all transactions.
- ❏ Test equipment as soon as you get home.

Mail-Order

Buying computer equipment by mail is convenient only if you don't run into problems later. The following checklist can steer you clear of disasters, fights with your dealer, and financial plundering.

Background Check

❑ Record with local Better Business Bureau is clean.

❑ Full street address appears in the ad.

❑ 800 numbers are available for sales, tech support, and customer service.

❑ Unconditional 30-day 100 percent money-back guarantee is stated.

❑ Advertising history has been steady over several months.

❑ Return policy is printed in the ad.

❑ There are no restocking fees.

❑ There are no credit card surcharges.

Service and Support

❑ There is a one-year (minimum) warranty.

❑ Warranty is honored by the dealer.

❑ Tech support is accessible.

❑ Turnaround on basic repairs is under one week.

❑ Terms of onsite service (if included) are clarified.

Closing the Deal

❑ Final price includes shipping, handling, other fees.

❑ Confirm delivery date.

❑ Be sure that explicit return and refund policy is clearly stated.

❑ Confirm exact model number and configuration.

❑ Record salesperson's name.

❑ Record order number.

❑ Keep records of all transactions.

❑ Test equipment as soon as it arrives.

Depending on the interpretation of this gaseous legalese, the "original purchaser" might be your dealer. Unless it offers a separate warranty, this system may not be covered at all.

Few manufacturers will break out a soldering iron to repair a cheap video card. Many will want to "recondition" a hard drive, a motherboard, or a monitor, however. Throw a fit, if necessary, to make them replace components, not repair them.

Limited Warranty

(To the original purchaser only,) Paradigm Shift Systems warrants its products to be free of defects in materials and workmanship under normal use for the period of one year from date of purchase from Paradigm.

There are no other express warranties on the product. PARADIGM MAKES NO OTHER IMPLIED WARRANTIES OF (MERCHANTABILITY OR FITNESS FOR A PARTICULAR PURPOSE) ON THE PRODUCT. Under no circumstances will Paradigm be liable to the purchaser or any other user for any (damages, expenses, lost profits, lost savings, damage to or replacement of equipment and property, or costs of recovering, reprogramming, or reproducing any program or data stored in or used with the products.

For the duration of the warranty, Paradigm will, (at its option, repair or replace) any defective parts of the Paradigm products under this warranty.

This limited warranty (does NOT cover) any Paradigm products that have been damaged or rendered defective as a result of accident, (misuse, abuse, unauthorized modification or use of parts not manufactured or sold by Paradigm,) or as a result of service provided by anyone other than Paradigm or an authorized Paradigm service provider.

For warranty claims, the purchaser shall (properly package and prepay) transportation costs of the unit to Paradigm or an authorized Paradigm dealer. The purchaser assumes all risk of loss or damage to the product in transit.

This keeps the lawyers happy. If your machine breaks while using it to perform an unusual religious rite, don't tell the manufacturer about it.

Never return goods to a manufacturer blindly. Get a "return merchandise authorization" (RMA) number first. Also, make sure it's insured during transit.

Not to worry. No manufacturer can tell that you tried to turn your PC into a transmitter for contacting alien life forms. Just make sure you put it back the way it was when you bought it.

When your PC unexpectedly kicks in the middle of a project, this clause says, "Tough Twinkies." You can't recoup lost profits, billable hours, or Maalox expenditures.

CHAPTER 10

FIGHTING BACK . . . .

What to Do When You've Been Burned

Three weeks after you purchase a $2,800 PC, it begins wheezing. The sound is slight at first—barely a murmur—but it becomes more pronounced as the system warms up. Then, several days after you first noticed the rasp, you switch the machine on, and . . . nada. It's suddenly a very expensive, very ugly paperweight.

You call the mail-order house from whence it came and ask to speak with your salesman, who you know only as "Rudy." You are put on hold. Rudy doesn't recall you or your order, despite his warm inquiries into your work and family just weeks earlier. As he digs up the invoice, you are put on hold again. You then explain your problem to him in detail. Rudy makes several obvious suggestions, each revealing how little he actually knows about computers. He then switches you to technical support where you are put on hold.

The technician who takes your call is condescending and impatient. After asking you four curt questions, she sniffs that she'll have to examine the machine firsthand to diagnose the problem. You are put on hold and then switched to customer service where you are put on hold. A remarkably dimwitted clerk asks you twice to recount the problem and to explain the labyrinth of phone calls that landed you at his desk. You explain your problem and are put on hold. "You'll have to get approval from your salesperson for repairs," he chimes after a long pause, having arrived at the proper procedures as if by oracle. He switches you back to Rudy where you are put on hold.

189

Thus begins a too-typical phone odyssey that spans a couple of days. Once you've gotten the many heads of your mail-order Medusa to respond to your plight, you box up the PC, tote it to a courier, pay shipping fees, and wait. Two weeks later you receive a call from your technician, who officiously explains that your hard drive is defective, but that since you didn't report the problem when you first heard the wheeze, you will have to pay $690 for a replacement. Your blood pressure soars. In hacker's parlance, you have just been hosed.

All Is Not Lost, Cinderella

Such a predicament is hardly peculiar to mail-order outfits—or even to PCs, for that matter. The complexity and expense of computer technology, however, opens endless avenues for misunderstandings, complications, and outright fraud. When you think you've been burned, keep a cool head and a charitable heart. PC merchants contend with an endless parade of hostile nitwits. Approach your merchant in a civil manner with a legitimate complaint, and he may bowl you over with empathy and service.

Key to resolving a problem is, obviously, knowing when your grievance is legitimate. A PC that you ordered and paid for, but that never arrives is a defensible gripe. So is a computer delivered to your care D.O.A., a refund that hasn't materialized six months after the merchandise was returned, or a repair that can't seem to get completed—weeks after it commenced.

Sometimes the signs of a hosing aren't so conspicuous, however. How much buck-passing you should put up with, for example, is a judgment call. Hardware makers routinely blame all problems on software. Even when a flaw indisputably lies in hardware, system makers may point their fingers at the hard drive or video card manufacturers who, in turn, may accuse the dealer of incompetent installation. Always, it seems, responsibility for the warranty lies with whomever you're not currently leaning on. So turns the wheel. Too often consumers end up losing this shell game, through naiveté, technical ignorance, or exasperation.

It doesn't have to be that way. There are scores of ways to fight back. The sooner you act, the better your odds of forestalling losses. Most of the problems you're likely to encounter are the result of one of three scenarios:

1. **You paid for something you didn't get**. Not only does this include undelivered or defective merchandise, but also products that were misrepresented—that don't perform as advertised or as promised.

2. **You're getting a runaround**. Unfortunately the tendency is to recognize this just as your patience has expired. Rectifying a runaround is trickier than getting undelivered goods that you've paid for, but it's not impossible.

3. **The dealer lied**. It's hard to believe, we realize, but occasionally salespeople will exaggerate a technology's capabilities, fudge a delivery date, or misspeak a price. Oh, yes: some sales types might even occasionally—only when backed into a corner, mind you—lie. Getting justice requires tenacity, sometimes craftiness. Read on.

Proper Channels

When your gripe is certifiably legitimate, be realistic about what you can expect to recover. Try to weigh the expense of settling a grievance against the price of the merchandise, remembering that your personal time has a dollar value as well. Spending $60 and relentless torment on long-distance phone calls for a $45 refund on a bum software program doesn't make much sense. On the other hand, taking the time to write a thoughtful letter to the manufacturer about an inattentive dealer may take care of your problem right away.

Keep in mind that companies don't respond to complaints; people do. The most expeditious path to resolving a problem begins with the person who manages the right bureaucratic machinery within the company—the person who can authorize refunds, most likely a sales manager, customer service manager, or the proprietor. If necessary, spend some time finding who that is. You'll want her name, title, and phone number. If possible, also try to get her fax number, the name and phone number of her boss if she has one, and the name of her assistant.

Once you've secured this information, you're ready to seek justice. Begin in good faith by following proper channels. They're the easiest way to solve your problem, they protect certain legal rights, and they set the stage for more aggressive tactics should you need them. Credit card companies, consumer groups, and other third-party organizations won't intervene on your behalf unless you can prove that you've made some effort to resolve the problem on your own. Follow each of these steps in the order presented, and chances are better than naught that you'll get satisfaction.

Gather the paperwork. Before you pick up the phone, pull together the original sales receipt or shipping invoice for the software or hardware you bought or ordered, the number on the credit card you used, the name of your salesperson, and any notes from phone conversations you've had with salespeople, technicians, or customer service representatives. If you're trying to get the company to make good on a warranty or an advertisement, you should have those items handy, too.

Establish what you think would be a reasonable solution to the problem. In the unlikely event that the manager asks what you would like him to do about it, you'll want to have something concrete and well planned to throw on the table. If your printer shows no signs of returning from the repair shop after several months, ask the dealer to provide you with a loaner, for example. Or suggest that he keep it as a trade-in for a newer model. Keep your suggestions reasonable and even tempered, but don't be intimidated, either. You'll never recover the cost of reconstructing data on a dead hard drive, for example. Instead, suggest that the dealer replace a dead drive with one that has more capacity as compensation.

Document everything. You'll need to keep fastidious records of dates, names, phone numbers, return merchandise authorization numbers, details of conversations, and any information that's incidental to the problem, such as conflicting dates on documents, unsigned authorizations, and phone numbers you've been given. If you ordered by mail, these notes should start when you first dial the 800 number. If not, take a minute to jot down the details that you can remember in chronological order. It's a pain, but it protects your rights. Also, it'll go a long way toward establishing your credibility later.

Pick up the phone. Start by dealing directly with your stubborn salesperson. If the shop is local, you can either drop in, or save yourself a trip by calling. Politely explain that you have a problem with your purchase and you'd like to find out what you can do to take care of the situation. Avoid negative language ("misunderstanding," "mix-up," and "oversight" have a more genial sound than "problem," "screw-up," and other accusatory phrases). Ask what you can do to expedite the situation, emphasizing your willingness to help resolve the problem.

Push for specifics. Assuming your efforts haven't provoked a brush-off, pin your salesperson down on a solution. If he or she assures you that your refund is being processed, for example, ask for the date that the credit will appear on your account and who in the credit department you can call for verification. If the merchandise hasn't arrived, find out the day it shipped, or allegedly will ship. Record the dates and push for the names of people who can confirm your salesperson's promises.

Put your side of the story in writing. Outline the details of the mixup and your phone calls in a letter to the salesperson and to customer service. Keep a copy for your records. If you have a fax machine at work, fax a copy to customer service (or the proprietor in the case of a small shop).

Keep letters short and to the point. A ten-page single-spaced letter will languish in someone's in-basket—or get chucked right out of the envelope. Don't forget to include the obvious: the order number, your address, and a daytime phone number. Also, mention the names of all the people you spoke to about your problem. Send each of these people copies of the letter as well. (You needn't personalize each one, just get their names on it.) This protects you legally, and you'll typically get better results. People don't like their reputations sullied in front of co-workers.

Be persistent. Don't let more than a few days (a week at most) pass without checking the status of your order or request. If your letters and phone conversations fall on deaf ears, start working your way up the food chain with calls to the manager, vice president, or proprietor. The bored temp who answers your calls couldn't care less about your repeat business. Managers, on the other hand, take a less myopic view.

If you can't get through to the manager or owner, leave a message, get that person's name, then forward a copy of your earlier letter to him or her. From this point forward, copy that person on all correspondence between you and the company's middle-management slugs. If it's a local shop, this may also be a good time to pay a personal visit.

Reputable outfits will readily tell you the name of a manager, the president, or other person in charge. They'll also make some effort to resolve your plight. Oily outfits tend to hide the names of company brass, offer bureaucratic excuses for concealing them, and stonewall. In such cases, get the names from the Chamber of Commerce in the town in which the company operates; even if it's a toll call, the information will be valuable to you.

Henceforth those names—offered willingly or otherwise—should become the custodians of your problem. Unfortunately you'll have to enforce this arrangement yourself. It will require aggressive tactics.

Now that you've made a good-faith effort to solve your problem through proper channels, it's time to get tough.

Aggressive Channels

Think of your credit card company as a very loyal, somewhat feeble-minded bodyguard who travels with you through rough neighborhoods. When thugs try to harass you, snap your fingers, and MuscleCard roughs them up. That metaphor becomes strained when you consider that credit card companies make a lot more money from the merchants they're supposedly defending you against than from you. There's little ambiguity in where their true loyalties lie, but plastic is still your first defense against a serpentine merchant. Play it for what it's worth.

Act quickly. Most purchase and warranty problems appear within 60 days of the transaction. If you paid with a credit card (always, always, always), follow proper channels and then contact your credit card company before those 60 days expire (incidentally, most credit card companies start counting from the day you place the order, not the date of billing). Even if 60 days have elapsed, call the card's hotline; many companies will help you anyway—especially if you haven't paid the charges yet.

Put it in writing. First, file your complaint over the phone. Then ask how you can follow up with a letter. In many cases, a formal grievance is required. Once your gripe is set in motion, the credit card company withholds payment to the merchant until the problem has been resolved. Cutting off cash often has a miraculous ability to get tongue-tied computer merchants to finally talk to you. After 60 days, your credit card company will usually send you a form to fill out with details about your order. After that, you can generally wash your hands of the affair. It's remarkably effective.

Don't give up. Even if your merchant already has your money in its clutches, you can still enlist help. If an authorized dealer for a line of PCs gives you trouble, for example, contact the computer manufacturer. Because the computer maker can revoke a dealer's license to carry its product line, the dealer may decide to cooperate. Likewise, if you're having problems with a manufacturer (in getting technical support, for example), consult your dealer; you may at least get the name of someone who has authority.

Drum up grassroots support. Don't underestimate the influence of fellow nerds. Computer user groups have substantial, sometimes invisible clout within the industry. Some maintain close relations with hardware and software manufacturers and can often provide you with key contacts within the company. Also, many user groups will go to bat for members to arbitrate disputes. Incidentally, a local dealer that's giving you trouble is likely to be a member of the local user group. A little embarrassment before one's peers can threaten his or her livelihood. Confront the person directly at the next meeting.

Take your gripe on line. Modem owners can tap into an online universe of millions of people who have bought computer equipment, a surprising number of which can recount similar tales of merchandising sleaze. Local electronic bulletin board systems and national online services such as CompuServe and Prodigy are excellent places to air your quandary. Most PC manufacturers pay close attention to online discussions about their products; if the company spots a consumer complaint in a public forum, it may try to resolve the problem quickly. Some companies even sponsor their own forums—terrific places to lodge a complaint.

Seek consumer advocates. You can also enlist the help of advocacy groups. Consumer protection organizations, Better Business Bureaus, and even some local papers and television stations investigate consumer complaints. None guarantees success, and you certainly shouldn't hold your breath even if one agrees to help solve your problem. However, the more help you get, the better.

Whenever you correspond with any of these organizations and services, be sure to send copies to your friends at the company that's caused you so much grief. Even underhanded operations recognize that it's typically cheaper to capitulate than to suffer bad publicity and suspicious scrutiny from consumer groups.

For listings of state, city, and county government consumer protection offices, the federal government publishes a free booklet called the *Consumer's Resource Handbook* (see "Consumer Police" for the addresses of the organizations mentioned in this chapter). It lists all state chapters of the Better Business Bureau and industry associations that resolve consumer complaints. It's useful not only for quarrels with computer manufacturers and dealers, but for any consumer problem. Every household should have a copy.

One of the largest of these organizations is the Better Business Bureau (BBB), a national organization with more than 180 offices across the country. You should file your complaint (either in writing or by phone) with your local BBB office even if the company operates several states away. The local BBB scrutinizes your complaint and forwards it to the branch closest to the offending company's offices. The BBB then tries to mediate the dispute.

As anyone who has traveled this road knows, it is slow and bureaucratic. The BBB represents *all* businesses, from car dealers to lute stringers. As you might imagine, the tide of complaints it receives is overwhelming. Weeks, sometimes months can pass before your letter even gets read. The BBB has no enforcement power, either, so you won't always get results. Filing a complaint with the Bureau is as much a civic duty as an act of self-interest. You should feel compelled to do it whenever you've been ripped off. Just don't wait for the phone to ring.

Grievances against mail-order houses can be filed with the Direct Marketing Association, which will arbitrate a dispute on your behalf. Many, if not most, mail-order computer dealers are members. Like the BBB, however, the DMA also has no enforcement power.

If you bought merchandise based on a mail-order advertisement in a magazine, drop a letter to the publication about your problem. Most computer magazines will make at least a cosmetic investigation into the matter (if only to protect themselves from sticky liability lawsuits). Some magazines even feature consumer advocates or ombudsmen who solve readers' problems, then write self-congratulatory articles about it. Keep in mind that publications have no enforcement power, either. Also, these services are largely token—the same PC manufacturer that bamboozles a magazine's readers pays the magazine's bills.

The Electronics Industries Association operates a little-known but effective Office of Consumer Affairs that handles complaints against manufacturers of any electronic equipment. It mediates disputes and will even lean on a PC manufacturer to discipline an under-handed dealer.

Consumer organizations can browbeat merchants, but without high-dollar lawyers, they lack legal muscle. You'll have to turn to government agencies for enforcement. Begin by filing a complaint with your city or county consumer protection agency. Look for these numbers in the government listings of your phone book; if you can't find them there, check the listings for the attorney general or the governor's office. They're included in the *Consumer's Resource Handbook* as well.

Send a copy of any complaint you file to the Federal Trade Commission. The FTC investigates and prosecutes companies that are flagrantly breaking the law, but they rarely intervene on one person's behalf. A company has to burn hundreds of consumers to come under investigation.

If your merchant has skipped town or otherwise vanished, place a call to the bankruptcy court in the town or city in which it operated. A company in Chapter 11 rarely advertises its defeat to the customers it has bilked. To get your money back, you'll have to file a claim with the district attorney in the merchant's home town. Don't get too hopeful about recouping your loss. The chances are slim unless the merchant is bought up by a new owner.

Guerrilla Warfare

There are times when consumer rights, like civil rights, must be fought for. The authors and publisher of this book do *not* in any way advocate lawlessness, physical aggression, deceit, or even bad manners. Occasionally, however, you must stand up for your rights. If victorious, you benefit not only yourself, but consumers everywhere. If you fail, you're no worse off than when you started. That principle drives all revolutionary movements.

One universal truth of guerrilla warfare maintains that in stooping to the enemy's tactics, you become the enemy. In battling a recalcitrant merchant, make it your personal policy never to steal, defraud, embellish, or make idle threats. Also, terrorists and bullies are social maggots. Don't become one.

The variety of combat tactics available to you is nearly endless. The best require a little research, though as with proper and aggressive channels, you'll want to balance the dollar value of the computer or software against the time, trouble, and expense of fighting back. Attempt the following strategies in order—and only try one at a time.

Get personal. Quite often a call to directory assistance can get you the home phone numbers (and addresses) of the key employees who have authority to solve your problem (see Proper Channels earlier in this chapter). Phone on a Sunday afternoon or weekday evening (before 9:00 PM). When speaking, your tone should be humble and placating. Softly explain that you hate to impose, but that the money in question was intended for your daughter's tuition or some such purpose that illustrates the human dimension of your problem. Be aware that invading someone's privacy will more likely provoke ire than sympathy. Keep your call short. Do not argue—about anything. Be satisfied with even a vague promise for assistance.

Send a bill. Address it (by name) to the sales manager, proprietor, customer service manager, or anyone with "vice-president" as a title. Make it look official by including a billing date, a due date, and an account number (invent one). Use your phone or gas bill as a model. If possible, list a P.O. box as the return address (they cost as little as $20 a year). Make sure you include your phone number for inquiries.

If you get no response by the due date, fax the bill, with "Second Notice" in big, bold letters on it (you can usually find the company's fax number on an invoice or letterhead; if not, the receptionist will be happy to provide it). Begin faxing the bill three times a day, if possible. Be aware that some states have junk-fax and fax-harassment laws that could land you in trouble. Otherwise, your faxes will nag the manager and possibly embarrass him in front of underlings. In the mean time, they gobble fax paper and tie up the company's fax line, which will usually provoke at least a phone call from the cheese in the corner office.

Make a scene. This works only with retailers and only then if you are absolutely capable of controlling your temper. Public scenes are explosive. The moment you get swept up in your own drama and rage, you'll come off as an imbecile and a jerk. There are two secrets to pulling a good scene: do it when the shop is full (late Saturday morning, for example), and make it an appeal, not a rant.

Just slightly raising your voice within earshot of other customers threatens to scare off sales. Management will quickly try to shut you up—often by making a concession. When raising your

"Send a bill. Make it look official by including a billing date, a due date, and an account number (invent one)."

voice, appeal to fairness, reason, and decency. Do *not* conde-
scend, threaten, or chide. Name calling, sarcasm, and threats
shut down communication all the way round. They make you
look like a crank.

If a vocal, impassioned appeal to reason fails to stir management, spin on your heels, smile confidently at the other customers milling around, and pronounce loudly to everyone, "Better
think twice about doing business with this company." Then
leave. You are now lord of the moral high ground.

Sue. It's as American as apple pie, but don't even think about
getting a lawyer unless the value of the transaction is at least
$5,000. In fact, for any amount under $10,000, it's unlikely that
an attorney would do anything more for you than write a few letters and make a few phone calls. These can cost several hundred
dollars in legal fees. Keep in mind that sleazier merchants receive threatening letters from attorneys all the time and don't
exactly stay awake nights worrying about them. Still, legal
muscle can sometimes intimidate a merchant into settling with
you. Don't let legal fees mount to more than 20% of the money in
question. It's not worth the fight.

A cheaper, simpler solution is small claims court, many of which
arbitrate contested amounts under $10,000 (though this varies
between municipalities and states). You can usually file suit in
small claims court by mail (look in the government pages of your
phone book), and filing costs run as little as $5 to $50. You appear before a judge or magistrate (you don't need an attorney)
who will listen to brief arguments from you and your merchant
and then pass judgment on the spot.

Don't leap to the bench, however. Unless you live or work in the
same jurisdiction as the merchant, it's highly unlikely that you
can sue it in small claims court (thus ruling out most mail-order
outfits). Also, plan on spending a full day for your case to be
called. Even if you win, the merchant can appeal the decision—
or simply refuse to pay. Then you'll be faced with the problem of
collecting; it may send you to an attorney after all.

Filing a collective suit is another possibility. After talking to user
groups or friends, you may discover several other people in the

same boat. Class-action suits, lawsuits filed against a company by more than one person, can be a way to keep legal costs down by sharing the expense of hiring a lawyer. Still, the odds that you'll find several people with like complaints are slim. The chances that these other customers will consider entering a legal battle are slimmer still. Most people give up long before it escalates to this point.

Unfortunately you might have to give up as well. It's possible to sustain a private war with a company almost indefinitely. The tactics available to you are limited only by your imagination—and the law. However, it's not a very good idea. Your time counts for something, too. Know when to quit and chalk a bad situation up to experience. Just be sure to spread the word about your misfortune. Whatever you lost from the merchant, it will forfeit several times over in business.

CONSUMER POLICE

If you can't resolve a dispute with a dealer directly, consumer groups can often help. The Consumer's Resource Handbook is an excellent free booklet that lists state, city, and county government consumer protection offices as well as all the Better Business Bureau chapters and trade organizations. Also listed are headquarters for several consumer action groups.

Consumer's Resource Handbook
Consumer Information Center
Pueblo, Colorado 81009

Better Business Bureau (Headquarters)
Alternative Dispute Resolution Div.
4200 Wilson Blvd.
Arlington, VA 22203
703-276-0100

Council of Better Business Bureaus
National Advertising Division
845 Third Avenue
New York, NY 10022
212-754-1320

Direct Marketing Association
Ethics and Consumer Affairs Department
6 East 43rd Street
New York, NY 10017
212-768-7277

Electronics Industries Association
Office of Consumer Affairs
2001 Pennsylvania Avenue, N.W.
Washington, D.C. 20006
202-457-4977

Federal Trade Commission
Pennsylvania Ave & 6th St. N.W.
Washington, D.C. 20580
202-326-2222

ONE HUNDRED COMPUTER TERMS WORTH KNOWING . . .

A Streetwise Glossary

ASCII

BIOS **CPU**

DRAM

MTBF

VGA **OCR**

PCL

XT

SCSI

Access Time: Usually described in milliseconds (thousandths of a second), access time measures how long it takes your hard drive to find a requested piece of information and then load it to memory. The lower the number, the faster the hard drive (also see "Transfer Rate").

ASCII: Pronounced "ask-ee," this tin-eared acronym stands for American Standard Code for Information Interchange." It's a coding scheme for letters of the alphabet, punctuation marks, and other characters in written language that provides a kind of *lingua franca* for all computers and software. An ASCII file is one that includes only text and numbers, no formatting commands, graphics, or special formatting characters.

AT: IBM's successor to its PC XT was dubbed the "AT" for "Advanced Technology." AT has come to connote a whole set of standards that that machine put into motion. Thus an AT *computer* describes a PC powered by an Intel 80286 chip; an AT *bus* refers to a 16-bit Industry-Standard Architecture (ISA) variety; and an AT *drive* interface is compatible with the Integrated Drive Electronics (IDE) drive.

Benchmark: A benchmark is a test that purports to measure the "performance"—typically, the speed—of a piece of hardware or software. Benchmark tests, however, are overused and can be highly misleading. They seldom tell you anything about a product's practical value.

BIOS: The Basic Input/Output System, or BIOS in any PC is a set of instructions (usually) encoded indelibly in a chip and then loaded into memory each time the machine is started. It gives the computer basic instructions for communicating with the disk drives, memory, processor, video, and other components. Flash BIOS, a relatively new variation on this technology, lets you upgrade the encoded instructions without having to exchange the physical BIOS chips.

Boot: To boot a computer is to trigger its startup routine. A cold boot occurs when you flip the computer's ON switch. A warm boot (invoked by pressing the reset key if your system has one or by pressing the CTRL, ALT, and DEL keys simultaneously), on the other hand, simply clears all information from RAM, then invokes the PC's startup routine.

Buffer: A kind of memory for temporarily storing data, buffers are found on printers, PCs, and on many other hardware devices.

Bug: A bug is an apt noun for defects, glitches, and boo-boos in hardware or software design. Bugs owe their existence to the sheer complexity of computer technology, to rushed development, to sloppy craftsmanship, and to whistling in the dark.

Byte: A byte is a measure for a volume of information. One byte consists of 8 bits (a single letter in the alphabet equals 1 byte). Because a byte is such a small amount of information, disk storage capacity and memory capacity are often described in kilobytes or megabytes.

Cache: Used to increase system performance, a cache is a kind of holding trough for frequently used data. Software programs often fetch several scraps of information from memory over and over again. Transferring these scraps to a memory cache helps the CPU get to them faster. A disk cache plays the same intermediary role between the CPU and the hard drive.

CD-ROM Drive: Similar to a disk drive, CD-ROM (Compact Disc Read-Only Memory) drives read information off computer CDs (which look identical to your Barry Manilow audio CDs). Unfortunately PCs can only *read* this information; they can't change the data etched onto the silvery discs. Because CDs hold such vast amounts of information on a single disc (650 MB or more), they're ideal for storing references such as encyclopedias and almanacs as well as unwieldy 15-MB software applications.

Clock Speed: All computer CPUs have internal clocks that set the pace at which information races between the CPU and the PC's other components. Clock speeds are measured in megahertz, and bigger numbers mean faster computers. Keep in mind, however, that clock speed is only one component of the real-world speed you'll ultimately get; memory, disk speed, the sophistication of your CPU, and a host of other issues come into play as well.

CMOS: CMOS stands for Complementary Metal-Oxide Semiconductor. Arf. This is a tiny chip that stores information about how your PC is configured: the type of disk drives that are installed, how much memory it has, etc. If you change a component in your system, you often need to change the information in CMOS through your PC's setup routine. (Check your PC manual about how.) A tiny battery keeps the CMOS from losing this information when you turn off your machine. When that battery dies, your PC is stricken with amnesia. For this reason, it's a good idea to record the information in CMOS on a sheet of paper and squirrel it away in a safe place.

Com Port: Short for "communications port," this is a pathway by which information enters or leaves your PC. There are two basic types: parallel ports and serial ports.

Controller Card: This is a circuit board installed in an expansion slot that conveys instructions from the CPU to the disk drive, monitor, scanner, or other device.

Coprocessor: System CPUs juggle an unfathomable number of tasks. Coprocessors, chips that unburden CPUs of (primarily) graphics and mathematical chores, make certain software go faster. A program must be specifically designed to take advantage of a coprocessor to benefit from it.

CPU (Central Processing Unit): The CPU is a computer's main processor chip or brain.

Database Manager: Also referred to as "database management system," this is a software program that intervenes between you and a pool of records that you've created (a database). It lets you add and change records, search and sort through them, analyze them, and print reports. Database managers include everything from recipe filers to application development tools.

Desktop Publishing: A suite of technologies that enable you to publish professional-looking documents as elegant as the pages in this book. The software component, desktop publishing programs, lets you create these documents, bedecking pages with borders, multiple columns, pictures, fonts, and other graphic elements. Many high-end word processors are essentially desktop publishers—and cost far less.

Device Driver: This is a software program that tells a PC and other software programs how to talk to a hardware device such as a printer, a video card, or a scanner. To use a StarBrite's Zirconia video card, for example, either your software or, more likely, the video card maker must provide a device driver written specifically for that make and model of video card.

Dip Switch: A set of tiny switches that control certain hardware functions, dip switches are typically found on circuit boards, printers, or other hardware. Dip switches are a hassle to adjust and often require you to open your PC to get to them. Generally you need to reset them only if the circuit board, printer, or other hardware conflicts with another device in the PC. Better hardware designs allow you to change these settings through software, rather than resolving conflicts willy-nilly with mite-sized switches.

Diskette: Also called a floppy, a diskette is a flat piece of Mylar coated with ferric oxide and housed in hard or soft plastic. We've all seen them. Though your data is generally safer on a hard drive, diskettes provide the fastest, least obtrusive way to move information between computers. They're also terrific for archiving old data and for backing up a hard drive. (Hint: For ultimate protection, store floppies used for backups in a different building than the one that houses your PC. Keep them away from magnets, dust, liquids, heat, and smoke.)

DOS (Disk Operating System): Sometimes referred to as "MS-DOS" (for "Microsoft DOS"), DOS acts as an intermediary between your computer and your software. It manages how your software and data run and how the software communicates with a computer's many components.

Dot Matrix Printer: This type of printer produces characters and graphic images on a page as a pattern of tiny dots. A printhead bangs tiny wires against a ribbon, which transfers ink to the page. Dot matrix printers are loud, and their print quality varies widely. Even the best dot matrix printers can't approximate the print quality of laser printers, but for forms, quick drafts, and mailing labels, they're indispensable.

Dot Pitch: Dot pitch is the distance between the pixels or dots of light that make up the image displayed on a monitor. In general, the smaller the dot pitch, the sharper the image.

DRAM (Dynamic Random Access Memory): This type of memory chip makes up a computer's main memory. "Dynamic" means that as soon as you turn your PC's power off, all the data in memory vanishes.

DX2: The name for Intel Corporation's family of PC chips that run internally at twice the speed at which the rest of the system operates. Thus a 50-MHz 486DX2 is an 80486-based PC with a CPU that runs at 50 MHz but that communicates with the rest of the computer at 25 MHz. For this reason, a 50-MHz 486DX2 is not as fast as a simple 50-MHz 486DX, which runs everything at the faster speed.

E-mail (Electronic Mail): Electronic mail is a way to send and receive messages to and from computers over a network, the airways, or telephone lines via a modem.

EISA (Extended Industry Standard Architecture): Pronounced "eesa," EISA is a 32-bit system bus architecture developed by a consortium of PC manufacturers to counter IBM's MicroChannel (MCA) standard. Unlike MCA, EISA is backwardly compatible with expansion cards developed for the 16-bit Industry Standard Architecture (ISA) found in most PCs. EISA and MCA machines are generally more expensive than ISA systems, and few applications and expansion cards take advantage of their 32-bit capability; ISA is generally a better buy.

ESDI (Enhanced Small Device Interface): This is a moribund standard for hard drives. Stick with IDE or SCSI hard drives instead.

Expansion Board: Also called an "expansion card," "add-in card," or "add-in board," this is a circuit board that holds chips and adapters and that connects to a computer's system bus through an expansion slot. Typical expansion boards include internal modems, video cards, and sound cards.

Expansion Slot: This is a socket inside the PC designed to hold expansion boards. Most PCs come with two to eight expansion slots, but you should find out how many are actually *free* (not being used by video, I/O, or other expansion boards) before you bite.

Fax/Modem: This device lets you send and sometimes receive faxes and data files with your PC via a telephone line. Most models don't include scanners, which means that the documents and graphics you send have to be created in your PC. Beware of fax/modems that can only send faxes, not receive them; for the same money you can find one that does both.

Floppy Drive: This drive reads and writes to floppy diskettes. Floppy drives generally come in two sizes, 3½" and 5¼" drives. The world is heading toward 3½" drives because the diskettes to which this drive reads and writes hold more data, are smaller to store, and are less susceptible to damage.

Font: A font is a complete set of letters, numbers, punctuation marks, and other special characters from a single typeface. Fourteen-point Courier italic, is a font, for example; Courier is the typeface.

Graphical User Interface: Abbreviated "GUI" and pronounced "goo-ee," which is often how it feels to use one, this is a display format that uses icons, windows, and other graphical elements to execute commands. Microsoft Windows, OS/2, and the Macintosh are all GUIs.

Hard Drive: Also called a "hard disk," this is a device inside the computer that magnetically stores data on coated circular platters that spin. Hard drives are the safest, fastest way to store and retrieve data.

I/O Port: Input/output port. (See "Com Port.")

IDE (Integrated Drive Electronics): This is a type of hard drive interface in which the electronics normally found on a drive controller card are integrated right on the drive. For hard drives with less than a 200 MB capacity, IDE is the fastest, most reliable interface available.

Ink Jet: This is a nonimpact printer that spits tiny drops of ink at a sheet of paper to create text and images. Ink jets are an inexpensive way to get low-quality color images. For black and white printing, however, their ink cartridges are expensive, their pages tend to smear, and their printhead nozzles tend to clog. Laser printers do a better job with less fuss.

Interlacing: In this CRT technology, an electronic beam refreshes (renews or changes the image) first on odd lines down a monitor's screen, then on even lines. This can cause a subtle flicker on the screen—the stuff of migraines. Better monitors are noninterlaced.

ISA: An unofficial abbreviation for "Industry Standard Architecture," it is a 16-bit computer architecture that has been an industry standard design ever since IBM introduced the PC XT.

Joystick: A stubby pointing device with a silly name used primarily with computer games for better control and more fun.

Jumper: A variation on a dip switch, a jumper is small wire band that you can move to change the configuration of a circuit board.

Kilobyte: One kilobyte equals 1,024 bytes. (See also "Byte.")

Laser Printer: This electrophotographic printer uses a laser beam and rotating mirror to draw an image on a print drum. It then transfers the image onto paper. Laser printers are quiet and fast, and they produce high-quality text and graphics images.

LCD (Liquid Crystal Display): A display technology found on many portable PCs, digital watches, and solar-powered calculators, LCDs use a liquid that's squeezed between two transparent electrodes. An electrical current causes the liquid to form patterns of text or images. A polarized filter allows those patterns to reflect only nonpolarized light. To the human eye these patterns appear as shadowy text and images. Backlighting makes them much easier to see.

Local Bus: The local bus is a data path that connects the CPU in a 386- or 486-based PC to the system's memory and cache. Be-

cause the local bus is a wider path that lets data travel at a
faster speed than the system bus allows, information arrives
three to ten times faster. Many system makers are designing
their PCs with proprietary local bus expansion slots for video
cards, hard drive controllers, and other add-in cards so that they
can catch this express line to the CPU, thereby boosting overall
system performance. Nearly a dozen local bus implementations
are vying to become standards, and the performance gains vary
depending on the implementation, the software you run, and a
handful of other considerations. Don't pay extra for it.

Macro Command: In word processors, spreadsheets, and other
programs, a macro is a small script that automates a series of
commands. With a single keystroke or combination of keystrokes
that you assign, the macro carries out a series of commands that
would otherwise have you typing away like a pecking hen.

MCA (MicroChannel Architecture): This is IBM's proprietary system bus design that traffics data on a 32-bit data path.
It's an overpriced competitor to another 32-bit bus design, EISA.

Megabyte: A measurement for a volume of information typically used to describe how much hard disk space or memory a
program requires. Also expressed as "MB," 1 megabyte equals
1,024 kilobytes.

Modem: Akin to a telephone for your PC, a modem allows your
computer to send and receive data files to other computers over
ordinary telephone lines.

Motherboard: The main circuit board in a computer, the
motherboard typically holds a PC's processor, memory, and other
chips that drive the computer.

Mouse: A palm-sized object resembling the rodent it's named
after, the mouse connects to your PC and acts as an alternate
pointing device for controlling the PC's cursor.

MTBF (Mean Time Between Failure): This is a manufacturer's
conjecture, usually measured in hours, of the amount of time a
hard drive, video card or other electronic device will run before it
keels over. Manufacturers arrive at this number through black
magic, clairvoyance, and tribal dances. It's entirely meaningless.

Multimedia: A term used to describe a vague category of software and hardware products that combine sound, graphics, animation and/or video. Its practical uses and the industry standards that will win it acceptance are still largely incoherent.

Multitasking: A broad term for the process by which a computer works on several tasks simultaneously. There are several degrees of multitasking; the simplest form, context-switching, allows more than one program to reside in memory at the same time, though only one of these (the foreground application) can use the system's CPU. More sophisticated multitasking allows both background and foreground applications to grab the CPU's attention whenever the other is idle.

NiCad (Nickel-Cadmium) Batteries: The most affordable and common type of rechargeable batteries found in portable computers. To get a full three hours of power from a NiCad, you need to drain the battery completely before recharging it.

Nickel Hydride Batteries: The second most common type of rechargeable battery used in portable computers, nickel hydride batteries hold their charge longer than NiCad batteries and don't require you to deplete them completely before recharging. Unfortunately they tend to add substantially to the price of a notebook.

OCR (Optical Character Recognition): OCR is the process by which a PC converts a scanned image of a page of text (a magazine article, for example) into text characters that can be edited with word processing software. OCR is generally only 90 to 95 percent accurate, which means that roughly one in every ten converted characters is likely to be a blooper.

Optical Drive: Any storage device that uses light to record and/ or read data is an optical drive. Write-Once Read-Many (WORM), Magneto-optical, CD-ROM, and Erasable Optical (EO) drives are the most common optical drives.

OS/2: OS/2 is a graphical operating system co-developed by IBM and Microsoft (but now solely backed by IBM). OS/2, like Windows, provides multitasking and can take advantage of 32-bit system bus architectures such as MicroChannel and EISA. Its steep hardware requirements, stiff competition from Microsoft Windows, and lack of applications written to take advantage of it make its future uncertain.

Parallel Port: This is the connector on a PC to which you typically attach a printer or other parallel peripheral. Every PC should have at least one.

PCL (Printer Command Language): The internal instructions recognized by Hewlett-Packard laser printers and laser printers that emulate Hewlett-Packard's models. Several generations of PCL are available. All printers should support at least PCL 4; PCL 5 is currently the most advanced version.

PCMCIA (Personal Computer Memory Card International Association): PCMCIA a newly emerging standard for credit-card–sized memory cards and expansion cards designed primarily for use in portable computers. Theoretically, any fax board, memory card, or other expansion card that meets the specification would work in any computer with a PCMCIA slot.

Peripheral: This is a generic term for printers, monitors, and other external hardware devices that dangle off a PC.

Pixel: Short for *picture element*, a pixel is a single dot of light on a computer monitor. A monitor's resolution indicates the number of pixels it can display horizontally and vertically.

PostScript: This printer language allows you to produce pages that combine complex text and graphics. PostScript can scale fonts to any size, print text around a circle, render elaborate graphics, and handle other tasks that elude an ordinary PCL printer.

Power Supply: Found in all PCs, this device converts AC electrical current to a form a PC can use.

RAM (Random Access Memory): A com-puter's main system memory expressed in K (kilobytes) or MB (megabytes).

Refresh Rate: Also called "vertical refresh rate," the refresh rate is the speed at which the video card redraws the image displayed on a monitor. The faster the refresh rate (70 Hz or greater is optimum), the less flicker you'll see in the image.

Resolution: Resolution refers to the number of pixels, or dots of light, a monitor and video card display to create an image. The higher the resolution, the smaller the dots—and the sharper the image. Higher resolutions also allow you to cram more text and graphics onto the screen at once. The most common video resolution is VGA, which displays 640 by 480 pixels.

Scanner: A scanner acts as a kind of photocopier for a PC. Pass a scanner over an editorial cartoon or a newspaper article, for example, and the scanner copies it into your PC as an image file.

SCSI (Small Computer Systems Interface): Pronounced "scuzzy," this interface connects peripherals and hard drives to your PC.

Seek Time: Measured in milliseconds (msec), the seek time is how long it takes a hard drive's read/write head to find the physical location of a chunk of data on the disk. You can usually ignore this number. The more important number is access time—the amount of time it takes for a hard drive to *locate and retrieve* data.

Serial Port: This is a connector to which you typically attach a modem, mouse, or other serial peripheral to a PC. Every PC should have at least one; better models have two.

SIMM (Single Inline Memory Module): A wafer-sized circuit board that has memory chips on it and that makes up the main memory of most newer PCs.

Spreadsheet: A spreadsheet is a software program used for basic financial and numerical analysis. It presents a matrix of cells divided into rows and columns, into which numbers or mathematical formulas can be entered. Spreadsheets are great for building budgets and financial models.

ST506: This is an old, slow, low-capacity (10 to 20 megabytes) hard drive standard found mostly in 8088-based PCs and other dinosaurs. It's been supplanted by IDE, the interface found in most newer systems.

Super VGA: This is a catch-all term for any video resolution that improves on the standard VGA (640 by 480 pixels). It includes 800 by 600, 1024 by 768, and 1280 by 1024 pixels. Ask for specifics before you buy into it.

Surge Protector: An adapter that resembles an extension to an AC outlet and that intercepts power surges and high voltage spikes coming across power lines so that they don't fricassee your data or your system's delicate components. Some surge protectors (also called surge suppressors) include connectors for intercepting power spikes coming across telephone lines.

System Bus: The system bus is a data highway that connects different parts of a PC, including its CPU, video, and disk drive controller. There are three main system bus designs: ISA, EISA and MicroChannel.

Tape Drive: This device backs up data (making copies of it for protection). It reads and writes this information to magnetic tape cartridges, which are similar to audio tapes. Although prices on tape drives have dropped drastically, they're still slow and mired in a welter of incompatible recording and cartridge standards.

Toner Cartridge: This disposable container holds the powdery "ink" that a laser printer uses to print an image or text on paper. Some cartridges hold only the toner; others hold both toner and the print drum, the photosensitive device that places the toner onto the paper. Toner cartridges are expensive; over a printer's lifetime, the cost of toner cartridges quickly outstrips the original cost of the printer.

Trackball: A variation on a mouse, a trackball is a stationary cursor-control device that you manipulate by rolling a ball that's held in place.

Transfer Rate: This is the speed at which a hard drive delivers information from the hard disk to the CPU, measured in megabytes per second. Transfer rate is linked to access time; a fast access plus a slow transfer rate equals slow performance. Thus the higher the transfer rate the better.

TrueImage: A PostScript clone developed by Microsoft, TrueImage interprets PostScript files, PostScript fonts, and TrueType scalable fonts.

Typeface: Typeface refers to the design of a style of type characters (Times Roman, for example, or Helvetica) that includes all point sizes and text modes (such as bold and italic versions of these styles). A variety of fonts makes up a typeface, not the other way around.

Uninterruptible Power Supply (UPS): A battery-operated device that supplies electricity to your PC when the normal AC power from a wall socket fails. It generally gives you just enough time to save the data you were working on and then turn off your computer.

User Interface: A general term that describes a software's design, command structure, and appearance. A command-line user interface means the program receives commands as words typed in from DOS's C: prompt. A menu-driven user interface refers to a program that has multiple choice menus from which you invoke commands. A graphical user interface, such as Windows, uses icons to represent commands and invites the use of a mouse to manipulate information and invoke commands.

VGA (Video Graphics Array): The most common video graphics resolution, VGA displays 640 pixels horizontally and 480 pixels vertically on a monitor.

Video Card: Also called "video adapter" or "video controller," a video card is a circuit board that generates the video signals that are sent to—and displayed on—a PC monitor.

Virus: This is a computer program that insidiously attaches itself to other legitimate computer programs. When the virus recognizes some trigger event within your system, such as the current date (which PCs keep track of), it may do nothing more than display a political slogan or other dogma, such as "Legalize Marijuana!" Other viruses can do serious damage to your data files and software applications. For all the mayhem they wreak, their danger is greatly exaggerated.

VRAM (Video RAM): VRAM is memory designed specifically for video cards. VRAM is faster (and costlier) than DRAM, the other kind of memory found on video cards.

Wait State: This is a period of time when the processor is idle, waiting for the circuitry or other devices in the PC to send it data. Wait states slow down system performance somewhat. Their importance is overstated, but whenever possible, look for a system that has no wait states.

Whizzie: Used as noun or adjective, a whizzie includes any technologically splashy, yet gratuitous PC gadget, feature, or mechanism.

Windows: A graphical user interface from the Microsoft Corporation that runs on top of DOS and that provides for task switching (a rudimentary kind of multitasking), the ability to share data between various software applications with relative ease, and centralized control of peripherals, such as printers and video. To take advantage of Windows, an application must be specifically written for the interface. Beware of the term "Windows-compatible," all DOS programs are Windows-compatible; Windows programs are simply called Windows programs.

Word Processing Software: This software is devoted primarily to generating and editing words in documents.

XGA (Extended Graphics Adapter): Technically a term for the graphics adapter in IBM's 486 PCs, XGA is now used as a general term for any monitor and video card capable of 1,024 by 768 resolution.

XT: The name given to the first 8086- and 8088-based IBM PCs that included hard disks, XT stands for "Extended Technology." The term has since become a generic term for any PC that is built around one of these chips and that comes with a hard drive or similar storage device.

Index

U

UART 16550 standard, 152
Uninterruptible power supplies (UPS), 110, 212
Updating of antivirus software, 23
Upgradable PCs, 5
Upgrading, 136–137
  of drives, 145–148
  guidelines for, 140–141
  of laser printers, 79–80
  of memory, 45, 136, 143–145
  of ports, 152
  of power supplies, 138, 151–152
  of processors, 137–143
  before selling, 167
  of software, 4, 17
  of video adapters and monitors, 137, 143, 149–151
Used computers and peripherals, 157–158
  checklist for, 170–171
  insides of, 163–164
  negotiations for, 164–165
  portable, 168–169
  prices for, 158–160, 166, 170
  selling, 165–168
  testing, 158, 161–163, 168–169
Usefulness in product reviews, 11
User Friendly Exercises program, 31
User interfaces, 19–20, 207, 212
Utilities, 30

V

V20 processors, 35–36
V.22, V.32, V.42 modem standards, 101
Vertical refresh rates, 54, 63–64, 150, 210
VGA (video graphics array) standard, 51, 65, 124, 212

Video cards and adapters, 50–52, 212
  checklists for, 66–67
  color and monochrome, 52–53
  speed of, 53–54
  upgrading, 137, 143, 149–151
Video drivers in Windows, 20
Video RAM (VRAM), 53, 65, 212
Viewing of database records, 30
Viruses, 22–23, 212
VRAM (video RAM), 53, 65, 212

W

Wait states, 41, 212
Warranties and guarantees, 58–59
  in buying computers, 183–184
  and credit cards, 60
  for dot matrix printers, 83
  for hard drives, 148
  importance of, 34
  for laser printers, 78
  by mail-order firms, 178
  for memory, 145
  for portable computers, 126
  for portable modems, 129
  in product reviews, 11
  by retailers, 176
  for software, 16
  for toner cartridges, 74
  for used computers, 165
  for video cards, 151
  voiding, 152–153
Weight
  of portable computers, 117
  of portable modems, 129
Whizzies, 212
Width of printer carriages, 81
Windows, 5, 18–21, 212–213
  database managers with, 29
  memory for, 20, 43